DOROTHY HERBERT

of the Age!

Sensation

Riding

A Memoir

Dale A. Riker
P.O. Box 361
Tellevast, FL 34270-0361

FIRST EDITION

ISBN 0-9771621-0-9

Book design by Joanne Reckler Foster
Cover photo—Dorothy Herbert with Ringling Bros. and
Barnum & Bailey in 1934—*courtesy of Tim Tegge*

Printed in the United States of America

How It All Began

*M*any years ago a very nice gentleman by the name of Clarence Hastings happened to see Dorothy Herbert perform. It was love at first sight, Clarence being an equestrian teacher and horse lover with an eye for a pretty girl. They never met but did carry on a correspondence over many years.

Clarence's association with Dorothy resulted in the raising of the Dorothy Herbert Tent, a sub-group of the Circus Fans Association (CFA) of America, in Jackson, Michigan. My wife, Evelyn, and I were charter members, and as state chairman it was my honor to present the CFA charter.

No one in the tent had ever met Dorothy, so when Evelyn and I were scheduled to attend a wedding in California, we contacted Dorothy and asked if we, as members of "her" Tent, could meet with her. She said yes, and we had a very pleasant visit with her and several other circus fans in the area.

At the 1985 Circus Fans Convention in California, Dorothy was scheduled to speak at the Ladies' Luncheon; she attended, but asked Ernestine Clark Baer to read her speech. It was recorded, and when we got home, Evelyn transcribed the tape and we sent copies to Dorothy and to Ernestine.

Shortly thereafter, Dorothy mentioned that she had written a book and asked if we would type and edit her manuscript. We spent the winter in Tucson, and both of us took part in the transcription; Evelyn with her ten-finger typing skills did a great deal more than I did with my two-finger touch system.

We sent a copy to Dorothy and she, in return, asked if we could find a publisher. We shopped the manuscript around, but no one expressed interest.

We saw Fred Pfening III and asked if the Circus Historical Society would be interested in publishing it in the society's journal, *Bandwagon*. He indicated that every performer had a book inside and most of them did not write very well, but that he would like to see it. We sent him a copy, which he shared with his father, Fred Pfening Jr. After reading it, Fred III felt it was worth publishing. It ran in seven issues of *Bandwagon*, and Fred Jr. indicated that it caused more good comments than most of the materials they had published.

We were fortunate to visit Dorothy on several occasions, and she discussed with us her dream of a retirement project for circus people similar to the one for the motion picture industry. She asked what organizations would be proper for her to ultimately share her estate with in hopes of fulfilling her dream. I suggested that the motion picture project might accept it and use it for the accommodation of circus folk. I further mentioned that the Showfolks of Sarasota also had dreamed of a retirement project.

Upon her death, a check for $25,000 was sent to the Showfolks of Sarasota. With the cooperation of the Community Foundation, the Dorothy Herbert Fund was established to provide shelter assistance for deserving showfolks in Sarasota and Manatee Counties. A presentation about Dorothy's dream and the history of the Fund at the Community Foundation encouraged the Migrant Ministries of the Catholic Church to establish the Circus and Traveling Shows Retirement Project Inc. (CATS), a 501(c)(3) not-for-profit corporation.

The manuscript is finally a book, thanks to Joanne

Foster, and the proceeds will be added to the Dorothy Herbert Fund or to CATS. Contributions can be made to:

> CATS
> P.O. Box 2085
> Sarasota, FL 34230
>
> or

> The Community Foundation of Sarasota
> Dorothy Herbert Fund
> 2635 Fruitville Rd.
> Sarasota, FL 34247-5222

This is the first of Dorothy's dreams. The opening of a Circus Retirement Facility will accomplish the other.

—*Dale A. Riker*

Chronology of Dorothy Herbert's Career

1925—Gollmar Bros. Circus (late season). Manege; vaultage act with mule and cart with Ray Thompson.

    1926—At Dreamland Park, Newark, New Jersey. Manege.

    1927—Miller Bros. 101 Ranch Wild West. Manege; learned to trick ride.

    1928—Eldridge & Bentum Circus. Manege and Thompson's barnyard pets. Lewis and Zimmerman Circus (Columbus, Ohio). Howard Thurston Magic Show (winter). Disappearing horse.

    1929—John Robinson Circus. Manege; novel three-horse liberty act.

    1930—Ringling Bros. and Barnum & Bailey. High-school waltz and rear; high jumps; broad jump sidesaddle.

    1931—Ringling Bros. and Barnum & Bailey. Center-ring manege. Presented Satan; jump over hurdle of fire without reins while blindfolded.

    1932—Ringling Bros. and Barnum & Bailey. Liberty horse act; zebra act; high-school horse, finishing with ride down track.

    1933—Ringling Bros. and Barnum & Bailey. Manege; jumped Satan over two other horses in Madison Square Garden and Boston Garden; fire jump on road; Roman riding. Appeared in ad for Camel cigarettes.

1934—Ringling Bros. and Barnum & Bailey. Liberty horses; high-school horse; hurdle riding; leader of Tommy Atkins troop of women riders. Worked with John Herriott on cat act planned for next season. Appeared on program cover.

1935—Ringling Bros. and Barnum & Bailey. Hurdle riding and breakneck riding on track; hippodrome races; high-school horse and liberty act; led Tommy Atkins' military maids. Shrine date in Chicago during winter. Appeared on Wheaties cereal box.

1936—Ringling Bros. and Barnum & Bailey. High hurdles on Satan while blindfolded; prone riding while going over fire hurdles; flying swings from saddle horn as rearing horse spun on hind feet on hippodrome track; Mazeppa riding through burning hoops; commissioned Texas Rangerette.

1937—Ringling Bros. and Barnum & Bailey. Ten-horse hitch Roman standing rider; high school; hurdle rider; Mazeppa. Shrine date in Chicago during winter. First Dorothy Herbert Circus Fans of America (CFA) Tent organized in Freeport, Illinois.

1938—Cole Bros. Circus. High-school riding on Cimarron; waltzing, rearing, and fire leaping horse, Satan; specialty horse, Black Hawk; high-hurdle horse, Rex; leading equestrienne with riding and jumping exhibitions at fairs.

1939—Ringling Bros. and Barnum & Bailey. Over hurdles and through hoops of flame on Sir George; madcap equestrienne; high-school horse; waltzing, rearing, and leaping horses; exciting laybacks on rearing horses and fire hurdles; leader of seventy girl riders. Won *Billboard* poll as favorite outdoor performer.

1940—Cole Bros. Circus. Rider of jumping and reinless horses. Heroine in Republic Pictures' *Mysterious Dr. Satan*. Played fairs and rodeos with own horses, Black Hawk, King Kong, and Rex.

1941—Cole Bros. Circus. Sixteen-horse hitch; rider on reinless, prancing Major over fiery barriers amid a herd of leaping horses; high school. Made honorary Oklahoma Ranger.

1942—Lewis Bros. Circus. Six liberty horses presented without use of whip while movements synchronized to music; three-horse high-school waltz and rear; high jump. Fair dates in fall.

1943—Lewis Bros. Circus. Liberty horses; high school; trained another girl to work with her. Fairs and indoor dates during year.

1944—Bailey Bros. Circus. Early in season chewed up by large monkey and unable to continue with show. Ben Davenport offered her use of his Gonzales, Texas, winterquarters. Austin Bros. Circus. Dog act. Joined Harry LeRoy to form Roy Bros. and Dorothy Herbert Circus, which fell through.

1945—Austin Bros. Circus. Fire leap; dogs. C. R. Montgomery Circus. Liberty horse act. Marriage to A. W. Kennard.

1946—C. R. Montgomery Circus. Liberty horses; high-school horses. St. Louis Police Circus. Fair dates for Boyle Woolfolk office.

1947—Garden Bros. Circus. Liberty horses. E. K. Fernandez Circus (winter). Liberty horses and ponies; dogs. At Frank J. Walters' winterquarters in Houston. Fairs for Boyle Woolfolk office.

1948—Clyde Beatty Circus. Jumping horses; dog act; ballet. Did radio and TV publicity.

1949—Clyde Beatty Circus. High jumping and rearing horses; manege; elephant; dogs.

1950—Clyde Beatty Circus. Besides horses, worked Harriett Beatty's animals after her death.

1951—Clyde Beatty Circus. High school; elephant; dogs; bally. Radio and TV appearances.

1952—Rudy Bros. Circus. Liberty horses; pony drill; high school; manege; dogs; riding dogs; and monkeys.

1953—Clyde Beatty Circus. Liberty act; pony drill; high-school dog act.

1954—King Bros. Circus. Rode Cimarron; dog act; rearing horse, Silver King. Rudy Bros. Circus in fall and winter. In fall on TV series, "Dr. Satan," on West Coast.

1955—King Bros. Circus. Equestrienne.

1955–1961—Bird Wonderland and Zoo.

1961—*The Bird Man of Alcatraz.*

1962–1965—San Francisco Zoo. Rode high-school horse, Cimarron, and was in charge of the baby zoo. Taught circus skills to college students.

1965–1969—Spot dates, some for Rudy Bros. Circus. Fairs and indoors.

1970–1972—Gene Holter Wild Animal Show; spot dates, including ones in Alaska.

1971—At Old Milwaukee Days Parade with pony act for Holter.

1972—Retired.

1973—Sold pony drill, which had been leased to Parley Baer.

1974—Sold dog act to John Strong, traveling with unit long enough to train girl to work them. Spot date with Earl Tegge's Circus in Chicago.

1976—Second Dorothy Herbert CFA Tent organized, in Clinton, Michigan.

1988—Dorothy Herbert living in retirement in Newbury Park, California.

—Prepared by John Daniel Draper

PROLOGUE

$\mathcal{I}$ have been asked many times, "Why don't you write a book? You have many things to tell that might be lost."

"I do not wish to write a book," I responded. "I have so little time left here I would like to spend it doing what I want to do for me."

"But what about your fans, the people who put you on top. Do you owe them nothing?"

"I gave them all I had to give. Why can't I now just sit back and rest?"

"Maybe they have a right to know how it all came about, and maybe you have a duty to the here/now generation to pass on to them some of the things connected with horse training or riding that were yours alone."

"But what about me? I want to be left to myself," I continued. "In order to tell these things, I must tell more. I would have to recall memories, some of them very unpleasant. Just why should I do this?"

"Because you are a little part of history—a damn little part to be sure, but a part that the future riders of America have the right to know about. Many of the stunts you have perfected have never been duplicated. Much has been said about what you did, but nothing about how or why."

When I first decided to write this book I thought I would have a ghostwriter. Then it occurred to me that if someone wanted to read something written by a ghost, he or she might better consult a spiritualist and get the information firsthand. So, for better or worse, I did it myself.

   I am aware that some of my friends are going to say I forgot to tell about this, that, and the other; however, this is not intended to be an autobiography. It is just a real-life story meant to give our young equestrians some clues to training and riding that, I hope, will help them obtain the goals they are seeking, with a few anecdotes thrown in to help them stay awake in the process.

—Dorothy Herbert

☾

How Did You Learn?

Mother was born in Kentucky, and she was very proud of that fact. When I was a little girl, she told me stories of the Grand Old South: the big plantations there, the beautiful horses, the warmth, laughter, and the wonderful life the people lived. These were the tales that had been told to her by her grandmother. If only the South had not lost the war, this life could have also been hers. Mother was a lady, and she never let you forget it.

My father was a descendant of hard-working farmers from Illinois, who, through the sweat of their brow, had cleared and tilled the land until they saw the fruits of their labor, and prospered. My grandmother on my father's side is the only one I heard mention anything of note regarding her roots. She once remarked about her kinship with Victor Herbert, the composer.

I, too, was born in Kentucky, and that is where I lived when I was young. When people asked how I learned to ride, I used to like to say, "Oh, I was raised with horses."

Only they were not our horses; they belonged to someone else. I would spend hours exercising them, and the owner, Colonel Reagan, who no longer rode himself but was a well-known breeder, was pleased to have the free help. Then one day he hired a new trainer who did not like the idea at all. He asked if they were not afraid that I would ruin the horses. The owner said he could not see that I was hurting anything. The trainer replied, "And I can't see where she is helping anything either, but if she is going to continue to ride these horses, she is going to do it right."

There were no more romps around the track bareback and barefoot. I was given an English saddle, a two-rein bridle, and was obliged to wear boots. So, instead of just exercising, I learned from the trainer how to put the horses through their paces. Later on, when the trainer felt I was ready, he allowed me to ride some of them in horse shows. There is a real thrill in taking a horse through the five gaits without making a mistake.

Then we went to live in Detroit, Michigan. The only horses I ever saw there were those ridden by the mounted policemen.

My mother and father had separated, not divorced; just a parting of the ways. This was to happen to them many, many times. I was attending school and Mother was holding down a job as a saleslady in a department store. I was also going to dancing school, and I loved it.

One day, after the dance class, they announced that a big spectacle was coming to town and extra dancing girls would be needed for the production numbers. The following week a man would be around to choose, and anyone he picked could be in the show. Costumes would be furnished and the girls would also be paid a salary.

I was one of those picked, and Mother went with me to sign up. While there, she was offered a job as an extra in the mob scenes. The play was Duffield's famous *Rome Under Nero*. It was held in a huge stadium, complete with chariot races, and it finished with a spectacular fireworks display depicting the burning of Rome.

One of the numbers was a military drill on horseback by the Roman gladiators. They were short of riders and asked if any of us had ever had any experience with horses. I raised my hand.

Just before the show closed, the man who was furnishing some of the horses asked Mother if she and I would like to join his troop. He had several girls working for him whom he was teaching to ride trained horses, but he could use a couple more. Mother thought this might be more interesting than going back to the department store, so we went with this outfit to Ann Arbor, Michigan, where we went into training.

Every so often we would go off to play a date somewhere, usually a fair. My mother and all of the other girls rode the manege horses, but I was picked to ride the comedy mule. I had to wear a clown suit and clown makeup and perform what was called a "January Act." People thought it was very funny, but it wasn't funny to me. At one point you fall down and the mule backs up and sits on you. The number finishes with the mule jumping over hurdles, and you vault on and off as he goes over the jump.

I have never talked about my early training. I do not like to think about it. People like to hear pleasant things, and I learned long ago to tell them what they like to hear.

Fact of the matter, I learned the hard way from one of the cruelest of all trainers, Ray Thompson. He was also considered the greatest horse trainer at that time. He and his troop had twice been called to England for command performances before the king and queen. He had been an officer during the war, training men for the cavalry.

He would work a horse and rider until both were ready to drop. If a mistake was made, the lash whip would often miss the horse and hit the rider instead. He was a rather small man with a sort of a one-sided smile, rather like a sneer. One of his eyes was disfigured and impaired, causing him to squint sometimes when talking to you. A horse had reared up and hit him in the face with his front hoof—the same horse he had blinded in one eye while he was training it. People who disliked him, and there were many, called it just retribution.

His idol was James Fillis, who had been ecuyer en chef to the Central Calvary School at St. Petersburg. He was acknowledged throughout Europe as the greatest high-school rider of all time. He had the honor of giving private riding exhibitions before the emperor and empress of Germany, the tsar of Russia, the queen of Belgium, and the emperor of Austria. I was presented with a book by Fillis and had to study it every day. Ray himself had been trained by Rhoda Royal, a past master in the art of dressage.

Ray claimed that the bit and spurs in the hands of an amateur were like a knife and a sword in the hands of an idiot. My legs at that time were not quite long enough to touch the horse in the proper place to cue him right; nevertheless, the stirrups were kept long. The spurs that I used were taped so that I would not accidentally hit the horse with a sharp rowel. At first the stirrups were hobbled under the horse's belly to keep my legs in the right position.

My hands were another matter; they quickly learned to stay in place after a few cracks on the knuckles.

The extra-long stirrups were uncomfortable. When riding the gaited horses I had been allowed to have them at a comfortable length in order to post on the trot. In high school this was not allowed. For a very long time I rode horses that were also being trained. They learned to respond to the bit and spur as I learned how to use them.

When I was considered capable, I was given a horse that was completely trained, Black Artist. He was the second best horse in the stable. The best, Kentucky Man, Ray reserved for himself. No one else was allowed to ride him.

Looking over this chapter, I have a feeling you will get the impression that I was quite stupid to be so long catching up with the rest of the troop, and just now getting into the act. I feel then the necessity to explain at this point the difference between high school and manege.

Ray was breaking horses for circus and other trainers. They liked the results of his training, but did not like to have him on their shows on account of his fiery temper and his methods of training.

The manege horses were the ones that were being trained to go on a circus. These horses were broke to waltz, march, get on a pedestal, side pass, and lie down and sit up. They are cued with a whip, and anyone can learn to work them with a few days' instruction.

A high-school horse is a different matter all together, and this is what I was being trained for. The horse responds to bit and spur and the pressure of your legs. Distribution of your body weight also plays a part. In conjunction with all the things a manege horse is taught to do, a well-trained high-school horse will sidestep on the trot, do the Spanish trot, seesaw piaffe, the rock the forehand, the high extended trot, and rear with the front legs pawing in the air. All this is done without the aid of a whip. Even with one knee and the camel stretch, no whip is carried.

At this time I was also given two Shetland ponies to train so I might "learn from the ground up." This was good reasoning, for at that time I would not have been able to handle the big horses from the ground but would know how to do so later.

Now, I do not intend to make an ass out of myself by trying to tell anyone how to train a horse through the mail or by the printed page. Many books have been written on the subject—most of them stink.

When I was with the circus, many times someone would ask, "How do you train a horse?" Run through that again and you will see how inane it actually is. Still, it required an answer of some sort, and I am sure that the ones I gave were as silly as the question.

Then one day, while I was standing in the horse tent feeding my horses some apples, a man holding a little boy by the hand sprang it on me again.

"Pardon me, miss, but would you mind telling me how you train a horse?" Before I could think up a dumb answer, the little boy looked up at him and said, "Which horse to do what, Papa?" That was the answer I had been hunting for years.

But, back to the time I was first learning. The two ponies that were issued to me had to learn to get on a pedestal, waltz, change the ring, lie down, sit up, and rear. I was instructed what to do, but would break them myself. Later on, they were put into a pony drill along with six others. The girl who was riding the waltzing, rearing horse left the troop to get married, and each of us were given a chance to try out for her job. None of the other girls were very interested in learning to ride sidesaddle. It was not hard for me, as I had good balance, so I was taught to do the waltz and rear, and the layback.

Someone else had inherited the comedy mule, so I no longer had to put on makeup and take pratfalls.

I had seen jumping horses at the horse shows and, although I admired the courage of the riders, I could not help but think what a chance it was to take just to win a cup or a ribbon. I never dreamed that one day I would sit atop one of them.

As I said before, when Ray Thompson was not on the road with his own stock, he trained a lot for other people. One time he received an order for six jumpers. We were told when the horses arrived that three of us girls would be expected to train two apiece.

When I got up on my first jumper I found that my stirrups were up short. It gave me a feeling of safety. I rode him around for quite a while to get the feel of him, and he of me. When they put the hurdle up the first time you could have almost stepped over it. This was to give me confidence. I was shown how to bridge my reins (cross them over the horse's neck, lean on them, and thus not interfere with his head when he was taking the jump).

After my first time over the hurdle, like your first dive into the water, I felt no fear. We jumped a few more times that day, and each time the bar was raised a little higher, but not too high, I assure you. Nevertheless, when I dismounted my legs were trembling.

Before long we were going higher and higher, and I realized the thrill the jumping horse riders in the horse shows felt when they showed their mounts.

During these sessions I topped two horses, but I

will mention only one. People in my age bracket may remember Ten Minutes to Midnight, who went on to fame as a high jumper. What did I gain by all of this? Well, I overcame my fear of jumping horses and came to love them. The thrill of riding jumpers never leaves you. It is like a gambler, always taking one more chance.

There are two methods that I liked best to use. If possible, I always liked to train the horse and rider together. When training a horse for myself, I worked it from the ground with a breaking rigging first and then rode it after the trick had been completed using the long reins.

The book by James Fillis is excellent—if you have someone who knows what he is doing right there to coach you as you go along.

But I fear I am getting ahead of my story.

When the owners came to look over their jumpers they were quite impressed, not only with them but with Ray Thompson's trained horses as well, and hired the troop to travel with them. This is how we happened to join Colonel Zack Miller's 101 Ranch Wild West Show.

The show was presented in a huge portable amphitheater, with canopies over the seats to protect the customers. The cowboys, cowgirls, and the Indians were at the mercy of the elements.

The arena, seats, corrals, and so forth were put up by the working crew, but it was up to the personnel to get the stock back and forth from the trains. This meant getting up early, riding and leading horses to the lot. The steers and calves were herded down the streets by the cowboys. Let me interject here that, if one is inclined to learn from the bottom rung of the ladder upward, I can think of no better place than a traveling Wild West show to do so.

We ran into a problem right at the start. As with all railroad shows, space was at a premium. The girls were expected to double up in the sleeping cars. I had always been a restless sleeper and at the slightest touch would jump right up. Neither I nor whoever had the bad luck to sleep with me had a chance of getting any rest. I suppose the fact that I was riding a featured high-school horse, doing the waltz and rear, and topping their prize jumper, Ten Minutes to Midnight, had a lot to do with it, but I was given a berth alone.

Eight of us girls were in the manege high-school number. We were also required to wear old-fashioned wardrobe and to participate in the stagecoach holdup, burning of the covered wagon, and a couple of other numbers. It was new, it was exciting, but compared with future events it had little impact on my life.

The act I liked best of all in the show was the trick riders. I struck up a friendship with the one I most admired, and he offered to teach me. He had a beautiful black-and-white pinto pony with a gait as smooth as a flowing brook. I learned to vault, split the neck, do a fender drag, and stand in the saddle.

Ray, as a boss, usually did not come down to the lot until around noon. He would go to town in the morning for breakfast, go to a hotel and read the morning papers, and arrive after everything was in order for the matinee. Then one morning he came early to check one of his horses that had gone lame and saw me trick riding.

He said that, in his opinion, trick riding was very unladylike. I told him that I thought riding a mule had been unladylike, too, whereupon he informed me that I was engaged to ride horses, not to think.

After the show closed and we got back to winter-quarters, Ray booked several horses out to work on different dates. Mother was sent out with a single horse to play in a show that worked in theaters on the stage. While playing in Cincinnati, she and Dad got back together again. When the show date was over, she sent the horse back and stayed with him.

Because I was light and had a good seat in the saddle, it became my job to top all of the new jumpers. Besides being lonesome in quarters, I was getting fed up with riding all of the green horses that were in training, and the first chance I got, I left and went home to stay with Mother and Dad.

It was nice to be a family again. Dad had always been fun to be with and he went out of his way now as though making up for lost time. He taught me how to ice skate and how to use a bow and arrows. He continued where we had left off, with little thought that I might have grown up during the interval.

Then one day Mother said to me, "Pack up your things; we are leaving." No explanation. We went back to Detroit, just she and I.

︶

Howard Thurston

One day Mother decided she would like to visit her aunt who lived in Indiana. Mother's aunt had a little farm, and Mother just raved about it. "Oh, to get out of the city and have a home of my own like hers."

Because I was so close to Louisville, Kentucky, just twenty-eight miles, I drove over to visit my friends the Reagans, who had put me on my first horse. They were very happy to see me, and after showing me around, which included seeing their new horses and colts, they asked what I was up to.

I explained that the show had closed for the winter and that I was at liberty. They suggested that I contact Howard Thurston, the magician, who was looking for a rider to work with his show. The Reagans made a phone call and set me up with an appointment the following day. I stayed with them overnight and went to Mr. Thurston's hotel the next morning.

Howard Thurston was quite successful. He had his own railroad cars with sleepers; and two baggage cars, one for props, scenery, and other paraphernalia used in his show, the other for the animals used in his illusions.

A large number of people traveled with the show, including two sets of girl twins and a set of boy twins. Upon arrival in town the twins separated and went to different hotels; thus, no outsider would ever see a set together. There were also several sets of animals, but since most of them were kept in the basement of the theater, this made no difference as no one saw them there.

Abdell, a Hindu, was responsible for the success of many of Thurston's illusions, although he was never on stage. He did all of his work behind the scenes. Unless you were directly involved with a certain presentation, you were not allowed backstage; you stayed in your dressing room.

Thurston's show did not work on Sundays. Everything was packed and loaded after Saturday's last performance and moved to the next town. The crew, together with the local stagehands, worked all day Sunday getting things ready for the Monday show. It was said that no one else in show business cut up a stage like Thurston, with all the trapdoors necessary for his illusions.

The feature of the show this year was the "Vanishing Horse and Rider." The white stallion used in this production had been trained in Europe and brought to this country at great expense. It did what we today call a dressage act, but, at that time, it was better known as a high-school act. The horse had acted up during a performance and deposited the rider in the orchestra pit. The rider had suffered a broken leg and other injuries and would not be able to work for quite some time.

As arranged, I met Mr. Thurston in the lobby of his hotel. I was seated in a chair when he walked up. I may have been predisposed from having looked at the lithographs prominently displayed in the lobby, where he was shown wearing a long, black cape, staring straight ahead, his arms outstretched, and surrounded by bats and ghosts. When he first looked at me, I felt a chill. He had the most penetrating eyes I was ever to see. Several times during the performance he was supposed to hypnotize his subjects. I later learned that this was just playacting, but I never got over the feeling that, if he had so desired, he could hypnotize a person for real.

He asked me to stand up and turn around. I could see that he was disappointed. "I have been hearing from your friends how you are able to handle horses, but I am afraid that I will take a little more convincing."

It was plain to see that he had expected something more than a hundred-and-five-pound slip of a girl.

"However," he continued, "I will give you a chance. Go down to the stable and see what you can do with that horse and then let my manager know. I do not have the time to fool with all this, although I do have a lot of money tied up in the illusion and I wish to keep it in the show."

I got directions and drove to the stable where this unruly horse was being kept. They called him White Cloud. He was cross-tied in his stall and had hobbles on his hind legs, which indicated that he kicked. They had a muzzle on him, which meant he bit. He also had a big potbelly, which could only mean that he was very much in need of exercise. With great caution, and a lot of misgivings, I undid all of the bondages and led the horse into the exercise arena in conjunction with the stall they were renting. I put a bridle on him before I released him, and attached a long lunge rope to it.

When I let him loose, he went wild! He bucked and kicked and reared, but after a time, he lay down and rolled. I picked up the lash whip and kept him going for a long time, until all of the play was out of him, after which I went through the "let's be friends" bit with apples and carrots.

The groom appeared about this time. He did not

understand a word of English, and neither did the horse. I, of course, was anxious to know what the horse had been trained to do. The pantomime must have been hilarious. Picture, if you can, me marching like a horse, going down on one knee, and the groom nodding "yes." Then, I was suddenly waltzing, going through the side pass and the lay down, as he caught on to the game. We were both laughing like crazy when I motioned for him to put the saddle on the horse. The horse was frisky but willing to work, now that he had been exercised. I found that he did an excellent high-school act.

Early the next morning, we took the horse to the theater and practiced with him on the mat; then I called Mr. Thurston's manager and announced that we were ready for the audition. The manager and Mr. Thurston watched us go through the act and then called for the prop hands to bring out the crate.

"Now," the manager explained, "after you are finished with your act, you take a bow and ride the horse into the crate. You and the horse will be lifted to the top of the stage. After saying a few words, Mr. Thurston will fire a gun, and you and the horse will both disappear."

I was then turned over to the wardrobe mistress, who was instructed to put together a couple of costumes for me. The wardrobe was to be all black or all white, and I was required to wear a black wig. This was on Saturday and she agreed to spend all day Sunday working on my outfit.

It was arranged that I would meet them in their next town. I drove back and told my mother the good news that I had a job. We had not brought much luggage with us, because we had only intended to spend a couple of days. Mother said that as soon as she got back, she would go through my things and forward what she thought I might need. She drove me to the station, and I caught the train to join Thurston's Magic Show.

I never did understand quite how the stunt worked.

When Mr. Thurston fired the gun, a lot of white smoke, like a mist, was around us. The crate fell to the stage, and the horse and I were left dangling in midair. The curtain closed, and Mr. Thurston went out and took a bow. Then came an intermission, during which the horse and I were lowered to the stage. It took several men to crank the mechanism that pulled us up and down. One day, it failed, and they could not get us back down to the stage. There we hung, all through the third act. Needless to say, those below were nervous throughout the balance of the show. When the show was over, I was very happy to get back on the ground.

The accommodations were great, we stayed in the best hotels, signed for our meals, and the salary was ad-equate—but I was very lonesome. I did not know what to do with myself most of the time. The rest of the cast had nothing in common with me, and I was quite alone. When they traveled to the next town in the private train, they would all have a lot of fun, enjoy a few drinks, something to eat, then retire to their compartments. I would sit in the corner and watch all of the fun; after they were gone, I would pick up a couple of sandwiches and go to my compartment.

I was glad when the Thurston show closed its season.

︶

My First Car

Mother and I were living in an apartment in Detroit. Dad was sending Mother money to live on; they were separated again at this time. I was working in a department store to help pay the expenses. I was just a teenager; as usual, I was lying about my age in order to have a job, and I did look older.

I decided to surprise my mother and buy a used car. The salesman was very kind and took me out for a short drive and showed me how to shift the gears on the little car I had selected, a coupe with a rumble seat.

I shelled out all of my hard-earned cash, signed some papers, and the salesman promised he would deliver the car the next day. I had told him what time I would be home from work, and when he arrived I was on the front sidewalk waiting for him. I thanked him and, as he and another man who was following him in another car drove away, I rushed upstairs and told my mother that I had something to show her. After looking it over, we got in to go for a drive. Nothing happened. The salesman had showed me how to shift the gears but not how to start the thing. It was too late to get hold of him by then.

The next day I phoned him, and he gave me all of the necessary information. When I got it started and was about to drive off, Mother asked me if he had told me how to stop it. He had.

Came Sunday, my day off, and it was warm and sunny. Mother said she would like to go to the park to play golf. I told her I would take her and pick her up whatever time she wished. Golf did not interest me, so I never played.

After leaving Mother off, I started home. I was not sure which way I ought to go so I turned around and headed back the way I had come. Pretty soon an officer on a motorcycle pulled me over and asked if I could read. I was going the wrong way on a one-way street.

I told him I had seen the sign but hadn't the faintest idea what to do about it. He suggested I back up and turn the car around. I told him I had not learned to do that yet. (Wonder what would happen if something like that were to occur today?)

He parked his motorcycle on the grass out of the

way, got in the car, and taught me how to drive, including the hand signals used in those days. I never forgot him. What he never knew was, from that time on, if I was ever in any kind of difficulty, I always ran to the police for help.

One evening while I was reading *Billboard*, the showman's magazine, I saw an advertisement for people for several shows in Peru, Indiana. Not knowing what to expect when I arrived there, I, nevertheless, packed my bags, put them in the car, said good-bye for now, and started out. Before I left, Mother told me if I was lucky and landed a job that I would no doubt be gone all summer, so she would go to Cincinnati and live there where she would be near some of her relations.

On arriving in Peru, I checked into a hotel and the next day drove out to the winterquarters. After wandering around awhile I entered one of the offices. I didn't bother to look at the sign on the door to see which one it was, but it wouldn't have mattered. I didn't know one from the other anyway. Several men, looking important, were seated behind desks. One of them asked what I wanted. I told him a job was what I had in mind.

"Then the man you wish to see is Mr. Zack Terrell here," he said.

Mr. Terrell was a rather heavy-set man with a serious look. They called him Simon Legree (behind his back, of course), but I am sure he knew it and was secretly pleased. He was in no way lame, but he carried a cane at all times. It seemed like it was part of his wardrobe. He used it to emphasize any point he wished to make. It found its way to many heads, although I thought he might have chosen a better spot.

He could glare at a person and make him feel guilty whether he was or not. Nevertheless, I liked and admired him very much and we had only one disagreement all the time I knew him.

"Well, now," said Zack Terrell of the Sells-Floto Circus, as he pulled out some kind of a form, "What is your name and just what can you do? Can you sing?"

I told him my name and shook my head no to his question.

"Can you work on the swinging ladder?" Because I had never seen one, I reckoned that I couldn't.

"How about web or iron jaw? Ever work with elephants? Can you walk a wire?" I just kept shaking my head to every question.

"Not very versatile, are you? Just what can you do?"

I did not know at the time, but they were all just having fun. Mr. Terrell had heard of me and wanted to see what my reaction would be. "Well, I can ride horses," I flung over my shoulder as I headed for the door, "but I seem to be in the wrong place for that."

"Hold on there. Suppose you go out to the ring barns and ask for John Smith, our horse trainer, and see what he thinks about it."

Their laughter rang in my ears as I slammed the door behind me. When I presented myself to John Smith, I was so mad I decided I would ride whatever they put me on, no matter what, and that was my attitude for many years to come. I would show them, even if I broke my neck trying.

John and I got along just great. John was one of the best trainers, but he was fed up with having to break in every girl they sent to him; some had never been close to a horse. Then I came along, not only able to ride but willing to assist him in training the horses he was breaking. Needless to say, the best-trained horses were mine for the asking.

I soon made friends with the other girls who were there practicing. We all lived in town, of course, and because I was the only one who had a car, we all shared the ride. We split the expense of the gas.

The car was pretty old to begin with, so it wasn't long before it started to go to pieces. It became necessary to use a crank to get her started, and, because she was mine,

I had the honor.

Either because no one had told us or we did not have the money for it, we had no spare tire. If we had a flat tire, we used something called a cold patch and took turns on the hand pump.

The radiator began to leak, so it was necessary to carry a bucket of water and stop when we were halfway there to fill it. Then the brakes gave out and in order to stop it, we would throw it in reverse. However, we went merrily along.

Then, one day a man from the front office rushed into the ring barn where we were working. "Who owns that coupe parked outside? There isn't another car on the place and it is too late to call a cab to come out from town. Mr. Mugivan has to catch a train. Will whoever owns it get him there?"

I got into my car, drove to the office, and picked up Mr. Jerry Mugivan and his luggage. He was a rather large, imposing man, all business. Beautifully dressed, he was very out of place in my little rattletrap car. I know he must have remembered his ride for a very long time. Halfway to the station, the car was steaming so badly we couldn't see, so I pulled over to the side of the road, got out and put in some water, which bubbled up all over the place.

"Young lady," said he, as I stepped back into the car, "can't you hurry? We will miss the train."

I stepped on the gas, gave her all she had, and when the station was in sight and the train coming, I could not stop. I ran her into the signal light and threw her in reverse.

"Thanks for the ride," Mr. Mugivan gasped, "but have you never heard of a garage?"

"Have you heard, sir, that we don't get paid in winterquarters—just our meals?"

A few days later, one of the show mechanics came and got my car and took it into their workshop and gave it a complete overhauling. After that she drove like a dream, or, at least, less like a nightmare.

Why do I go on so about my first car? Because it was so much a part of all that happened.

Now, it came time to go on the road. All of us girls were advised to report to the office to sign a contract for the season. After reading mine, I said, "Mr. Terrell, there is only one thing that I would like added: I would like to have a lower berth alone. I have been told that due to a shortage of space, some of the girls are required to double up. This will not do."

"Of course," said Mr. Terrell, "we have been receiving great reports from John Smith in regard to your ability and we want you to be happy on our show."

The next morning I checked out of the hotel, put my car in storage and took a taxi to the train. I set down my bags and went wandering down the aisles of the sleeping cars looking for a berth with my name on it. When I located it, I found another girl was in it.

"Hi," she said, "we are to be roommates for the season. Which side of the berth do you want?"

I mumbled something and flew out to the runs, where they were having the usual trouble loading the train for the first time out. I located Mr. Terrell, and the following conversation ensued.

"Mr. Terrell, there is another girl in my bed."

"What's the matter with her?"

"Nothing that I know of, but I will not sleep with her."

"Why not?"

"Well, would you?"

"Certainly not! Wait. Just sleep with her tonight, and we will settle this tomorrow in the next town."

I went to some of the friends that I had made on the show and asked them to get my trunk out of the trunk wagon and see that it got to the railroad station. I went back to where I had left my luggage, found a cab, and returned to the hotel.

The next morning I went to the railway station to have my trunk shipped home. It had never been delivered to the station, so I got my car out of the garage and drove out to winterquarters to see if anyone there might know something about it. Zack Terrell's office was closed, of course, so I went to the next one and asked if anyone had noticed a stray trunk anywhere.

"Why, yes, young lady," said Mr. Jess Adkins, manager of the John Robinson Circus, "I am sure I saw one of my men put it in that big, red baggage wagon a while ago."

Jess Adkins. He was tall, white haired with twinkling blue eyes, and most of the time he was talking to you, you got the impression he was laughing at some secret joke he did not care to share. In retrospect, I would say that he looked very much like the now-famous Colonel Sanders, though I am sure he never plucked a chicken in his life.

"I understand," he continued, "that you are heading for Cincinnati. Did you know that it is the town we are to open in? If you like, you may ride there on our train. I am sure that we will be able to find a lower berth for you—alone."

I knew he could not come right out and offer me a job when I had just blown a sister show with no notice.

So I said, "Would I get the same salary?"

"Indeed," he answered, with a twinkle in his eye. "We might even do a little better."

"Well, then, suppose you keep my trunk and I will drive through and meet you there. My mother is in Cincinnati, and I think she might like to have my car."

I made the drive without incident, thanks to the man in winterquarters who fixed my car. I found where mother was staying, bathed, changed my clothes, and went to the show grounds. The tent was up when I went to report to my new boss. My trunk was in the ladies' dressing room, and it looked like I was all set.

I found Mr. Adkins under the big top, and he told me, "Our horse trainer should be here shortly. He has been playing some indoor dates. Tell him who you are and that you are to ride a horse named Lilly. You will finish the manege act with a waltz and rear. He will show you the cues."

Everyone was very busy rushing to get ready for the forthcoming show. I went and sat in the seats to be out of the way.

Rudy Rudynoff walked into the tent. He looked like something out of a men's fashion magazine—derby hat, white gloves, a smart suit, and, of all things, spats. It was plain to see that he was from Europe.

I walked over to him and gave him Mr. Adkins' message. His reaction was anything but what I expected.

"Oh, you are going to ride Lilly, are you? And do the waltz and rear? Well, I have spent a lot of time breaking that horse from rearing. Good luck to you!" And with that he turned on his heels and walked away.

Boiling mad, I went to the ring stock boss, whom I had already met in Peru at winterquarters and asked him if he knew of anyone who might help me. He suggested that I talk to one of the other trainers who worked the liberty horses and was also familiar with the manege horses. "Alabama" Campbell was lean, long, and lanky. He kept to himself and had little or nothing to say to anyone. He was a capable enough horseman, but too serious to ever be an outstanding showman. I never saw him smile. He was quite helpful, however. He went with me to a vacant lot behind the tent and we worked with Lilly. I must admit the outcome wasn't too good.

Later on in the day, when we lined up our horses to be issued our places in the manege number, Rudynoff assigned me to a spot at the far end of the tent facing the blues: a section that was last to be filled. With a small house on teardown nights, these seats were removed before the show was half over and you were playing to no one.

At the matinee I was boiling mad, and the more I

rode, the madder I became. When the number was at last over and I was scheduled to do the waltz and rear, I had not only myself but the horse in a frenzy. She reared all over the place. After a short bow, we dashed out of the tent and I started to jump off. Just as I did, she reared again and, of course, I fell—right at the feet of two gentlemen.

A short time later Mr. Rudynoff called me out of the dressing tent and said, "I want you to know that this is not my idea, but tonight you will work in the center ring. Also, at the end of the waltz and rear, you will jump your horse into the ring, dismount, and take a bow."

Mother and some of my relations came to the show that night, and I guess I hammed it up. Anyway, I got a nice hand and was feeling sort of smug. That didn't last long. Rudynoff caught up with me as I started into the dressing tent.

"That horse is just excited and worked up, but it won't last. She will stop rearing as soon as she quiets down; and, as for you, anyone would think that you were deliberately trying to break your neck. You don't even look to see where the poles are on the track. If I were you, I would quit while I was still in one piece. You are not much of a rider."

I flew into the dressing room and started to bawl. I was in the midst of packing my trunk to leave the show when Eva Lewis, wife of the famous clown Joe Lewis, came running over to me. "Dorothy, who do you think wants to talk to you? Pat Valdo."

"Well, who is he? I never heard of him. Besides, I don't want to talk to anybody."

I walked out of the tent and there he was, standing where he could not have missed hearing everything that was said. "Miss Herbert, we would like to have you with the Ringling brothers' circus. I guess you have heard of them, even if you haven't heard of me. Now there is someone out here who wishes to meet you. May I present Mr. John Ringling."

I remembered him at once.

He was one of the men who had been standing at the back door when I had taken my buster off Lilly at the matinee; then Pat Valdo must have been the man who was with him.

About that time my mother walked up and said she was ready to go home. I introduced her to them and told her I would only be a moment while I closed my trunk. When I came out of the dressing room, Mr. Ringling and Pat Valdo were still there. I told Mother to wait until I got the car.

"I heard you say you have a car," said Pat Valdo. "I wonder if you would be kind enough to drive us to the railroad station? We could talk on the way."

Before I could answer, Mother, who was all agog over meeting John Ringling, chimed in, "We would be glad to."

She didn't know what I had done. I had removed the cushion from the back seat in order to have more room to take my things to the show train. When I returned with the car, Mr. Valdo had somehow gotten Mr. Ringling and himself into the rumble seat and I delivered them to the station. With the top down and the wind blowing, there was no chance for conversation.

Before they left, Pat Valdo pointed out all the advantages of being with the "Big One." I, in turn, explained that if I was unable to cope here, I sure did not wish to try it there. I wasn't sure I wanted to stay in the circus business at all. He told me to stick it out, learn all I could, and when I felt I was ready, to let them know.

We played in Cincinnati for three days and when we left town, the car stayed with my mother. She later traded it in on a new one. Throughout the years I have had many cars, cars that I cannot even remember, but your first car is like your first love—you can never forget it.

Neither could John Ringling. I recall him saying one day many months later as he stepped out of his chauffeur-driven limousine, "Dorothy, do you still have that car of yours with the lovely rumble seat?"

The John Robinson Circus

My horse, Lilly, continued to work well. I had also become very good friends with Rudy Rudynoff. I made it a point never to mention any other trainer's name to Rudy, or that someone else had taught me to do it a different way. I did this not only with Rudy, but with every trainer I worked with over the years.

After we had been on the road for a few weeks, Mr. Adkins called Rudynoff into his office and told him he would like me to work the palomino liberty horse act. Inasmuch as no women in the country were working liberty horses, Mr. Adkins was eager that I learn.

Rudynoff was very exact in his teaching.

"First," he said, "you have to learn how to handle whips."

We spent many hours in the ring with the whips. Rudy would place pieces of paper at different points in the ring and I would have to hit them from the front or back, high or low. Rudy explained that the horse must be hit on the chest, the back, or under the belly. This training paid off, as I never hit a horse in the eye with a whip in my life, which cannot be said for many trainers.

The act Rudy taught me was a takeoff on the old Johnny Agee "brewery act," which traveled all over the country advertising beer, as do the Budweiser horses today. It consisted of three palominos. Three barrels were placed in the ring and each of the horses would jump in a barrel, stop, turn around, go the other way of the ring, and then back again. The next time when they had reached their respective barrels they waltzed three times, then out and around again. This time, when they were in their respective places, they would lie down and sit up. This was quite effective with their heads and necks sticking out of the barrel. For the finish they all stood on their hind legs in their barrels.

Late in the season, one of the men who worked a liberty act in the end ring while Rudynoff worked his spotted liberty horses in the center ring was injured, and Rudy asked me to take his place. I was quite flattered and made it a special point to work the horses just like he taught me.

Rudynoff was considered the foremost liberty horse trainer in the business. He was very flashy in the ring, and his showmanship was superb. As a former bareback rider, he would often end his act by jumping from the ground to the back of the last liberty horse and turning a back flip to the ground.

One day the riding act was short a whip-master and one of the principal lady riders asked if I would help out by being the whip-master. After watching her for several days, I decided that I wanted to be a bareback rider. I told this to Rudy.

"Fine," he said. "When we go into winterquarters, I will find a suitable horse to train for you and I will teach you. My wife, Erma, was a great rider, and I know she will be happy to help teach you." Erma was not traveling with the show as they had a young son, and she was staying home while he was in school.

I thought I was very lucky to have such excellent teachers, but it was not to be.

In those days a few weeks before the show closed, management put up a small tent in the backyard, called each act in, and signed those they were going to retain for the coming season. By ones and twos the acts filed in and out. I waited and waited, but I was not sent for, and soon the little tent was no longer in the backyard. So, a couple of days before the show closed I went to see Mr. Adkins. "Tell me what is wrong. Wasn't I good enough to be asked back?"

He looked at me, and, for once, there was no twinkle in his eye. He said, "Dorothy, you know better than that. I would love to have you back; you have been great. I will have a long talk with you later."

That very day I received a wire from Ringling Bros. and Barnum & Bailey, signed by Pat Valdo, offering me a job with that show. I went straight to Mr. Adkins and showed him the wire.

He shook his head and said, "So, now you know."

I said, "Well, I certainly don't want to go there. I would like to stay here."

"Sit down, Dorothy, and let me tell you what happened. The Ringlings have bought out the American Circus Corporation. We do not know which of the shows they will continue to put out on the road. From now on, the performers will not be able to pick and choose which show they would like to be with. They will go where they are put. Rudynoff, by the way, is being transferred to the Sells-Floto Circus, and he is not a bit happy about it. You had better do as they say if you want to stay in the circus business."

The season had gone by all too quickly. I had made many friends, and they were now all busy making plans for the winter months. Most of them had their own acts and would continue working. I did not answer Pat Valdo's wire, and walked out of the tent on closing day without looking back.

I bought a ticket for Cincinnati. As the train pulled away, I started to cry; I had a feeling that things would never be the same again. They never were.

∪

Early undated photo of Dorothy Herbert. *Courtesy of the John & Mable Ringling Museum of Art, Tibbals Digital Collection.*

Ringling Bros. and Barnum & Bailey

It seemed like the train ride from Cincinnati to Ringling's Sarasota winterquarters took forever. I rode in the coach. After sitting up all the way, I was very tired and dirty when I arrived. Pat Valdo met me at the station and said he had arranged for me to room with a private family, as hotels were in short supply and very expensive.

I spent the rest of that day getting cleaned up and resting. The next day I was taken out to winterquarters and introduced to Frank Asher, who was in charge of the manege horses.

Frank informed me that all of the good horses were already taken, riders from the past season having first choice. They finally gave me some sort of a mount, who balked at every trick. When I put the pressure on to try to make him work, he took the bit and ran away with me. When I saw that I could not stop him, I let him run; then, when he got tired and tried to stop, I made him run some more. When we got back to the practice arena, the horse was in a lather. All of the other riders were lined up having a big laugh.

For the next few days I fooled around, doing nothing. Then they sent for me to report to the office. They asked why I was not practicing with the rest of the girls, and I told them there did not seem to be a horse available.

I was told to go back and look over all of the horses and let them know which one I would like to have. Mr. John Ringling had brought me there himself, and he intended to feature me.

Of course, word of this soon got around and I was about as popular as the seven-year itch. I did not blame the girls at all: I wanted so much to make friends, and this was sure not the way to start. I just would not even look at someone else's horse.

A couple of days later, not knowing what to do next, I began wandering around the winterquarters. I happened to pass by a corral where a bunch of skinny horses were penned up. I asked one of the hands what the horses were used for and he said that was the "bat pen." They were slated to be fed to the lions. I felt so sorry for them.

As I looked closer, I was sure I recognized one of the horses.

"The big bay over there: Where did he come from?" I asked.

"Oh, he is one of the horses from the Sparks show that they brought in here. He's no good, though; he's an outlaw."

I had heard that Ray Thompson had run into hard times and had sold his stock to the Sparks Circus. I was sure the horse was one of his, and I hoped it was the one I thought it was.

I went to the ring stock boss and asked if I might ride that horse. He didn't care one way or the other. So I had a groom saddle him up and, sure enough, though he looked like a plug, he was the same old Kentucky Man.

Now, unless you had ridden for Ray Thompson, or some other bit-and-spur man who used the same method, it was a pretty sure guess you would not be able to ride one of his horses.

I didn't ride him very hard the first day, nor did I try to work him. When I came back, I told the groom to put him in a box stall, feed him well, and try to get him brushed and looking like something.

From then on, I took Kentucky Man out on a back road, where no one was about, and gave him a workout every day. After a week or so, I was again called to the office, and this time seated at the desk was Mr. John Ringling. He was heavyset, thick-jowled, and, for some unknown reason, reminded me of an English bulldog I had once had as a little girl. Mr. Ringling was not smiling.

"My, my, if it isn't the young lady who falls off of

all the horses," he said, recalling the first time we had met.

"Not quite, sir; most of the time I get thrown off."

"Well, now, what is this I hear about you riding a horse taken out of the bat pen? Are you trying to be funny? I know you want to go back to the John Robinson show, but you are not going."

"Look, Mr. Ringling, I am not being funny and I do need a job. If you will have someone come down to the ring barn, I would like to have him look at something."

A short time later, he and Pat Valdo, along with several other men whom I had not yet met, came to the barn.

Kentucky Man, when ridden right, was one of the best high-school horses in this country, and he worked his heart out for me. Besides the regular routine, he did the swinging piaffe, rock the forehand, and a beautiful high trot. In fact, he did about everything. They were well pleased.

"One more thing, now," said Mr. Ringling, "you are going to have to get with one of our trainers and have him find a horse for you on which to do the waltz and rear. I believe Tex Elmlund is the one for you to see."

"Don't worry about that," I answered, my confidence restored. "As soon as Kentucky Man gets his strength back, he will do that also." (The first pictures I had taken on the Ringling show were with that horse.)

Now that I had a horse of my own and time on my hands, I again started to wander about the winterquarters. In those days the show was so big and carried so much stock it had trainers for all of the different types of horses.

Doc Webber was in charge of the jumping horses. After watching him and his girl riders practice them for a few days, I asked him if I might ride one of them. He said I would have to get permission from the office.

◡

Ringling-Barnum Zebras

It never occurred to me that they would not say to go right ahead; but, when I asked, they told me they did not want me to get hurt. After all of the jumpers I had ridden, I had an idea I was pretty good. However, there had not been a jumping horse number on the John Robinson show, so they had no way of knowing.

"We do have something else in mind for you, though," said Pat Valdo. "We know that you work liberty horses. You worked one of Rudynoff's acts."

"I sure did." Me and my big mouth!

"We have decided that you will work the zebra liberty act."

(They wouldn't let me ride jumps because they thought I might get hurt, so they put me in with a bunch of zebras. This just goes to show how little the front office knows about what goes on backstage—or, ought I say "backyard.") Since this was somebody's last-minute idea, there was very little time to rehearse.

When we got to Madison Square Garden in New York City, I found that the three liberty horse acts were to work in the rings, with a pony act on one stage and the zebra act on the other. The rings and the track were dirt, but the stages were covered with canvas.

The liberty horse trainers wore tuxedos and the lady handlers dressed in evening gowns for the pony and zebra acts. This also called for high-heeled shoes. The canvas was slippery, and it was difficult to keep your footing.

During the rehearsal I had all kinds of problems. When the zebras got to running around the ring they all looked alike to me, so for the opening show I had a bright idea. I bought a calendar with large numbers and, before we went in, I had the horse trainer line them up and I pasted the numbers on their harnesses. That show they worked fine; the next show—utter chaos.

When the act was over, I went down to the basement where the zebras were kept and asked one of the grooms, "Are you sure you had the right harnesses on those zebras?"

He replied, "Listen, lady, we can't tell them apart either."

In case you think I might have been overreacting, it was necessary to put muzzles on them, otherwise they would get into a fight and be at each other's throats. There were times when the grooms did not get the muzzles on the zebras right and they would come off. Disaster! I often wonder now why they ever kept the act in. It was not worked like a conventional liberty act; instead, you used a bull whip to keep them going, and a gaff to keep them away from you.

For this number I wore a black evening gown with rhinestone straps over the shoulder and a very low bare back and, since in those days we did not have strapless bras, nothing underneath except my panties. There came a day about the middle of the second week when a couple of zebras came into the ring without their muzzles. They got into a big battle and I stepped in to try to break it up. One of them reared up and put his hoof down the front of my dress and ripped it down to my waist.

I dropped my whips and ran back to the dressing room, leaving them to settle their differences in whatever fashion they saw fit.

Somehow I managed to work them all that season, but when it came time to sign up again I was ready to say, "No way!"

By that time a great many things had happened, and working an act of that nature was no longer required.

◡

Ringling-Barnum Jumps

While still in winterquarters, as soon as I saw that Kentucky Man had gained strength, I switched him over from astride to sidesaddle so I could also use him for the waltz and rear. On the Ringling show the riders all furnished their own wardrobe. Everyone wore whatever struck her fancy. I had very little money, so riding habits were out of the question. Why not evening gowns?

After arriving in New York City and getting settled in a hotel, I went to Macy's to shop. I had heard a lot about this store, but it was bigger and busier than I had ever dreamed a place could be.

Macy's had a bargain basement where you could find most anything at very low prices. I found several evening gowns with really full skirts that would do for riding sidesaddle.

I cannot deny that I was very bitter and resentful. I had so wanted to be friends with the other girls, but I just was not accepted. I made up for it by showing off. In the manege act I tried to steal the act at every show. Of course, this just made matters worse.

We went from New York to the Boston Garden. During the New York engagement, first one and then another of the jumping horse riders had been injured. By the time we reached Boston, only three riders were left in the number. Let me explain here that in the Garden they have dirt hauled in, pack it down on the cement, and it is quite dangerous when it starts to loosen up and wear through. Now, three riders were not quite enough to make a display.

I was told to report to the office, that one of the bosses, George Smith, wished to see me. It seems that every time I saw him he was chewing on a cigar, but I don't recall ever seeing him light it.

"I understand that a while back you asked to be in

the jumping horse number. Would you care to go in now? Just for a few days, that is."

Certainly, each of the horse trainers was anxious for his presentations to be a success. Tex Elmlund was in charge of all the liberty horse acts; Doc Webber had the jumping horses, but several were involved with the manege and high school horses. Frank Asher was the trainer of the manege horses, and in charge of all their riders. Tex Elmlund was also the boss over the high-school horses from the Schumann Circus, which had come over from Europe; and Frank Miller had three high-school horses of his own.

No one seemed to be in charge of Kentucky Man and me.

After my conversation with George Smith, I went to see Doc Webber, the jumping horse man.

"Mr. Webber, I am here to ride one of your horses."

He was in a very ugly mood. "Look, just one more rider going over a hurdle is not going to add much to this number," he said. "Now, if I only had someone to ride Rover over the broad jump, that might help. He will take a broad jump over five hurdles, but he usually loses his rider. He is very hard to sit."

"What if I were to ride him sidesaddle? I have quite a grip from riding waltzing and rearing horses."

"Well, we can give it a try."

Everything worked out great; the horse was a wonderful jumper. It was just that the broad jump was so long that it was hard for a rider to grip for that distance, but, with riding sidesaddle, it was okay.

I bought a red hunting coat, a black riding skirt, and a black hat. The number was well received, and when the other riders recovered and they again had a full crew, no one suggested that I stop riding in the number.

Now, at last, I was part of a group and had someone to talk to.

There is always competition in the circus business; everyone likes the sound of applause. Some of the riders would wave their hand in the air as they were going over the jump. I, being strictly horse show where jumping was concerned, rode in a very straight-laced manner. I began to take a lot of ridicule from the other riders about it. So, one day when I had had enough, I said, "What is so great with all of your styling? Why, I could go over a jump with both hands in the air, if I wanted to."

They bet me I could not do it. So, the next show, when it came my turn to finish the act with the broad jump, I threw both hands in the air, dropped the reins, and Rover was on his own. Doc Webber and Pat Valdo were both right behind me as I headed for the dressing room.

"What are you trying to do," yelled Pat, "break your neck?"

"Of course not, I just won a bet. Why, I could ride a horse over a hurdle blindfolded."

"Well, you better not try it," snapped Pat.

So that night I did just that. The audience gasped, and I was so thrilled at the impression I was making that I pulled the blindfold off, vaulted to the ground, and took a bow. The rest is circus history.

Ringling-Barnum on the Road

A great deal had happened in a very short time. I was now getting a special announcement for my reinless blindfold jump. The indoor engagements were over, and we were now going on the road.

When I arrived at the circus train, I found that I had been given a section in the single girls' car. Quite a few stories have been written about car 89, and I am sure there could have been a great many more, what with the number of young ladies who, at one time or another, re-sided there.

We had a woman porter named Helen who re-minded me of Patsy Kelly, only heavier. She was like a mother hen with a few too many chicks. She babied us and spoiled us, but could be as hard as nails when the occasion arose.

There was a certain set of rules that had to be followed. The main one was being in by a set time. If one showed up after the door was locked for the night, she had better have a darn good excuse for being late—and Helen had the only key.

She kept law and order, and she did it well. The washroom was at one end of the car with only three washbasins and three mirrors, and it was up to her to see that all shared them equally.

In the morning she would serve us coffee and rolls or doughnuts in bed, and at night she would have some sort of snack and cold drinks waiting for us. She had only a two-burner portable stove, and how she managed it, I have no idea. At the end of each week, on payday, she would give us our bill and, when we paid it, we would all give her a tip.

She listened to all of our troubles and gave us advice, though no one ever seemed to take it. Still, we had someone to turn to. The girls all loved her, and we tried to make her job a little easier by making up our own berths and keeping things tidy.

My section was next to that of Helen Kreis, and we became good friends. She later married the famous Karl Wallenda and became top mounter in the high-wire act.

When I reached the circus grounds for the first day under canvas, I did not know what to expect, but certainly nothing like what I saw. Today's generation could not even picture what it was like; I am glad that I was there and a part of it. There were so many tents—forty-one in all, large and small—you could not help but wonder what they were all for. The menagerie tent was as large as the average circus tent today. They had their own blacksmith shop and a harness maker. It took three women to care for the wardrobe used in the production numbers and specs. The doctor and nurse had a tent, and some of the acts had private tents. There were dressing room tents for the men and women, a huge sideshow tent, along with tents for the horses and ponies.

The dining department had three tents, plus the wagons where they did the cooking. They served three full meals a day. The meals were comparable to those served at a leading hotel. They even baked their own pies and cakes. The dining tent was divided into two parts, one side for the workingmen and the other for the performers. How in the world could they ever manage to move this thing? I found out later: The show moved in four sections.

The first section carried the cookhouse and dining room equipment, the draft-horse tent, the menagerie, and the sleepers for this part of the crew. As soon as it was loaded on the train and flats, it was on its way to the next town. It was called, aptly enough, "The Flying Squadron."

The second section carried the big top, the props, and also the sideshow on flat cars. There were sleepers for the workingmen, and horse cars for the draft horses that helped load and unload the train.

The third section was all sleeping cars, and carried the sideshow personnel and some of the staff who needed to be in town early in the morning.

In the fourth section were the performers and all of the performing animals and their keepers. In all, the train carried 1,600 people and some 1,000 animals.

I had thought the Garden was big, but here you could hardly see from one end of the tent to the other. I counted seven rings and stages, and usually something was going on in all seven at the same time. How on earth could I ever manage to do the waltz and rear around this track?

I found the dressing room and my trunks. I was

delighted to discover that I had been placed across the aisle from the Reiffenach family, bareback riders; on one side of me was Marie Maximo, wife of the well-known comedy slack-wire walker, and on the other side, Vera Bruce of the Alfredo Codona flying act.

The Reiffenach family members were all wonderful to me. How I would have gotten by without them, I'll never know. Mama Reiffenach took me under her wing and ordered me about, the same as she did her daughters. She taught me how to pack my wardrobe properly and how important it was that everything be put right back in its place as soon as you were finished with it.

One by one I started making friends with the other riders. It began with them asking questions. When they found that I was more than willing to help them with their horses by offering suggestions, they accepted me as one of them.

Of all the girls, I liked little Ann Pickle best, and we soon became pals. She was small and very dainty, with a winsome smile, quite clothes-conscious, something I was not. I loved pretty wardrobe for my acts, but as far as street clothes were concerned, I was inclined to be careless. Way ahead of my time, I would have been happy to wear blue jeans back and forth to the lot, which, in those days, you would not have dared to do.

Ann saw to it that I bought the proper clothes, and she taught me how to shop and get the most for my money. Before long, I found it was important to dress well at all times. It did matter.

About mid-season we arrived in Chicago, where we played on the lakefront in Grant Park. It was here that the management sent for Harry Atwell, the action photographer, to take pictures of Rover and me going over the hurdle. Everything was set up outside the tent on a grassy part of the lot. He took quite a few shots, but none of them were any good. The broad jump did not photograph well, and neither did I. I had worn my black and red riding habit.

They said I looked like something out of the Gay Nineties. They were right; I did.

One of the show press agents suggested that I borrow a pair of tights and a leotard from one of the girls in the flying act. I asked Vera Bruce to help me out, and she was quick to oblige.

This time we had Rover take a high jump. Of course, for the photos I did not use the blindfold, as they wanted my face to show. Our press agent, feeling that he was on the right track, requested that some more pictures be taken of me on my rearing horse in the same regalia, so we sent for Kentucky Man.

Three bareback acts were with the show. One was Orrin Davenport. He, together with Eddie Stinson, produced the Shrine indoor shows in Detroit and Cleveland during the winter months. Most of the acts were individually owned, but the big animal presentations were from the American Circus Corporation, now the property of Ringling. They consisted of the elephants, liberty horses, manege horses, and any other animal acts belonging to them.

When Mr. Stinson came to look over the acts, I was one of those he picked to play his dates. He made me an offer, and I accepted. Just before the show closed, Orrin Davenport came around handing out the contracts for the Shrine shows. I called his attention to the fact that his figures and Mr. Stinson's differed, but he said this was what I would receive; I said no more and signed.

Closing day came and I had my ticket to return home, only this time I would not have to sit up all the way there—I had a sleeper. Some of my friends came to the station with me to see me off. Of course, I had been hired for the following season, so it was not "good-bye"—just "so long for now."

♘

Scottsburg, Indiana

*A*fter arriving at Mother's home and resting for a few days, I told her I would take her back to Indiana to visit her aunt again. After I got her settled, I went house hunting. I found what I thought might be to her liking and then showed it to her; it was just what she wanted. I made the down payment on the little farm for her. It was not so little at that, thirty-six acres, but farms at that time were usually quite large. We went back to Cincinnati and arranged for a truck to take all of her things to Scottsburg, and then we drove back.

It was primitive: We bought kerosene lamps and a lantern, and an oil-burning stove to cook on. There was running water in the house, but you had to pump a handle to make it do so; this gadget was mounted on the kitchen sink. The toilet was in a separate building and was called an outhouse. On the circus, the toilets are in separate tents and they are called donnikers—I never found out why.

We had fun playing at being farmers; I bought some chickens, a German shepherd puppy, and, of all things, a cow. Mother thought it would be great to have all of the butter and cream we could use. The folks thereabouts were very helpful, and a farmer sold me a really gentle cow. When he delivered her he brought along a small calf—hers! I had not bargained for that, but he said it went with her.

Next morning, bright and early, my mother sent me out to get some milk for breakfast. The cow was in the pasture, and I had a pail, but she would not stand still long enough for me to set it under her. Then I took a teacup and followed her around for quite some time, but she would not cooperate. I drove to the farmer's house and he came back to the house with me.

"First, you put some feed in the manger, then you get on the right side to milk her." (I was used to mounting a horse from the left side.) "But, before that," he continued, "you let the calf nurse for a while so she lets her milk down, then you tie the calf up until you finish milking, then let him back with her again. After he is through nursing, you then separate them until time for the next milking. Thought you knew a little something about critters, or I would have told you right off."

It was fine to have all the butter and cream we could use, but there was so much buttermilk we did not know what to do with it—so I bought a little pig. He had an idea he was a dog and became quite a pet. The calf and I got along quite well at first, but as he got bigger and stronger he became quite a handful.

However, about this time I was ready to leave for the indoor shows. I let the land out to a farmer on shares and hired a girl to come by and help Mother a few hours each day. The girl had been raised on a farm and knew just what to do.

♀

Indoor Shows

The first indoor show was the Shrine Circus in Detroit. They laid out the high-school horse number the same as it had been presented on the Ringling show. Ella Bradna had her "Act Beautiful" in the center ring, two riders were in each end ring, and the rest of us were working on the track.

Ella's act consisted of one horse pulling a large cart and another horse standing in the back of it with huge, white wings suspended from its back—Pegasus. Ella rode in the front seat with the driver, and six ballet girls, each leading a big white dog, walked on either side. Ella would alight and mount the horse, from whom the wings had now been removed. She would then go through the manege act in unison with the rest of the riders. At the end of her act, while her horse was lying down, assistants would let loose a flock of pigeons that had been dyed various colors, and they would fly to her, landing on an umbrella she carried and had now opened.

After she left the arena, we would proceed with the specialty horses, and I would finish the number with the waltz and rear.

Mr. Stinson and Orrin Davenport called me out of the dressing room after the first show was over.

"Dorothy," said Mr. Stinson, "from now on, during this engagement, you will be in the center ring. Set the routine you will be using; get together with the horse trainer so he can instruct the rest of the riders and also the band leader."

"But, what about Mrs. Bradna?" I asked.

"We will continue to pay her her salary for the rest of the dates, and we are sure she will understand. After all, we have used her act for several years and we need something different."

I wasn't so sure about how she would take it. I felt awful.

Then, too, Fred Bradna was the equestrian director with the Ringling show, and I was worried about his feelings. When I told him, he had already been informed.

"That is show business, kid; it happens all the time. Ella held down the center ring with that number for a very long time. We will let her continue to ride her horse in one of the end rings, and everything will work out just fine." If Ella was upset she never showed it, and later on we were to become the best of friends.

At the end of the week we lined up outside Mr. Stinson's office to get paid. I was very worried. I had received a phone call from Mother; she was in need of more money than I was going to be able to send her, what with my hotel bill and all.

As I picked up my check, I turned to Mr. Stinson and said, "I sure wish I had signed up with you instead of Mr. Davenport."

As I started out the door, Mr. Stinson called me back. "Let me see that check." He turned to Mr. Davenport, who was seated beside him. "Orrin," he said, "I offered this girl twice the amount of this check, and you must admit she is worth it."

Orrin laughed and said, "We try to get them as cheaply as we can."

I was given another check for the original amount agreed upon. To say it was welcome is putting it mildly.

Then, during the second week of the indoor shows, Pat Valdo called me from Florida. "Dorothy, I don't know how to break this to you, but Rover is dead. No one seems to know what happened; they just found him dead in his stall. The trainers here tell me that we have no horse that can replace him. Have you any suggestions?"

U

Satan

I recalled that when I had been in winterquarters I had watched the trainer trying to replace a horse in his liberty act. The horse he was working with gave him nothing but trouble. At one point he jumped out of the ring barn window and over the fence before running back to the stables.

The trainer finally gave up on him and had him put back in the pasture. He was a beautiful, long-legged black and he held his head high. (I will explain why this is so important later on.) If he was still there, he was the horse I wanted.

Pat called me the next night and said that the horse was still there, but Doc Webber was no longer with the show, and the man who was replacing him as the jumping horse trainer did not think much of the horse. He was disinclined to waste time on a horse that he felt would not work out, let alone maybe having a rider hurt in the process. I had not yet met the new man and, while I understood he was a fine trainer, I had something quite different in mind.

"Mr. Valdo, I do not want the new man to train the horse. I want Tex Elmlund to break him for me." Tex was in charge of the liberty horses and three school horses and had nothing to do with the jumpers.

"Dorothy, this is unheard of."

"Never mind. Have Tex call me tonight after our show, and I will tell him just what I would like for him to do."

When Tex called, I told him I wanted him to break the horse to come to him when he whistled, using the lash whip and getting a little farther away all the time; then start putting him over the hurdle at liberty.

"Don't let anyone ride him!" I told him.

As soon as the last show was over in Cleveland, I took the train to Sarasota.

Tex was flattered that I wanted him to work on my jumping horse and must have spent a great deal of time on him.

Satan! I thrilled when I saw him; black as coal was he, and someone had sure been grooming him—he shone. Tex showed me how he had him taking the jump at liberty and, sure enough, he jumped freely and willingly, with his head held high. I had a groom put my saddle on him, and he did not like it one bit. He kicked and bucked and reared and snorted, but after a while he calmed down, and we put him over the hurdle. This time when Tex called him to come to him, it was I who gave him his treat first. While his attention was on the food, Tex held his head, and my groom gave me a foot up. I quickly wrapped my leg around the horn and put my foot in the stirrup, and none too soon; he really let loose. He bucked and pitched, but did not offer to rear. I called to Tex to help me to get him running. Tex cracked the lash whip, and Satan took off. I ran him until he settled down to a nice easy lope, and then slowly pulled him to a stop, talking to him all the time.

The bar was on the very lowest pegs the first time I took him over the hurdle. I used the reins as little as I dared, yet still be able to guide him. Tex stood at his accustomed place by the side of the hurdle. I nodded, and when he whistled, Satan took off like a shot. He made no attempt in that open field to go anywhere but over the jump, and I just held the reins limp in my hands with no cue whatsoever.

I knew then that we had it made. Now, it was only a matter of getting him to go higher and higher, and that he did. It did not occur to me at the time, but looking back I believe Satan must have been one of the greatest jumping horses that ever lived. For seven years in a row he jumped more than six feet, twice a day. In order to make the jump more sensational, we added fire to the top bar. The hurdle was six feet, so in order to clear it, he had to go a little higher than that.

Unknown to us, the bosses were keeping a close watch on our activities. They sent for me to report to the office, and when I arrived, Charlie Cannely, their head designer, handed me a sketch. The girl in the picture was wearing a leotard of gold; on her head she had a red spangled cap; on her feet, red shoes; and from her shoulders were long, flowing chiffon drapes of yellow, orange, and red, bespattered all over with shimmering spangles—depicting flames. Instead of telling him how beautiful I thought it was, I flew into a rage.

"I will not wear such a thing on a horse," I cried. "Why, I would as soon go out naked!"

"But, Dorothy," said Charlie, "you did not demur

when we had those photos taken of you in Chicago. Why now?"

"That was different. After looking at the first pictures taken in my red jacket and long, black skirt, anyone would know that they would not do for publicity. But to ride a jumping horse in a show in such regalia is out of the question. I can just hear people saying, 'Where is the net? She thinks she's in a flying act!'"

Charlie merely shrugged his shoulders. Designing was his job, not arguing with dizzy dames.

We always spent several days in Madison Square Garden in rehearsal. When it came time to lay out the high-school number, I found that the show had so liked the way it looked on the indoor shows that they wanted it the same way. That meant I was to have center ring.

As I mentioned before, at that time everybody furnished their own wardrobe, except for the specs and production numbers. The first year after I joined the show, I had a couple of outfits that I had worn on the John Robinson show, and I had bought several evening gowns in Macy's basement in New York. But, if I were to be featured in the center ring, I felt something flashier was in order.

Con Colleano, the great wire artist, wore the most dazzling costumes of anyone I knew. I went to his wife, and she told me she would go with me to Con's costumer in New York, but she doubted if they could get an outfit ready in time for the opening.

They did though, and it was beautiful beyond my dreams. It was a deep pink top covered in rhinestones; a long circular skirt of ostrich feathers, ranging from light pink to deepest rose; and a headdress of variegated feathers to match. It was out of this world—and so was the price: several weeks' salary for one costume.

When Tex learned that I was to be in the center ring, he insisted that I ride his horse Ottoman for part of the number. Ottoman was a lovely gray, which had come with him when he had been brought over from Europe by

Schumann. At one point, the rider was on foot, and he or she and the horse danced down the track together—rock the forehand on foot. Tex thought it would be more effective for a lady to dance with the horse. Of course, I continued to use Kentucky Man for the specialties and the waltz and rear.

Opening night went off very well until time for the jumps, which were next to the closing number in the show. My costume for this number had arrived in all its glory, and I had had several days to boil over it. Instead of being grateful that the show was furnishing it, I was angry at the thought of wearing it.

The jumping horse number was under the direction of Carlos Carron, with the exception of Satan and me; Tex Elmlund was working with us. This year the show was furnishing the wardrobe for the number. The riders were attired in bright red hunt coats with black lapels, white pants, black riding boots, and black caps. They looked nifty. Maybe I was supposed to be the fox!

Now, don't ask me why I did what I did—I have no idea what I had in mind at the time. Nevertheless, I had gone to Brooks Costumers and rented a long, blonde wig. I bought a flesh-colored leotard, and I sewed gold leaves on it, at points where I thought they would do the most good. Over this I wore my long, black velvet cape, which completely covered me. We had to sit in the back entryway until time for the number and, as it was very cold there, no one thought anything about me being all bundled up.

When the other riders had completed their jumps, my announcement came. The flames were lit, I dropped my cape, and Satan and I dashed out. I heard quite a few gasps from the audience, and immediately after the act, without waiting to take a bow, I ran to my dressing room—at this point I rated a private one. Pat Valdo, Tex Elmlund, and several men whom I did not know, were not far behind me. I had locked the door, and now I refused to open it. I was scared.

George Smith, the assistant manager, assured me that I was in no immediate danger, so I opened the door and let everyone see that I did, indeed, have some clothes on. They then told me that, with the lights, the long, flowing wig, and the speed at which we had been going, it looked as if Lady Godiva had returned.

I think the only thing that saved me that time was the fact that the newspapers made a big to-do about it, and the show welcomed the free publicity. Anyway, Satan's debut didn't go unnoticed. I was to recall this event at a later date when I was, again, in such a situation.

Needless to say, I returned the rented wig the next day and was happy to wear the outfit they had ordered for me. Incidentally, the costume turned out to be very appropriate for the fire jump.

Many things were to happen to me that season. When I had joined the show the previous season, I had been assigned a section; now I was to have a stateroom. I was seated not at the star table, but at the staff table in the dining tent. It was suggested that I have a private wagon in which to dress, but I would have none of that. I wished to be in the dressing tent with all of my friends.

At this point, I would like to explain why all of this attention was lavished on me. I was good copy. Most of the performers were imported from different countries and spoke little, if any, English. I liked to entertain the press and would go out of my way to see that they got all of the pictures they wished, not only of me, but of the other acts as well. It made a good impression when I would invite someone from the press to lunch or dinner and we dined at the same table with the bosses.

This brings to mind a certain incident that had happened early in the season. The place was New York City; the time, a week after our opening there. It was at a party given for some of the stars on the show, and although I did not figure I had yet attained that status, I had been invited to attend the dinner.

Mr. John Ringling was seated at the head of the table. I was somewhere far down the line. Drinks were being offered before the meal. Mr. Ringling was in poor health at this time and always had a nurse by his side. He turned and said something to her, and she arose and came down to where I was seated.

"Miss Herbert, Mr. Ringling wishes to speak with you," she said. I managed to jump to my feet without turning over the table. I sort of side-passed down the aisle, well aware that all eyes were upon me and, for once, I did not welcome the attention.

When I arrived at my destination, Mr. Ringling told me to sit down in the seat that had been vacated by his nurse. He held out his glass and offered me a drink of what I learned a long time later was scotch and soda. I thanked him and said, "Sorry, sir, but I do not drink."

He replied, "No one refuses to drink with John Ringling."

At that, I grabbed the glass and took a good, long drink of the stuff and I came up choking.

"Now," continued Mr. Ringling, "you have had your first drink, and what I hope will be your last during the time that you are with my show. It is obvious that you are ambitious, and I will help you to become a star. There are three things from which I shall ask you to abstain: liquor, cigarettes, and men. The first two can ruin your health; the third, your reputation. The last will be the hardest to cope with. You are quite an attractive young lady and there will be propositions, and some may be tempting. Never get the idea that you always have to be nice to someone in order to get ahead; that is the surest way there is to lose everyone's respect, including a man's. Now, eat your dinner."

Mr. Ringling then turned his attention to the others seated around him.

It was as though I was in a trance. I had been taught how to act at the dinner table, but now I felt as though I ought to be seated in a high chair with a bib around my neck.

The first course was raw oysters on the half shell, which I had never had the displeasure of coming in contact with before. Not wishing to draw more attention to myself, I devised a method whereby I could get rid of the slimy things without actually chewing them. I accomplished this by filling my mouth with crackers and then swallowing the thing whole. There were six of them in all. I could not tell you, if my life depended on it, what the rest of that dinner consisted of, but the oysters and John Ringling, I never forgot.

If he had lived a little longer, I am certain my story would have been quite different.

∪

Stunts

No one else was doing the reinless jump, to be sure, but riders on other shows were doing the waltz and rear. I wanted my act to be more sensational than anyone else's, so I dreamed up the idea of throwing one leg in the air while my horse was rearing.

"No one else has ever done it," I explained to Tex.

"I don't think you should, either," said Tex. Nonetheless, he agreed to help me.

Now, I am not going to say that it was easy—no one has ever done it since. Other than the ride of Mazeppa, it was the hardest trick I ever learned to do, and I took more spills trying it than anything I ever attempted.

The first thing you have to do is learn to lift one leg from the saddle horn at the same time the horse is going into the rear, and bring your leg back down as he also comes down. Again, the most important thing is timing; otherwise, you will go on over and land on the ground, as I did quite a few times before I got the hang of it. Balance plays a big part in all of this type of riding. Later on I was able to do a full-body layback and throw my leg in the air.

When taking the high jump sidesaddle, I was able to lean forward in the saddle so that the horse felt little of my weight. This was true of the regular jumps. In the ride of Mazeppa, with my body dragging over the side of the horse, he was carrying all dead weight.

U

Danny Dee

It was now my third season with the Ringling Bros. circus. The show had hired a new announcer, Danny Dee. He was formerly of the "Did You Know?" radio show, which dealt with little-known facts. He was peculiar, and the circus public relations staff felt that he would be a big asset, not only announcing but, especially, handling the radio publicity.

For some reason, he singled me out, perhaps because so few of the performers spoke English; nevertheless, he asked me to appear with him on his radio broadcasts. I liked the challenge of something new, even though it meant getting up earlier in the morning.

Danny worked out a radio program where he would ask me the questions, rather than the studio announcer, and this put me at ease. We had made quite a few broadcasts by the time we reached Boston, and the same old questions and answers had become boring.

No one had ever told me that I was not adapted to writing, so I decided to write a play. Danny was used to innovations, so he did not veto the idea. For my subject I chose the love affair of Fred and Ella Bradna. Ella had told me all about how she had met her husband, Fred. I liked the story, so this was to be my first radio drama.

It seems that this lovely, young bareback rider was performing in a circus in France. Every night a certain handsome cavalry officer would occupy the same box, and every day she would receive a bouquet from him, but he never got up the nerve to sign his name, nor would she have known who he was if he had. One night, as she was standing on the back of her horse, he stumbled and fell, and she was thrown over the railing and into the seats. The handsome cavalry officer picked her up in his arms and went with her to the hospital. This was how Ella and Fred met.

After she recovered from her fall and went back to work, Fred continued to see her and to wine and dine her every night after the show. They fell madly in love.

Ella and her partner in the bareback act were booked to go to America to join the Barnum & Bailey Circus. Before they left, Fred and Ella were married. In order to be with her, Fred gave up his commission and, as soon as he obtained his release, sailed to America to join her.

When the directors of the Barnum & Bailey Circus discovered that he spoke seven different languages, they offered him the job of interpreter, which he accepted. Since so many of the acts were importations, his was an important position. Before long, he was made equestrian director. At the time, on a show that large that job did not include the announcing. He blew the whistle for the acts to start and stop, and saw to it that they all finished at the same time.

But, back to the love story of Fred and Ella Bradna. I put the story into a radio script; very dramatic. In the story, when she comes to in the hospital after the accident, Fred is right there by her side.

Now for the players: Danny took the part of Fred, and I played Ella; the catcher from one of the flying acts, who had studied drama, was the doctor; our prima donna, who had a lovely speaking voice, took the part of the nurse. We rehearsed for several days between shows.

We were playing in the Boston Garden when we first aired our little drama. It was cold and snowing hard, and we were laughing and joking as we climbed into the warm taxi. Even with the windshield wipers going full blast, it was possible to see only a short distance ahead. We were not far from the radio station when our cab was hit by a huge truck. I was seated next to Danny, and he must have seen the truck coming, for he pushed me to the floor of the cab just as we collided.

I was not hurt, but we were all rushed to the hospital. While the others were getting patched up, knowing that a great many of the show people were intending to tune into our program and that the radio station would be anxious when we did not show up, I went to a phone. I called the station to tell what had happened and say that we would not be able to make it. The man I talked to was very concerned and he told me that if it was possible for us to make it at a later hour, the station would hold for us and put us on anytime we could make it. Of course, the station broadcast that we had been in an accident but would endeavor to get there as soon as possible.

Recalling this incident now, I can better understand the concern of our bosses for their prima donna, their announcer, the catcher from the Concello flying act, and a kookie blonde (me) who was featured in three numbers.

When we arrived at the radio station (thank goodness it was not TV), both men had their heads bandaged and blood all over their shirts. When it came time for the big love scene, Danny looked so silly I had all I could do to keep from laughing. The play went well, and the radio staff was kindness itself.

Fred Bradna's real name was Frederick Ferber; he changed it to Bradna after coming to the States. He looked every inch the officer, the height of dignity with a tiny, well-groomed black mustache. Danny looked like one of the East Side Kids who had been in a street fight.

When we got back to the Garden, we were met not only by our bosses but newsmen and some lawyers as well. The lawyers were from the truck company's insurance agency. Word had sure gotten around fast about the accident. The newspapers latched onto it, and there was quite a bit of publicity. The powers that be in the front office were well pleased with the play and we used it in other towns, but never again to this kind of reception.

Danny asked me to write more plays using stories about other performers on the show. Some were good and others were bad, but the directors of the radio stations liked the idea. It was different from the regular interviews.

Before the season had ended, Danny received an offer from his old boss in New York, and while he had enjoyed his experience with the circus, he felt it was too good a job to turn down. I had liked working with him—when he left, I figured that was the end of my radio career. However, when the show opened the next season, I discovered that not only was I expected to continue with the radio show, but I was to go it alone. From that time on, whichever show I was with, this was considered part of my job. Later on, when TV advertising became the rage, this was also included.

∪

Our Club

We had a lot of free time between shows, and some of us would spend it playing bridge. Just before the night show, one of us would go out and bring back coffee. In the morning, if a bakery were anywhere close to the radio station, I would pick up a cake or some cookies so we could have a snack before dressing for the last performance. In the backyard was a stand where we could buy coffee, milk, or cold drinks.

The third year on the road, after we were back under canvas, some of us girls formed a club. Our dues paid our expenses for the refreshments.

The circus lots were almost always a long way from the town. The railroad cars were usually much closer, so the performers would go directly there from the train.

It was difficult for people, unless they made a special trip by taxi, to pick up any small thing they might need. I got into the habit of making out a list of the things the club members wanted and, if it was possible, I would pick up the items for them after the broadcast. Because this service was for club members, I hit upon an idea: Why not have the members run a little store? We would sell the items for a few cents over our cost and put the extra money in the kitty.

We got together and made out a list of the things we most often ran out of: soap, towels, Kleenex, and the like. Because we would have to carry all of this stuff in our personal trunks, we agreed that each member would stock and sell different items. Soon we added cigarettes, candy bars, and gum. The rest of the girls in the dressing room were quite enthused over the idea of our little store and asked us to include a personal shopping service, with a fee of five or ten cents. Danny Dee may have thought this entailed a lot of extra running around town in the morning, but he never said anything and cheerfully helped me carry the packages. This might sound like a lot of extra work, but actually it was fun.

Our club made money, and near the end of the season, about a week before we were to close, we would rent a dining room in the leading hotel in the town in which we would be playing, and arrange a banquet for all of the members. Each girl could bring either her husband or a friend as her guest. A local band would be hired, and after dinner there would be dancing.

Several times during the season we also had little parties in the big top, between shows. On the Fourth of July, we would invite everyone on the show to attend, and we would put on entertainment and serve refreshments.

The first year we were the Pirates Club. In all of the following years we called ourselves the Manege Club.

Johnny

or quite a few years the jumping horse act was the next to closing number in the show; the closing act was Hugo Zacchini's cannon. The other girls who rode jumping horses could partly undress and get away from the lot quickly, but with the type of wardrobe I was wearing, it was another thing. I had to strip completely and then dress in my street clothes.

Later, the show had a personnel bus to take us to the train, but at that time it was a mad scramble to get to a taxi. We tried to share the cabs, but as soon as they were full, the driver being anxious to get back for another load of passengers, often left, leaving me behind. By the time one got back to pick me up, I would sometimes be the only one there.

Upon arriving at the railroad yards, quite often you would find that you had a long walk down the tracks to the coaches. One dark night, while walking alone, I was accosted and my purse taken. I was not harmed, but my bosses thought that I ought to have some protection. Pat Valdo assigned Johnny Grady, who worked with Pat's wife, Laura, in a boomerang act and also clowned in the show, to be my guardian. He could not have made a better choice. Johnny became my shadow, always there.

I fell in love with him and, I think, he with me. However, this was not to be. Johnny, who was honesty itself, told me from the first that he was married to a girl in Boston. He asked me not to mention this to anyone, and I never did. He never said why, and I never asked.

Johnny was big, broad-shouldered, and proud of the fact that he was Irish. Instead of Dorothy, he always called me Buddy, and buddies we were. Everyone took it for granted that we were going steady, and we let them think so. This had many advantages for me, one being that it discouraged others from trying to date me, and I liked that, because I was so tied up in my work I didn't wish for outside involvements. This arrangement continued all of the time that I was with the show.

∪

Scottsburg

It was the end of my third season with the Ringling Bros. and Barnum & Bailey circus. When the show closed that fall and I went home to Scottsburg, I was very happy to discover that my father was there for a visit. I was hoping that Mother and Dad who, through all the years had had their separations and reunions, could get back together for good.

Dad, who had been raised on a farm, was enthused about our little place and saw all sorts of improvements he could make on it. He also liked the town and the people he had met there. He said he would enjoy staying there, if only he could find a way to make a living.

Now I must explain that when Mother and I moved

to Scottsburg, we never mentioned the fact that I worked on a circus. Mother felt that the townspeople might not accept show folks as their friends. Without anyone ever saying anything, they just assumed that when I went away I was off attending school, and no one told them any different. This led to some odd situations.

This was before the days of television, of course, and people resorted to all sorts of recreation for amusement. Now that there was a man on the place, we were invited to all of the doings. Socials and square dances were the main source of entertainment. Mother insisted that I attend those functions, and I felt the fool when some farm boy would bid on the box lunch my mother had prepared so that he could share it with me.

I recall one day when three boys on horseback came by, leading an extra horse, to take me riding. They did a lot of showing off: riding backward, vaulting, and one of them even standing up on his horse. When I told Dad about it, he laughed and said, "Wonder how they would feel if they knew what you really do?"

A few days before Christmas, a messenger came with a notice that I had a package at the railway station; we had no phone out there in the country. I drove into town to see what it might be.

In a crate, with a big bow tied on it, was the most beautiful pony I had ever seen—a little bay stallion with a black mane and tail. One of the circus fans had sent him to me as a gift. I named him Barney and spent a lot of time teaching him tricks. He was smart and easy to teach, and became a terrific hind leg pony.

Dad found a restaurant in town that was up for sale, and he thought he could make a success of it if he could get the backing to keep it going until it proved itself, but he was unable to swing it. I offered to go in with him if he would stay, although I wondered how long I would be able to keep it up because I still had to make the payments on the farm. Anyway, we pooled our money, and Dad took over the restaurant. I helped him with it until it was time for me to leave for the indoor shows, or rather I ought to say, to the Peru, Indiana, winterquarters to practice for the indoor shows.

The Ringling show had booked the Shrine Circus, as usual, but it was not sending any stock from Florida; instead they were using animals from the shows that they now owned in Peru.

When I arrived at the ring barn, I was greeted like a long-lost daughter. The Al G. Barnes show and the Hagenbeck-Wallace show each had a waltzing and rearing black stallion. The trainers from both shows pointed out the merits of their horses. I rode them, and they were both good, but I could not make up my mind which one I liked best. They ended up by sending both of them to the indoor dates. Later they realized their mistake.

When Pat Valdo and Sam Gumpertz, who was now the manager of the Ringling show, came to visit, they liked them both so well that they had them shipped to the Sarasota winterquarters after the engagement. Their names were Sir Christopher and Lindy.

◡

The Vaultage Act

I had asked the officials on the show several times if it might be possible to raise my salary, but no luck. Perhaps if I were to come up with another act?

I had heard about this act from people who had seen it in Europe. I went to Mr. Gumpertz and told him about it. He was quite enthused with the idea, as he had also seen the act while abroad. He said he thought it would be a fine feature for the Wild West concert. I gathered up all of the information I could as to how it had been pre-sented, and Tex and I set about to get it broke.

Now, for the benefit of you young riders who, per-chance, may wish to copy this number, I will go into it in detail.

You enter the ring, Roman standing on two horses; they circle the ring and another horse gallops in, going the opposite direction as it comes toward you. The team on which you are standing separates and the third horse goes through. It repeats this maneuver twice, then turns and comes up between the two on which you are standing; once around, and all three come to the center of the ring, and rear. (Let me say, at this point, that the hardest part of this act for me was standing on the three horses while they were rearing.) The extra horse then leaves the ring, and the two upon which you are standing jump over a hurdle of fire. There are two of these hurdles, one on either side of the ring. The horses jump them three times and you leap off to the ground. These two are then led from the ring.

The third horse now returns, this time wearing a surcingle. You do a few cross and side vaults, circle the neck, place your foot in a loop, and do a drag over the side of the horse, ending the act with May Wirth's finishing trick—the vaulting rollover and somersault. My training in trick riding stood me in good stead here.

Tex Elmlund and I worked hard at breaking this number. We used three of the horses from the gray liberty horse act. The harness department made bright red trap-pings with brass studs for the team.

I had one of the Indians who worked in the concert make me a very elaborate headdress. I ordered an Indian dress from a costumer to go with it. Both Tex and I were to receive extra money for the act.

In the Garden, they do not hold an "after show." Certain parts of the concert are included midway in the show. The first three days went great; the act was fast, the public liked it, and we got a warm reception, but the show was running too long. On the fourth day, they cut the time allotted to the concert. We had come to the part of my act where I was jumping the two horses, Roman-standing, over the hurdles of fire. It had not occurred to them that this might distract my team (they were merely trying to save time). Nevertheless, they sent in the trick riders on the hippodrome track. In they dashed with much whooping and hollering. One of my horses jumped the hurdle, the other stopped, and I lit astride the hurdle.

They carried me to a nearby hospital. I was pretty badly burned, and when I returned to the show the number was scrapped, along with my dreams of a raise.

As it so happened, all of that hard work was not for naught, after all. I later re-created the act on a different show and was well rewarded for my efforts.

U

The Tommy Atkins Military Drill

The Ringling Bros. Circus was always looking for something new. While in winterquarters, Tex and I broke Sir Christopher and Lindy to work high-school tandem. Certainly they were both trained to do high school, but it was quite a job to ride one horse and work another on the long lines at the same time.

This was the year of the Tommy Atkins Military Drill. The high-school number had been the same for several years; now it was to have an all-new look. For the first time, the show was going to furnish the wardrobe for this number. All of the girls worked on the track in unison. A smart salute would be our way of styling. They wore red coats, blue pants with a yellow stripe, red and blue hats, and black boots. My outfit for the center ring was white and gold, with the trappings on the horses matching my wardrobe. Very striking.

As usual, something was bound to go wrong for me in Madison Square Garden. The costumes had arrived for the act, and the wardrobe ladies were busy fitting the girls into them; mine was missing. After several phone calls, it arrived, and when I opened the box I found a pleated skirt, but no pants. Anyone who has ever been inclined to wonder what the Scotsmen wear under their kilts ought to ask me.

The skirt did have a bush brush dangling down the front, but this in no way took the place of pants. Fact of the matter, the darn thing kept bouncing up and down on my lap with every movement of the horse, making it impossible to concentrate on what I was trying to do. One of the wardrobe ladies hastily made a pair of underpants for me and I, just as quickly, discarded the brush.

After the first part of the routine, Sir Christopher would be taken from the ring, and I would complete the act riding Lindy. At the climax of this number, after the specialty horses were through, we would all side-pass, first down the back track and then down the front. When we got to the backdoor, my horse and I, which were last, would then dash around the hippodrome track doing the waltz and rear and layback, which now included the one leg in the air.

The first matinee, everything went fine. Then, at the night show, someone got the bright idea that the waltz and rear would look better with the house lights off and just the spotlights on us. Of course, both the horse and I were blinded. When we got to the far end of the track, Lindy took a step backward while he was rearing. One foot went inside the ring curb, he lost his balance, tripped, and fell over backward. I hit my head and was stunned for a moment or two; then I stumbled over to the ring curb, sat down on it, and started to bawl. I thought for sure Lindy had broken his neck. Everyone rushed over and got the

Rodeo days, location unknown. 1929. *Courtesy of the John & Mable Ringling Museum of Art, Tibbals Digital Collection.*

horse back on his feet, and me back on him. The house-lights were back on by now and we finished to a big hand. This usually happens when you take a bad spill, but who needs that.

Satan, as usual, was great; our club was a success; and it was a pleasant season—over much too soon. When the show closed and I got home that fall, I found that my father had left and that Mother had sold both the restaurant and the farm. I had been sending money home each week, but was too involved in my own affairs to know what was happening. Mother had bought a lot in town, if you care to call two acres a "lot." It was a beautiful piece of property. She had contacted her brother, who was a builder in Cincinnati, and he had put up a two-story house, with a full basement, on the property. The money from the sale of the farm and the restaurant had paid to get it started—now all I had to do was keep up the payments on it, plus new furniture bought on credit.

I was frantic.

U

Dramatic School

Some of the executives from the Paramount Studios had an idea that I might do well in motion pictures. They had offered to send me to their dramatic school in New York, but I had been too busy to go.

For some reason, the owners of the Ringling Bros. Circus were not allowing any of their people to play the indoor shows that winter, nor were they sending any of their stock. I contacted the studio officials, and they offered to pay me a salary to cover my expenses while attending the school.

Evelyn Cook was living in New York with her husband, Frank, who was the legal adjuster for the Ringling Bros. Circus. She was the sister of Jack Joyce, who was later to become famous not only as a horse and camel trainer but other animals as well. She and I had become good friends before her marriage to Frank. She, too, had been a rider with the show and, of course, a member of the Manege Club; all of the riders belonged to it. She had retired from the circus to be with her husband, as he did not travel with the show but conducted its legal work from his New York office.

Frank was in poor health, and Evelyn had to be with him most of the time. They had a penthouse apartment atop one of the leading hotels. When Evelyn heard that I was to be in New York, she suggested that I get a room in the same hotel so we could keep each other company. I spent most of my time with her when I was not attending school. They had all of their meals sent up from the dining room, and I usually ate the evening meal with them, after which Frank would retire. Evelyn and I would then either practice my script for the following day or play cards until bedtime.

Somewhere along the line as legal adjuster for the show, Frank had gained custody of a little old man named

Clico, who was billed as "The African Bushman." He was a great sideshow attraction, but a pest to have around. He was quite hard to handle when cooped up with nothing to do. He was very short, dark skinned, and so wrinkled he looked to be a hundred years old.

Evelyn would get me to take him for walks down the avenue, which would not have been so bad (even with people often staring), but he had an awful habit of suddenly running up behind ladies and pinching them, then jumping up and down laughing. Most of the ladies did not find it funny. Neither did I, so I learned to keep a close watch on him. Another annoying habit was his cigars. He smoked almost constantly, and the ones he liked most were black and smelly.

Because there was no television in those days, the only pastimes were reading books or listening to the radio while in your hotel room. I was sending part of my allowance home to Mother, so I did not have anything extra for picture shows.

Every few weeks some of the big shots from the Hollywood studios would visit, and all of us young hopefuls would go through some of our scenes for them. On those occasions when we knew they were coming, Evelyn would insist that I wear one of her fur coats to the studio; she had two, a mink and a leopard. I never forgot the feeling of luxury they gave me when I wore them.

Mother kept writing, urging me to come home, so I finally left New York and went back to Scottsburg. When I got there things were far from compatible. It was obvious that I was going to have to find a job, and I was not adept at too many things.

︶

Show Horses

Shortly after arriving home, I drove over into Kentucky to visit with my friends the Reagans. Naturally, they asked what I was doing, and I told them I would not be playing the indoor shows that winter. We had a nice, long visit, and I returned home.

A few days later a rather heavyset, middle-aged lady pulled into our driveway, got out of her car, came to the door, and introduced herself as Mrs. Anderson from Auston, a small town close by. Then she said, "I understand from our mutual friends in Louisville that you are pretty good with gaited horses. Could I get you to teach me to ride?"

I invited her into the house and explained to her that I did not have any horses, nor did I have a place to keep any if I had.

"There is an empty barn down the road which I am sure could be rented," said she, and then asked a lot of questions. When she left, I thought I had seen the last of her. This happened on a Friday, but the following Tuesday a truck and trailer pulled in, with two outstanding saddle horses, and Mrs. Anderson was in her car right behind them.

"I picked up two," she quipped, "figuring if I couldn't ride one, I could ride the other." She had already made arrangements to rent the barn. When I explained to her that we did not have a proper place to train, she brought in a couple of men and they put up a practice ring on my property. I will say one thing for her—she would not take "no" for an answer.

The trainer where she had bought her horses had made out a list of the things that might be expected of them, so I began to teach her to ride. Word of my new venture soon got around, and before long I had other pupils. She brought some of her friends, and my old friends the

Reagans sent others.

One of the first to join my class was Marion Morgan. Her father owned the Scott County Canning Company, and all of her family members were to become my close friends. I think she originally came because she thought I needed the work, but after a few lessons she was impressed and told others. She was especially interested in jumping horses, so I started a class in this also. Because everyone owned his or her own mount and had the expense of the upkeep, everything that I made was clear. Strangely enough, I was making more money than I did when I was with the circus.

I should have stayed right there, but when they called for me to report I went right back. As the old saying goes, "The circus is in your blood."

Dexter

Because of the monthly note on Mother's house, plus what I was sending her to live on, it was becoming harder and harder to make ends meet. The radio shows—while I did like doing them and meeting all of those interesting people—required a certain amount of decent street clothes. It was plain to see that the people who had their own acts had the advantage.

It was while we were playing in San Antonio, Texas, that I met Jack Sellers. He was later to become known as the palomino king of Texas. He took me out to show me his stables. He was eager at that time for publicity, and wished to get his string of horses noticed. Among his horses was a lovely white stallion. He told me that he had played a little at being a circus trainer and asked if I would care to see the horse work. After he put the horse through all of his routine, I admired the horse and told Mr. Sellers what a nice job I thought he had done in training him.

He then asked, "Would you like to have him for your very own?"

I told him that I could not afford to buy the horse, though it was obvious that it was an outstanding animal. He assured me that all of the publicity he thought he would get from my showing his horse would compensate for the small price at which he intended to sell him to me. He delivered him to the lot the next day.

Now I had something of my own! Every day between shows I worked with him. Dexter Fellows, the show's leading press agent, saw him and remarked, "You know something, I was named after a horse. If you have not named him, I would like it if you were to call him Dexter." So that was how he got his name.

At that time I was using different horses for high school, jumping, and rearing. My horse would have to do it all. In order to get the best out of a dressage horse, you need to ride astride. Kentucky Man was an exception as he worked just as well sidesaddle as astride, but he was never jumped.

My horse would indeed have to be an exceptional mount. He would have to do high school, sidesaddle, the waltz and rear, and jump over the hurdles as well. I had been told by booking agents that if I had stock of my own, they would be able to offer me dates to play during the winter months when the Ringling Bros. show was closed. Tex offered to help me from the ground while I topped the horse, and by the end of the season we felt Dexter was ready. I was anxious to get started on my own.

The first agent I can recall was George Hamid. He booked me into the Royal Winter Fair in Toronto, Canada, for my first engagement. What an experience that was. Horses from all different countries were competing in the various events.

A few days before the end of the season I called my mother in Scottsburg and asked her to pick up a one-horse trailer, have a hitch put on my car, and meet me on the show's closing date.

I packed what wardrobe, street clothes, and horse equipment I would need and arranged with Tex and his wife to take the rest of my things home with them when the circus train got to Sarasota. As horse trainer, Tex worked for the show year-round, so, of course, they spent the winters in Sarasota.

Mother arrived on time and, instead of taking a train home, decided to go to Canada with me. Jimmy, my groom, went along to care for the horse.

In the Garden and on the indoor shows, I always had a private dressing room and, on this date, it was also included in my contract. At horse shows, everyone dresses at the hotel; however, they had built a special dressing room for me. On horse shows, the grooms stay quite close to their charges, so I was given two box stalls: one for my horse and one for my groom.

After getting everything put away and Jimmy settled, I went to inspect the arena. It looked huge. It was probably no larger than Madison Square Garden, but with no rings or stages or anything at all in it, it sure looked big.

The next afternoon we rehearsed with the band. The first show was that night, and I will not forget it as long as I live. The Grand Opening was also society night; all of the elite, including the Duke and Duchess of Windsor in their flag-draped box, were there. The ladies and gents were all in evening clothes, and it was beautiful. The women were bedecked in every kind of fur coat imaginable. They came not only to see but to be seen.

As an added flourish to my act, two men rode out ahead of me and gave a bugle call. The curtains opened, and I made my entrance. So many lights were on me that I had difficulty finding the center of the arena. I was wearing a long, flowing evening gown. I went through the first part of the act without mishap.

Now, it would have been impossible to do the waltz and rear and the fire jump in this getup, so I had arranged for my groom to enter the arena while my horse was doing the laydown. I would step back and hand him my large feather headdress and the skirt from my costume, then one-knee the horse, mount, and continue the act. When I dropped my skirt, you could hear gasps all over the house. (You must remember that this was back in the 1930s.)

I continued my act and then went back to the dressing room. Almost immediately thereafter, a messenger came to inform me that the act had been canceled. Mother and I went back to the hotel and I cried all night.

Here was my first date with my own horse, and I had been fired.

Very early the next morning, while we were packing our things to go home, the phone rang. It was the big boss himself, the show's director.

"Miss Herbert, I would like to see you right away."

I told him that would not be necessary; I understood.

Then he asked, "Have you seen the morning newspapers?"

Of course I had not and told him so, to which he replied, "How about you having breakfast with me while we talk it over?"

Well! Dexter and I had not only made the papers, but headlines: "American Girl Shocks Canadian Society." Once again, I had been saved by publicity, and I was discovering that, good or bad, that was what counted. I could not help but recall the stunt that I had pulled on the Ringling Bros. Circus when they had first suggested the scanty wardrobe; this time it had happened accidentally, but with much the same result.

This incident led to my meeting Bertram Mills, the great showman from England. Not only did he own his own circus, but was a noted horseman as well. He was there as a judge for some of the events. He was a tall, gray-haired, distinguished-looking gentleman. In one hand he carried a cane with a gold top. He came to my dressing room, tapped on the door, and when I opened it, he offered his services to revamp my act. I was flattered to think that a man in his position would offer his help.

We took Dexter into the arena for a rehearsal, where Mr. Mills made some changes in the act so that it would look less like a striptease on horseback.

Several days later, Mr. Mills offered to take me to London with him to feature me in his show. He told me of the wonderful trained horses he had there, and I would love to have gone; however, I would have had to stay with his show for two years. Mother had her new home in Scottsburg and she was not about to leave it, and she would not hear of my going that far away and leaving her for so long.

Before the Toronto engagement was over, I had been offered a contract to play the Chicago horse show, which I accepted. No one in her right mind would have done such a thing at that time of the year and with the type of equipment I had.

After the final show, the horse show people who were also going there loaded their horses in baggage cars, went to their berths in the sleeping cars, and so to bed. Not us. We loaded Dexter into the trailer and started out.

We crossed the border and then on to Detroit. It was snowing hard, the road was slick, and while going down a steep hill, I discovered that the trailer was no longer behind but was alongside the car. Suddenly, the trailer broke loose and went rolling down a hill alongside the road. I pulled to the side of the road and stopped the car. Jimmy and I jumped out and went sliding down the hill after the trailer.

The trailer had rolled over and back upright again. We managed to get Dexter out, and there we were, all three of us, belly deep in snow. Mother flagged down a passing motorist and asked him to go for help. After what seemed like a very long time, he returned and told us that a farmer and his tractor were coming to pull us out. The farmer, after getting the trailer back up the hill and back on the road, towed it into a nearby garage. Jimmy rode Dexter, and I followed close behind in the car. We waited at the garage while they fixed the broken hitch and added safety chains to the trailer.

By the time we got to Detroit, I was very tired and we were all half frozen. The car had no heater, and we were relying on blankets to keep us warm. To top it off, the windshield wiper was not half doing its job. I pulled into a filling station and called the police. After being assured by the filling station attendant that this was not a prank call and that a horse was involved, the police said they would send someone to try to assist us.

When the officer arrived, I explained that I was too tired to go on any farther and figured I would be a menace on the highway. The horse had been in the trailer far too long and needed to be watered and fed. I did not know what to do.

Never have I met a nicer person. He called his chief, then turned back to me and asked if an empty garage would do for the horse.

"Of course."

When Dexter had been watered, fed, and bedded down, he suggested that we leave the car and trailer there in the driveway, as it might be hard to find a place to park it, and he would drive us to the hotel. We had a bite to eat before checking in and renting a room for Jimmy and one for Mother and me, and then we turned in.

The next morning, we were just finishing our breakfast when the officer came to take us back to Dexter and our rig. We couldn't thank him enough and, as you can see, I have never forgotten him.

When the horse show in Chicago was over, Mother went back to Scottsburg by train, and Jimmy, Dexter, and I drove on to the Sarasota winterquarters.

Tex and his wife, Yetta, were anxious to hear how I had made out on my own, and the first night I arrived we sat up until all hours while I told them of my adventures.

Dexter had a habit of nipping. Both Jimmy and I had warned the other grooms time and time again not to encourage this habit, but they continued to tease him. We were playing a date in Texas about the middle of the season. At that time, eight horses were in the string that I used. All of them belonged to the show, except Dexter, and all were stallions with the exception of Satan, my jumping horse.

It had been a long run from the last town, and they were late getting things set up that day. It was also beastly hot. The horse tent was up, so I went in there and sat down on a bale of hay, waiting for the dressing tent to be put up. Most of the grooms were in the cookhouse having a late breakfast.

In front of my string of horses was a rope net, six feet high, with a sign hanging on it: "Beware—these horses bite!" Their feed had just been placed before them when a man with a little boy in his arms walked up and lifted the boy so that he could reach over the net and pet the horses. A couple of the other stallions also had a habit of nipping, but the child reached for the only white horse, and Dexter bit him. An ambulance was called, and the little boy was taken to the hospital. Later in the day I was called to the office and told that I would have to get rid of the horse. He had bitten the tip off of the youngster's ear, and the father was suing the show.

Colonel Zack Miller from the 101 Ranch happened to be visiting the show at the time. He said that he would like very much to have that beautiful stallion and promised to give him a good home. I hope he did. I could not bear to have the horse put to sleep.

Colonel Miller sent a truck to pick up Dexter, and I never saw or heard of him again.

◡

Troubadour

Shortly thereafter, Mr. Gumpertz and Pat Valdo went to visit the Al G. Barnes Circus. While there they espied this terrific rearing horse, Troubadour. They lost no time in having him sent to the Ringling Bros. show. They also sent along his trainer, Mark Smith. He remained on the show for several weeks and showed me all that I would need to know about the horse.

Troubadour was truly a sensational rearing horse. He would make as many as three revolutions while standing on his hind legs, pawing the air all the time. He was a coal black stallion, chomping at the bit and frothing at the mouth, with his nostrils flaring red, all of the time he was working. There was no doubt that he made the waltz and rear more thrilling than ever to the audience; you could tell by the response to the number.

I had an idea that one reason Mr. Gumpertz had had the horse transferred to the Ringling Bros. show was to help me get over the loss of Dexter. But it wasn't the same at all. Dexter was the first horse I had ever owned. He had been mine to do with whatever I pleased and to take wherever I wanted. He had somehow given me a feeling of freedom. The plans that I had made . . . but the dream was over.

Your first horse, your first car, and your first love— the memory stays with you forever.

◡

Jimmy

Jimmy. As I go along, I find myself speaking of him so many times I feel I ought to say something about him, but there is so little to tell that I know about; yet I wonder how I could have managed to get along without him.

He was about the same age as my father and had fought in the same war. He had suffered shell shock, and it left him with a slight affliction that only seemed to affect him when he was upset—he would twitch. I acquired him in my second year on the Ringling Bros. show; he was put on my string of horses by the ring stock boss, and there he stayed. Strictly a loner, he said little to anyone. He shaved every day, but would only go for a haircut when someone sent him. He would have fit in nicely today.

He never seemed to leave the circus lot, so I got into the habit of buying all of his clothes for him, which suited him fine. He loved to eat, and as long as he was well fed and had a place to sleep—always, of course, near his beloved horses—he was happy. In all the years he was with me, I never knew where he was from, and in all that time he never received a single letter. He would do just as he was told and would never enter into a conversation or offer any suggestions.

When it came to caring for the stock, no one was better. This was the one thing he took pride in. After the first time he was assigned to me, he went everywhere my horses went; when I bought my first horse, he attached himself to it and, thereafter, all of the others. I do not recall him ever asking where we were going, and when I would go someplace without him, he showed no concern either. As long as he had his horses to take care of and plenty to eat, he was happy.

One winter while staying at my home, he picked up a habit that annoyed me very much. My mother called me "Dot"; I preferred "Dorothy," but never said anything. Then, parrot-like, Jimmy began calling me "Dot," which I did not think was very dignified.

Maybe I was lucky he had not been around my father, for when I was very young his pet nickname for me was "Snippy."

∪

Ringling Bros. Circus Liberty Act

During the start of my fourth season with Ringling Bros. circus, we were going through our rehearsals at Madison Square Garden in New York City and, for some reason, one of the horse handlers left the show.

I was called to the office and the assistant manager, George Smith, asked if I would work one of the liberty horse acts until they could find a replacement. I suspect they didn't try very hard, because they never found one.

Because I was in the show in so many other numbers, George thought I should wear a gaucho outfit and cover my blonde hair with a hat; then I would not be quite so conspicuous.

Tex had broken a new act for himself to work that winter, so he turned the grays over to me. This act had been broken in Europe by the renowned trainer Earnest Schumann. He had come over with the horses when the show first bought the act, and he also brought Tex and Yetta with him. Schumann did not like it here and soon returned home, turning over the act to Tex.

The act consisted of ten horses. Besides the usual change of the ring waltz by twos, fives walk the ring curb, all rearing at the end of the number, they did a trick that I have never seen in any other liberty horse act: At one point they all lined up and bowed down on their front knees. Each ring had an excellent hind leg rearing horse for the finish trick. These horses were so well trained that it was a real pleasure to work them.

Opening in Madison Square Garden was always hectic, and this was to be no exception. Animals would work in the ring barns perfectly, but when you put them all together in all three rings at the same time, in a building with strange sights and smells, bright lights, and, above all, the sound of music, problems always resulted. There were usually some replacements in the horse numbers and, as a rule, the replacements caused the trouble.

I was assigned the end ring nearest to the back door from which the horses all entered and left the arena, Tex was in the center, and the other trainer in the far end ring. His act consisted of ten horses, all blacks, and four of them were new. Tex was working eight bays and all of them were green; so far, however, they had been doing fine.

We were midway through the number when two of the horses from the far end left the ring, and the others followed. A couple of them jumped into the center ring with Tex, scaring his eight, and they also left. The back door was closed, blocking their getaway and, with everyone running after them, quite a number of them jumped into my ring—so many that I felt there was no room for me, and I also left!

Tex and I both felt it would be better if the acts were switched around; thereafter I worked in the far end ring and had no more trouble.

U

My Second Horse

Seven horses were in the string that I used, all belonging to the show, and it was necessary to have two grooms to care for them. One day the ring stock boss introduced me to a very handsome young man, Robert, and told me he had hired Robert as Jimmy's assistant. Robert was overly polite with his "Yes, ma'am" and "No, ma'am." Often when I would tell him I wanted something done, I would notice a sly grin on his face. It soon became apparent that he knew a great deal about horses. I also noticed that the show's veterinarian would call on him if he needed assistance when doctoring a horse.

He stayed with the show for several months and then, one day, he told me that he was leaving right away. I was indeed sorry to see him go. I offered to go with him to see the paymaster, as he had several days' salary coming and might not be able to get it before payday without an explanation. He said to never mind, he would not need it.

Some weeks later, as I was about ready to leave the train, my porter informed me that some people were waiting for me in a car. As I stepped off the train platform, out of this big Lincoln jumped my former groom. He took my arm and escorted me to the car. In it sat a beautiful girl and a very elegant gentleman.

"Miss Herbert," said Robert, "I would like you to meet my father and my wife."

They took me to a hotel dining room for breakfast, and while we were dining, Robert explained his reason for running away with a circus: He and his wife had had a misunderstanding, and to teach her a lesson, he had run away. Because the thing he knew the most about was horses (other than the business he was in with his dad), he took a job as a groom. He, like many others, as a little boy had dreams of running away with a circus; as a big boy, he had actually done it.

After we had breakfast, they drove me to the radio station, waited until the broadcast was over, and then drove me out to their stables. They had a groom lead the horses from their stalls for my inspection. There were quite a few of them, and all of them were gorgeous. When they asked me which one I like best, I couldn't choose. Then they told me why; one of them was to be mine.

At some time or other, Jimmy had told Robert about Dexter and how heartbroken I had been when I had to give him up. I was overwhelmed. The horse I finally chose was Count DeGraceland—even his name was elegant. His tail dragged the ground, his long, wavy mane hung almost to his knees; he was sleek and black as a panther. He handled himself like a ballet dancer, so graceful was he.

When the show closed, I left him in Sarasota in the able hands of Frank Asher, the manege horse trainer. I had made a deal with him to teach the horse the laydown, one knee, and the march. I would put the other tricks on him when I got back to winterquarters after playing the indoor shows, where they were again using the livestock from the shows in Peru, Indiana.

In the meantime, it was necessary that I go home to Scottsburg.

As a young girl, my mother had spent a lot of her time in the summer swimming and diving, and once, while diving into the Ohio River, she had struck her head on a rock. Other than a very sore head at that time, nothing else had resulted from it—until now. A large lump had appeared on the top of her head and would have to be removed. We waited until after the indoor shows so that I could be with her for the operation and be home to take care of her. Therefore, I did not go back to winterquarters, but met the show in New York for the opening.

Madison Square Garden had always been a jinx for me, and this year was no exception. When I arrived there I found my horse, the Count, had a very bad cold, as did several of the show's horses. The show vet and a couple of others worked hard and did everything possible, but mine was the one that died. I cried and cried and cried.

∪

The Book

Elizabeth Brody, the daughter of Irvin S. Cobb, the writer, had made arrangements to travel with the show as its guest. Her intention was to write a circus story, with me as the key figure. It was to be her first book (maybe with a little help from her father). She was given a stateroom in the same railroad car as I. She spent quite some time with the show, forever asking question and making her own observations.

After she left the show and returned to New York, where her book was completed and published, she sent me a copy of it. I was far from pleased with it. To add spice to it, she had added things that were not true; however, it had been written as a novel and not a true story. But the girl in her story looked like me and did all of the things that I did, and there could be no mistake the girl was modeled after me. Later, the book appeared in serial form in one of the leading magazines.

Elizabeth's book was written early in my career, when I was just starting out. It is a shame she could not have written her book a few years later, when I had done a lot more daring things that were worth writing about. In case you might be wondering, the title of her book was *She Was A Lady*. I never quite got the connection.

∪

Nugget

When you are traveling across the country with a show like Ringling Bros., you receive many invitations from horse people to look over their stock and offer your opinion. Most of the time your tight schedule makes it impossible to spare the time. This time, however, there was a difference. Some of the equestrians and horse trainers had been invited to an after-show dinner party and a tour of the stables where a group of horse people kept their mounts. The show was there for a two-day stand, and as I had no broadcast the next day, I was happy to go.

Nugget! I fell in love with this beautiful golden stallion the moment I saw him. He was the color of a newly minted penny, with a long, white, wavy mane and tail, four white stockings, a white star on his forehead, and the tip of his nose was also white. The next morning I took the ring stock boss and the show's vet to examine the horse to be sure he was sound. Both agreed that he would be a good horse for me, and although it took every cent I had, I bought him. In the 1930s five hundred dollars was a lot of money to pay for a horse. It was a lot of money, period.

Ella Bradna had just lost her horse, and I, of course, knew just how she felt. While at the radio station one day I heard about a white stallion that was for sale and, after the broadcast, I went to see him. As soon as I got back to the lot, I went to her and told her about him.

After hearing about the horse, Ella replied, "I am sure that he is lovely, but he is untrained, so of what use would he be to me?"

I advised her that I was going to spend most of the winter in Sarasota working on my horse, and I was sure that she could make a deal with Tex to help, and he and I could break her horse at the same time. She was really thrilled and could hardly wait until between shows to go and look at him. The moment she saw him she cried, "Mine

Eagle," and that became his name.

When the show closed, I went home to Scottsburg and told Mother of my plans to go to Florida. She thought she would like to go along to get away from the cold weather. I went to a loan company and borrowed some money on the house to see us through. We arranged with a neighbor to look after the place for us, packed our things—including Patsy the dog—into the car, and set out. In Sarasota we rented a small apartment.

It would be necessary to forgo working the indoor shows, as we would need to put in all the time we could on the two new horses. Tex, of course, was working for the show breaking horses, and when he had finished for the day we would work on Nugget and Mine Eagle. Each of the horses had good action—I knew that when we bought them—and they were willing workers. Then, too, both Tex and I were trying to prove ourselves. The results came up to our expectations.

Fred and Ella Bradna had gone back to Europe on business, so she did not see her horse for quite some time. When she did, she was very pleased with him, and she kept asking if there was not something she might do for me.

I confided that I had always had a desire to learn to ride bareback, so when we were back on the road she proceeded to teach me. There were a couple of horses available that we could use.

I already knew a few of the basics from the vaultage act, but that had been a rather wild sort of Cossack thing. She taught me to stand up on the horse and to do all of the movements in a ladylike manner.

I was glad of my ballet background, which was a help. Her teaching was to come in handy later on.

♘

The Big Hitch

Knowing that the show was always on the lookout for new acts for me, Rudy Rudynoff went to them with an idea he thought they might like: "The Big Hitch"—Roman standing. He would teach me, and they could use the horses from his liberty act.

The first thing I heard about when I got to Sarasota, after playing the indoor shows, was the plan for this new act. Practice would start on it as soon as trappings could be made. They had their own harness shop, so they had the whole thing made right there and fitted to the horses.

The actual act was not too long in the making; the horses were used to working together in the liberty act, and I was no novice to Roman standing. To be sure, the number of reins that had to be held at one time was a little difficult at first, but I got used to that. When the management saw that the act was going to be a winner, we were advised that it was to have a featured spot in the program.

I went to the office with what I thought was a just complaint. This was an extra number that would require more wardrobe, and I did not feel I could afford it. They agreed that I was right and sent me to the dressmaking department with an order for three costumes. The wardrobe ladies were busy making last-minute changes and alterations on other costumes; they tried hard, but they were swamped. Although they got the outfits finished, they had no time to sew on all of the trimmings, which had to be put on by hand. I called on some of my girlfriends and made them a deal.

The train trip from Sarasota to New York was always long and tiring. The train would have to stop several times to unload and feed and water the stock. Most of the people working with the show would join in New York. Those now riding the train were either the ones who stayed in winterquarters all winter, or some of us who had to go there to practice for the coming season, plus the animal trainers and attendants.

When on the road with the entire personnel aboard, a privilege car served short-order meals and snacks, but this would not be added until later on; it did not operate for just us few. On this trip, the show furnished everyone with box lunches, which consisted of sandwiches, fruit, coffee, and doughnuts and the like—but no hot meals.

I was the only one in my gang who had a state-room. I told the girls that I would do the cooking for all of us if they would help with the sewing; they thought it was a good deal. I bought all kinds of food, and we not only had fun all of the way there, but my wardrobe got finished as well.

We always rehearsed in the Garden for several days before the opening. Everything seemed to be going all right. Opening night I was nervous; call it a premonition if you will. It seemed more than my normal aversion brought on by memories of former experiences there.

Tex Elmlund and his wife were not with the show. Yetta was going to have a baby, and Tex had left the show and gone to work in a riding academy so that he might be with her.

Rudy Rudynoff was going to help me with the fire jump, so that was all right, but I still had a strange feeling. The high-school number was warmly received, especially Troubadour with the waltz and rear. Instead of the usual thrill I normally felt when a number was well-received, it left me cold.

The Big Hitch consisted of ten horses. First came a horse and rider carrying a flag, which was a guide for the others. Behind her were two horses; next, three abreast; and then four. I stood upon the two middle horses of the four as they raced around the arena at a full gallop.

A new importation to the show, from France, was the Marcellus Troupe. They worked in all three rings at the same time, twelve girls in each ring. The ones in either end ring were painted gold, and in the center ring they were covered with silver glitter—living statues. They worked on huge, heavy tables that revolved.

Came the time for the Big Hitch, and it was almost over before it started. Halfway down the back track (all numbers started in the back and ended up on the front track) was this table, sticking part way across the track. The first two horses cleared it, then one of the three abreast hit it, tripped and fell, and all four of the ones I was standing on went down. Those still on their feet continued to try to go, dragging the rest behind them and, of course, they started kicking. When they went down, I fell astride one of those on which I had been standing and I grabbed him around the neck. Blood was everywhere.

Somehow attendants and grooms got the horses and me out of there, and when I regained my senses, I was in the doctor's office. In the Garden it was located close to the back entrance. Mr. Gumpertz and Pat Valdo had left their box seats to see how serious my injuries were. I was quite concerned about my new costume, which was a total wreck. After being assured they would buy me another to replace it, I went to my dressing room. I had been told by both the doctor and Mr. Gumpertz to go to my hotel, but this was opening night. All of the press was there, and after the disgrace of my smashup and being carried out of the arena, I felt I had to do something to redeem myself.

I asked one of the wardrobe ladies if she would help me clean myself and change wardrobe. I sent word to my groom, Jimmy, to saddle Satan. Then, when the time came, I made the blindfold fire jump, took my bow, dressed, and went to the hotel to be laid up for four days. I was black and blue all over. Our doctor said I had been hit or kicked eleven times, but, luckily, never with a shod hoof. The blood all over me was from the horses cutting each other.

I went back to riding the Big Hitch, of course, as it was in the program, but it continued to haunt me. As time went on, I took spill after spill, and I usually had a bandage on a knee, an ankle, or both.

It seemed that I would do all right on the straight-away, but on the turns the horses would sometimes separate so far apart that I would do a split and then fall off.

One day as I came limping out of the tent, far behind the horses, I passed by an old-timer seated on a bale of straw. He was an old teamster, a leftover from the days when they took the wagons to and from the train with horses; they had recently modernized and now used tractors for most of the hauling, though at the runs they still used horses. My stand-up team had again separated on the turn and I had hit the dust.

"You know, girlie," he drawled, "if I were you I would put a set of breechin' on them horses and cross-couple the stand-up team."

I sat down beside him and asked him to explain just what he was talking about. When he was through, I said, "Don't go away. I'll be right back."

I hobbled over to the office and got an order to the harness maker to stop everything and make the changes in the harness. I took the old man with me, and when they were finished, it was so simple. The team I stood on was coupled together at the belly, then all four of them had wide straps across their backsides, keeping them together on the straightaway or the turns.

In just a few days I was able to place all of the reins in one hand and hold the other hand in the air. The act went over so well with the public that they increased the number of horses to sixteen; later on, when I joined the Cole Bros. Circus, I would drive twenty-four.

I finished the season with no further mishaps, except perhaps an occasional spill due to a wet, muddy track, but that is to be expected. When the season was over I went home to Scottsburg, as usual, and then on to the indoor shows.

I've Got a Big Mouth

Sometimes it was fun to reminisce about some of the silly things I was prone to do. We were playing in New York City, and I stopped to look in I. Miller's window as I was walking down Broadway. They carried the best and most expensive shoes. There I saw a pair that I would love to have owned but, of course, it was out of the question; I could not afford them.

I walked into the Garden, down the hall, and opened the door to my dressing room, and there on the vanity table was a very long, narrow box with a bow on it. In those days, many people sent flowers to the performers, and sometimes other gifts as well. As a rule, you had no idea who they might be from, even though they included a card. When I opened this box, it held not one but six orchid corsages, each a different color. They were beautiful, but what on earth would I do with them? When the show was over at night, I went directly to my hotel and to bed. Because I was in so many different numbers, I always had some sort of early morning rehearsal and seldom left the building after that, except to grab a bite to eat, so where would I be going to wear them? I never knew who sent them, but I did know that the money that had been spent on them would have paid for a couple of pairs of shoes.

As I tell this now, I once told it to Marion Morgan and her mother. I then, of course, forgot about it. Every year when the show played Louisville, some of the Morgan family would drive over from Scottsburg to attend the matinee. Always, at the end of one of my acts, when I took my bow, I would be presented with a basket of roses from them—I had come to expect it. This time I knew the Morgans were in the audience; I had spotted them in the first row. So after each of my acts, when I took a bow, I hesitated—but no flowers.

After my final number, when I went back to the

dressing room, I expected to find them there. Instead, I found a note saying they were picking me up and we would go to dinner. They would be waiting for me in the backyard of the circus, and to meet them as soon as I was dressed.

Later on, as I was getting into their car, Mrs. Morgan handed me several boxes. They contained a beautiful new purse, several pair of hose, and a bottle of perfume.

"I remembered the story of the orchids," she said. I felt like two cents and told her so.

"No," she replied, "you were perfectly right. Flowers are a lovely thought, but in a few days they are gone; these things you can enjoy for some time and remember me when you use them."

♘

Fox Hunt

It was during the winter, and I was spending some time at home in Scottsburg with my mother. Roger Johnson, a friend of mine, raised hunting dogs, of which he was quite proud. He invited me to attend a meet. With open space becoming more and more scarce, and the wood rail fences being replaced with something more durable, the old fox hunt is becoming a thing of the past, and I am glad I was fortunate enough to be included in a few of them. Even then they were not like in the old plantation days, but fun they were.

We went to the stables by truck; the red fox was on the front seat in a box and the back end was filled with dogs. At the barn we were met by the other hunters and their dogs. A lot of jolly kidding was going on, and I could see that bets were being made as to whose dog would be the first to pick up the scent. The main objective was to test the ability of the hounds.

The cage with the fox was brought forth, and he was turned loose. He lit out and disappeared before you could blink your eyes. My friend Roger now led out a little bay mare. He assured me she would jump any obstacles we would encounter on our cross-country run. Roger then told me that for me to enjoy the sport and join in the fun, he had entered a dog for me, Old Red. He didn't make many of the hunts anymore, as he was getting old, but he had a howl that was different from all of the others, and Roger thought I might get a kick out of trailing a dog of my own.

A rider with a bugle announced that the hunt was about to begin. The dogs were turned loose, and away we went. The ground had a light covering of snow. After riding a while we were becoming quite cold, and someone suggested that we dismount and exercise a little to warm up. A game of leapfrog followed, and it was a lot of fun. When we heard the hounds baying, we quickly mounted and joined in the chase. We caught up with the hounds and found them circling around the bottom of a tree, with the red fox clinging to one of the branches. The dogs were gathered up and their leashes put on them; the fox was shaken loose from the limb, placed in a sack, and then put back into his box and taken home until next time.

Back at the stables, after turning our mounts over to the grooms, we went to the lodge where the caretaker's wife had a huge breakfast awaiting us: thick slices of hickory-cured ham, eggs, hot biscuits, coffee with thick cream, homemade jam, and butter—all cooked on a wood-burning stove and eaten at a long table near the fireplace. The conversation was mostly about dogs, and I am afraid I was not too interested.

The next time I was invited to go along was quite a different story. It was a lovely moonlit night, but every so often the clouds would roll by and there would be a few moments of darkness.

Now, I had been warned during the first hunt to stay close to the other riders, as I was not acquainted with the territory. The little mare I was riding was a good jumper and had taken all of the fences willingly and very smoothly, and I became overly confident.

We hadn't been riding very long when one of the dogs let out a howl. There was no mistaking that call; it was my dog, Old Red. He was in the lead, and the other dogs were respecting his point. I became so excited I urged the little mare forward for all she was worth.

Looming ahead I espied a little stream; assured that she would take it in stride, although the moon was behind a cloud at the moment and it was quite dark, I gave her a touch with my spurs and we landed, kerplunk, in the middle of a pond. The rest of the gang came along and fished me out with a pole; the mare scrambled out on her own.

I remounted and was rushed, posthaste, back to the cabin.

Sarah, the cook, shooed everyone out of her room and dragged in an old washtub, which she placed in front of the fireplace and filled with hot water. After my hot bath, she wrapped me in a blanket and seated me before the fireplace, where my clothes were hanging to dry. When the hunters returned from the chase, I asked that Old Red be allowed to come into the cabin so that I could make a fuss over him. He wasn't greatly impressed, and curled up by the fire and went to sleep.

On the way back to town, I happened to ride in the truck where the fox in the box was on the front seat. It was probably the aftereffect of the hot toddy that Sarah had fixed for me to take away the chill, but I could have sworn that he looked up at me and winked.

♘

Auction

It was the middle of the season and time was hanging heavy on our hands. What to do for excitement? We had already had several treasure hunts, where we ran from one place to another picking up clues; a box of candy was the prize. Why not an auction?

You must understand that most everyone on the show was interested in our Manege Club and was willing to lend a hand. We enlisted the aid of one of our banner men. I will take a moment to explain for anyone who might not know what a banner man is.

The advance crew sells advertising to different merchants; then, when the show plays in their town, banners are strung all around the tent with their ads on them. The ads are painted on oilcloth by the banner men—painters versed in the art of lettering. Most of them held down another job with the show, and this was a sideline to earn extra money.

We asked one of them to paint a banner for us announcing that the Manege Club was bankrupt (which was far from true), and we were going to hold an auction on a given date. The club members were instructed to gather up whatever junk they no longer had any use for and bring it to the sale; others on the show joined in the fun and contributed other things.

Came the day of the sale. The wardrobe ladies cleared off the tables where some of the spec wardrobe was usually placed, and, after arranging our things on them, we were ready for the sale. On a show of this size you were bound to find someone who had done something else at other times, and we came up with a first-rate auctioneer. Everyone was all set for a lot of fun and laughs. What we had not counted on was the reaction. Many of the performers were in this country for the first time and were unable to do much shopping in town because of the language barrier, and they were eager to buy many of the items offered. Further, we had not expected the workingmen to attend; however, they were in the market for used clothing and shoes.

When the husbands of some of the members saw what was happening, they went to their trunks and pulled out a lot of things they no longer wanted. Fred Bradna, our equestrian director, came up with the hit of the day: He brought forth a case of imported wine that a circus fan had presented to him, which made more money for the club than anything else.

Our club made a lot of money from this sale, and we felt guilty about it. Why not give a party for the entire show on the Fourth of July? We made a deal with the cookhouse steward to order the refreshments for us because we did not know how to go about it; the Manege Club would provide the entertainment. Merle Evans, the leader, agreed to have some of his musicians furnish the music.

∪

Washington Blowdown

Tex Elmlund had rejoined the show, but his wife and baby had remained in New York. Ella Bradna had been having some sort of trouble with her horse, Mine Eagle, so Tex and I were going to practice him between shows. Just before I left the dressing tent, Mama Reiffenach called me back and told me to close my trunks as it was going to rain.

We were in the ring a short time when the wind started to blow. We could hear the big top crew outside pounding down the extra stakes. I suggested to Tex that we stop, but he thought we ought to keep on until we had won our point. Suddenly, there was a big gust of wind, and Tex yelled, "Run!" Mine Eagle and I made it outside just as the big top blew down; then came the rain, in torrents. Not knowing which way to go, I rode down an alley. Seeing an empty garage, and figuring no one would mind in a storm like this, I rode the horse inside.

After a bit, a lady motioned to me from her kitchen window to come into the house. I found a place to tie the horse and went in. She went to her bedroom and came back with a robe, showed me to the bathroom, and advised me to take a warm shower. She put my wet things in her clothes dryer. When I came out, she made us some tea and brought forth a dish of cookies to go with it. We sat and talked until the storm was over. I got dressed, thanked her, mounted Mine Eagle, and went back to the lot. When I rode up, I saw quite a few people digging around in the rubble.

"What are you looking for?" I asked.

Without looking up, one man said, "Dorothy Herbert and a horse."

Everyone was glad to see us safe and sound, but no one was as happy as Ella Bradna.

Where the dressing tent had once stood was now waist-deep water. Clothes of all sorts were floating around in the mess. Somehow or other, the gallant working crew had managed to get most of the trunks and rigging onto the wagons. Tow trucks were sent for, and the show tractors, with the aid of elephants and their handlers, took the wagons to the railroad flatcars. The performers who were not needed to help (the women) were told to go to the coaches and keep out of the way.

When I got to the train my porter told me a chauffeur and limousine were waiting for me. In the excitement, I had forgotten I was to have dinner with Senator Walsh. I had met the senator a few years before, and ever since, when the show played Washington, D.C., he had taken me and a girlfriend out to dinner after the show. But not under these

Famous glamour photograph by H. A. Atwell, 1933. *Courtesy of the John & Mable Ringling Museum of Art, Tibbals Digital Collection.*

circumstances; I told my porter I just could not go. He returned and said the chauffeur had orders to wait for me, and he was going to do just that; also, as usual, I was to bring a girlfriend with me. One of my pals who happened to be standing nearby made up my mind for me.

With a sad look, she said, "Here we could be having a nice dinner someplace, and you want to stay here on the train with nothing to eat. I'd be more than glad to help you get dressed."

Was I ever glad she had talked me into going. As usual, we dined at the senator's club. The senator knew I loved lobster thermidor, and that, along with a lot of other food, was waiting for us when we arrived. The floor show was lovely. And regardless of how bedraggled we looked, the senator introduced us to any of his friends who stopped by.

The following morning I had a broadcast in the town where we were showing, so I was late arriving at the lot. It was a sight to behold. Clotheslines were stretched from guy line to guy line, so you could hardly get through; it was pathetic, all of the beautiful things that were ruined. I went into the dressing tent, unpacked, and added my tears to the others. The show's wardrobe was hung and carried in wagons, so it sustained little damage. How we managed to get enough of our things together to put on a show is a mystery, but we did.

∪

Mazeppa

After playing the indoor shows, I had just arrived in Sarasota when Mr. Gumpertz sent for me to come to his office. As usual, they were looking for something new. He told me about a spectacle he had seen produced in Europe. He suggested that I go to the public library and get the book so I would be familiar with the story, and then get together with the horse trainers and see what we could come up with.

The story took place during the Roman days. It seems there was a young girl who was fair to look upon. The king had been casting eyes in her direction; the queen got wind of this and demanded that the girl be offered as a sacrifice in one of the forthcoming games. Not wishing to arouse the queen's displeasure any further, the king gave the order. The girl was strapped to the back of a horse and turned loose among a herd of wild mustangs. A young gladiator, who was enamored of the lass, rode up on his mount and raised his sword, indicating he would like a chance to save her. The king turned thumbs up, which meant that if the soldier could save her, he might claim her as his own. He dashed off and, eventually, caught the horse she was tied to. The story ended sadly, for when he placed her on the ground she was dead.

There was no shortage of horse trainers that year; besides Tex Elmlund, there was Rudy Rudynoff, and Gordie Orton had also joined up. We practiced the number for weeks and weeks. Thirty-two head of stock were used, not counting the one on which I rode. Horses of all colors were used, with a few ponies mixed in to make it look like colts running with their mothers. All were running at liberty, with nothing on them, as they were supposed to be a wild herd; and with everyone cracking whips and chasing them, they sure acted like they were.

Many of the things that I had done had not been easy, but this was the hardest I had ever attempted. All of the horses and ponies had to be taught to jump a hurdle of fire, which had been added to make the act more effective. But the bad part was the way the horses would crowd each other, plus their biting and kicking.

I finally chose a mean little stallion named Diablo

for my mount. He would bite any horse that came too close to him, which gave us a little space of our own.

The main difficulty was that I had to lie across the horse's back sideways with my hands dragging and one leg in the air, as if I were about to fall. On the straightaway it was all right, but going over the hurdle in this position was quite another matter. My arms and legs were black and blue, and my midsection, back, and stomach were taped up like an Egyptian mummy.

Months later, on the road, when the act was a proven success, I remarked to Mr. Gumpertz one day, "The girl who did this act in Europe must have been quite a rider."

He laughed and said, "Now that you have it licked, I'll tell you something. When they came to the part where they tied the girl on the horse, they used a dummy." As you may have guessed, I felt like one.

The wardrobe for this number was a flowing white and gold toga, gold sandals, and a gold cord worn around the waist, which they were supposed to have used to tie the girl onto the horse. We had been told that this act would close the show and be featured, but no one told us to what extent.

When I arrived at Madison Square Garden, the first thing I saw was my name in lights on the marquee. The figures, from a full-size lithograph, had been cut out and mounted on plywood, with flickering lights around it. It was fantastic—it looked like real flames. Of course, I was thrilled, and all of the pain and hard work were forgotten.

Because the fire was one of the main features of this act, and they were not about to cut out the blindfold jump, another means of presenting Satan had to be devised. The high-jumping act was moved to the middle of the show, and, instead of Satan jumping fire, we trained him to jump over two horses standing side by side. We used two of the grays from the liberty act for him to jump over, and, as usual, I was blindfolded.

○

Rex

The management had told me that I should start look-ing for a horse as a stand-in for Satan. Suppose he were to get hurt or go lame when he was being fea-tured. I asked them how much money they were prepared to spend. I had in mind an Irish hunter, which was not cheap. When they told me that they would go as high as three thousand dollars, I was astonished: That was a small fortune in those days.

I asked our press agents, who were ahead of the show and who made the arrangements for my broadcasts, to make inquiries and if they heard of a good jumping horse in some town, to make an appointment for me to look at it when I got there. I looked at a lot of horses, but one trip stands out clearer than all the rest.

This unshaven, seedy-looking, tobacco-chewing farmer met me at the radio station with a truck. It was hot, and the road was bumpy and dusty. We turned off the main road, if you could call it that, and went a long way down a country lane. He parked the truck, went into the barn and came back leading a horse that looked like he had forgotten his plow. I told him I was sorry, but the horse would not do. That is where I made my mistake, and one I never repeated.

He walked into the house and came back with his milk pail. I asked him if he was going to take me back to town, to which he replied, "You didn't buy the horse, did you? I'm late fer my milkin'."

When I asked if I could pay him to take me back, he answered, "Nope." Becoming more nervous by the minute, I asked if he might have a phone that I could use and, again, his answer was, "Nope."

Now, I had on a white dress and white high-heeled shoes. I hobbled back to the main road and hitchhiked for the one and only time in my life. I told the man who picked me up and drove me into town what had happened.

"Now, there is where you weren't very smart," he said. "Don't ever commit yourself on the spot. Next time say that you need to think on it for a spell, or that you have to talk it over with your boss, and get yourself back where you started from."

Believe me, I took that advice.

After the show closed and I had gone home to Scottsburg, I kept recalling one horse I had looked at when we were playing in Ardmore, Oklahoma. I was not really sure he would fill the bill, and he was not black but was bay. He was, however, the only horse I had looked at that jumped in a manner that made me think he might be suitable for the reinless jump. Moreover, the rancher had asked only two hundred dollars for him, and if he did not work out I could always get that back for him.

I phoned the rancher long distance and asked him if the horse was still available. When I had ascertained that he was, I told him I would be there shortly. I still had the one-horse trailer I had bought to carry my unforgettable Dexter, so I went to Ardmore, picked up the horse— Rex—and brought him home. After he had a few days' rest, I started to train him.

Breaking Rex was a far cry from what I had been used to. At Ringling Bros. winterquarters, horse trainers had always been available to help from the ground; now, I had to do the training all by myself, plus caring for him. Jimmy, of course, was in Sarasota with the horses I used on the show.

Thanks to Mrs. Anderson, I did have an arena in which to practice and a few of the hurdles from the old jumping class, but it was not easy doing it alone. If the horse knocked down a bar, I was obliged to dismount, tether him, replace the bar, remount, and try again. Nonetheless, I got the job done and decided to keep Rex. The Ringling show would send their baggage horses to the Peru, Indiana, quarters for the winter, so I arranged for Rex to go back with them when they rejoined the show.

An Honor

The year was 1936. We were playing in Madison Square Garden, which I had come to believe was a jinx for me. Something always seemed to happen to me there.

This time, not only did I have a bad cold but I suffered a fall and was on crutches. The show doctor thought I ought to stay in my hotel room for a few days, but my employers pointed out that I was doing so many solos in the show that it would cut quite a few minutes from the program if I did not appear. They told me to take it easy, but do as much as I could.

Would you believe it? This, of all times, had to be when the governor of Texas flew into New York to commission me an Honorary Texas Ranger and to present me with a beautiful silver-mounted saddle and bridle, along with a large, white Stetson hat.

They stopped the show and, for some reason known only to our press agents, we met in the center ring while mounted on elephants. Jack Earle, our sideshow giant, who had been born in Texas, made the introductions. The saddle was brought out and placed on my horse. I was assisted down from the elephant, mounted my horse, and, as the rest of the riders joined me, we went through the high-school number. Then I changed horses for the waltz and rear. At the finish, I was presented with a large bouquet of flowers and another kiss from the governor. Of course, the whole thing was a publicity stunt. It was the year of the Texas Centennial, and our show would be playing there later on. I was invited to be a judge at their horse show. The show's manager had told them that I would be there, and, sure enough, they let me off to do it.

The saddle was, indeed, a work of art. Made by the Harnley's Saddle Shop in Pendleton, Oregon, and different from any other: It was half Western and half English. It was black hand-stamped leather with a white quilted seat. It was trimmed in silver with my name in gold on top of the silver. The bridle was white, trimmed in silver, with the horse's name on it.

Two other people were awarded this honor at about the same time in other places in Texas. Clyde Beatty was one: They presented him with a lovely silver mounted gun and holster. The other person was Ginger Rogers, the movie star. I have no idea what her present was, but I am sure it was something very fine.

∪

Trapeze

The powers that be who ran the show were forever searching for something more sensational for me to do. The Big Hitch was still going over big and would be kept in the show another season. It was the second year for the wild horse jump, but they thought a new thrill should be added. Someone came up with the idea that if a rope were to be suspended across the track in line with the hurdle and I would grab it as my horse jumped, it would look like I had accidentally been dislodged. Then I could come down astride one of the other horses in the wild horse jump.

They thought it would be a sensational stunt.

In order to do this, I would have to learn to handle myself in all sorts of positions on the rope. I would start off by learning a little trapeze. Gordie Orton, a star in his own right and the teacher of many fine aerialists, was given this job. Because Gordie was also a horse trainer, he was the logical choice.

At the time they had a separate tent for the ponies and other smaller ring stock away from the main horse tent. Gordie selected this as the place to teach me single traps. He would hang the trapeze there every day, and we would work out between shows.

Now, all that I was supposed to do was to learn to handle myself for the jump from the horse I was riding to the rope, and then alight on the back of another horse. This was not much fun, and Gordie discovered that I was, as he put it, "very adaptable to the air." He grew more enthusiastic as we went along and proceeded to teach me a complete trapeze act.

"If you ever find yourself without horses," Gordie explained, "you can still made a living working in the air."

I loved it. Certainly there is a feeling of accomplishment when riding or presenting an animal, but there you are depending on something else to reach your goal; there is a real thrill in flying high in the air, depending on yourself alone. That wonderful sense of freedom and control of your own body—nothing else can compare.

I had mastered the heel catch along with the various other tricks, and Gordie now felt it was time for me to get off the ground and into the air. So, one afternoon between shows, he put my trapeze up in the main tent, and we began to practice.

Now, whether someone went and told them, or if they just happened to be walking through the big top, I never knew. All I know is what Gordie told me later. Pat Valdo and Sam Gumpertz came down the back track and stopped by the end ring where we were working out.

Mr. Gumpertz, who was nearsighted, asked Gordie, "Is that Dorothy Herbert hanging up there like a monkey? If it is, get her down from there and don't ever let her go up again."

That was the end of the trapeze for the time being. However, I took it home with me when the show closed and worked out on it most every day. I found it an excellent way to keep in shape.

When we practiced the stunt that had instigated this in the first place, we found, after much hard work, that the thing was impossible. They used a rope so that it would look like I was pulled off by accident. If I did manage to grab the rope as my horse jumped over the hurdle, then none of the others would come under at the right place for me to land on him. I never was able to do it without a safety belt. All I ended up with was quite a few rope burns for my trouble. Anyway, they finally scrapped the idea.

∪

Failures

*T*his was the only time we failed when trying for something new. We would often spend a lot of time breaking something in winterquarters, only to have it axed when we hit the road.

One such fiasco called for two men on horseback to be riding side by side with a hurdle between them. They would gallop down the track, I would approach from the opposite direction, and my horse would jump the hurdle.

It was a dangerous trick to expect a horse to jump a

moving obstacle. In retrospect, I doubt that anyone other than a few horse people who might attend the show would be aware of the difficulty. Nevertheless, we had been told to break it, and that we did.

Luckily, it lasted just the first two days in Madison Square Garden. To be sure, the people in the balcony and other higher seats could see what was happening, but those people in the boxes and the reserved seats saw only three people going in opposite directions. The hurdle, unless you knew it was there and were looking for it, was nonexistent.

Another time I tried to jump three teams, two abreast, Roman standing on the last two. Now, this sounds like it would be fairly simple. However, the difficulty is that while you are trying to maintain your balance on the last two horses you are standing on to take the jump, the two teams ahead of you are apt to lunge forward too fast and pull you off, since you are holding the reins to your team in one hand and the reins to the other two teams in your other hand.

I remember one number that took up more of everyone's time than any of the other ring barn failures. The trainers were called upon to produce a musical horse number. They enlisted the aid of any of the riders who might be standing about. One horse, with bells on all four ankles, stood on a board doing a standing piaffe. Another pushed a cart on which a drum was mounted, around the ring, close to the curb. He was required to hit the drum with his front feet; in order to do this he must go into a high trot. Two horses were bedecked with chimes, which gave off a loud tinkling sound when they jumped the ropes that were handled by the two riders atop them, jumping rope in place. One of the trainers was on foot in the center of the ring with his hind leg horse, who, while rearing, was to bring his front feet together, causing the cymbals attached to his front legs to give off a fearful clatter.

Everyone worked very hard. It was no easy matter

to get the horses used to all the gear, to say nothing of the awful racket. It was the custom that when the trainers send word to the main office, the bosses would come down to the barn, look the number over, and give final approval.

That day arrived. The act was shown, and after it was over Mr. Gumpertz summed it up with these few words: "It looks like a damn clown number," referring, I suppose, to the clown band.

The only thing they liked in the whole number and would use in the show was the horse beating the drum. And guess who was riding that horse? Yours truly. I had no business in this number at all and had been riding the horse only because it had a hard mouth and was tough to handle; also, you had to use a lot of leg pressure and spur to keep it going. Tex had thought that I would be able to handle the horse, and now I was stuck.

But you haven't heard the worst part yet. There was no spot in the show for this in the program, but the powers that be insisted it be in the show, so the only place they could find was in opening spec—riding just ahead of Merle Evans' band, which led the parade.

It was a mess as far as I was concerned, and Merle felt the same way about it. Here we came down the track—bang! bang! bang!—completely out of time with the band or anything else, yet they kept it in. When we got out on the road, I bedeviled Tex until he got someone else to ride the horse.

Another time I became involved in a similar deal. This one was not a failure, and I was chosen for the job, and was not in it by accident.

At the conclusion of the liberty horse act, a large turntable was placed in the center ring; four tubs were also placed in the ring; four girls riding on camels would mount pedestals, then an elephant would get on the one in the center. All of the horses from the liberty acts would now enter the ring, going in three different directions; the two troops of Shetland ponies would then run around the outside on top of the ring curb; the lights would dim and the elephant would stand on his hind legs, the table started revolving, and colored lights came on. I would then stand on the elephant's head waving a lash whip in the air. Trainers were stationed at various locations in the ring and kept the horses moving. I was in no way directing anything, just standing there, smiling.

A side issue, which will be of no interest to anyone except those directly involved (but ought to go into the record) concerns how I spent those many hours perched on the elephant with nothing to do while they were breaking the horses: I crocheted a tablecloth, one medallion at a time, and in the evenings, at home, I would put them together. This, along with some other mementos, I am leaving to the Circus World Museum in Baraboo, Wisconsin. So, in the event that the information gets lost, the thought has occurred to me the museum folks might like to know they have the only tablecloth ever crocheted by someone while on the back of an elephant.

$\cup$

Ring Barn

After all of the hard work I had put in, and all of the hurts I had suffered breaking in the Mazeppa number, it had become clear to me that I was getting no place. Although it seemed to be a big hit, I did not receive a cent more.

Obviously, I was going to have to do something; I would have to take a chance. I was able to make money teaching riding, but because my time off was during the winter months—plus the fact that the weather in Indiana would only permit outdoor riding in certain seasons—I could not do much of that. I figured that if I had an enclosed arena I would be able to teach. I had paid back the loan I received when Mother and I went to Florida to work on Nugget, so the building and loan company was willing to make me another loan.

My good friends in Scottsburg were a big help, offering all sorts of suggestions, and assuring me that they would see to it that I had enough pupils to keep me busy.

When it was finished, the barn was lovely: stalls down two sides, a circus ring in the center, and a track around it. The barn had an upstairs where the hay and feed were kept, and an observation platform where guests might sit. I had not planned to go in for anything quite like this, but everyone assured me it was the thing to do.

There was a lounge room, a tack room, and a bunkroom where two grooms could sleep. I was afraid I had taken on too much, but true to their word, my friends saw to it that all of the stalls were rented. People were glad to have a place where they could ride, despite the weather. They told me they would continue to handle the rentals for me while I was gone and, thus, keep up the payments.

I settled down to teach in earnest. Dressage was just starting to become popular among the horsey set, and I found I could do really well with this. I was sorry when it was time to go back with the show, but now, at least, I would have a place to bring my horses.

Sixty-Four Horses

Sam Gumpertz continued to seek new or rehashed ideas for acts for the big show. Either he or an associate had been digging through old circus programs and posters looking for acts that had been presented in the past, and got the idea of a big horse tableau from an 1896 Barnum & Bailey lithograph. This bill showed fifty horses in the ring at once.

During the winter of 1936–1937 a number of animal trainers, four girls, and I assembled in the ring barn, and the training began. A huge revolving table was placed in the center of the ring on which stood the largest of the show's elephants. I was seated on its head, the trainer standing at its side.

Four camels with the other girls were placed on four other pedestals. Ten liberty horses were turned loose and circled the elephant tub. A concealed trainer kept them in line. Two ten-horse liberty acts were then brought in to circle in the opposite direction. In addition, a number of ponies entered the ring; they ran the other way on the ring curb. At this point, the elephant trainer cued the elephant to stand up on its hind legs. Meanwhile, I stood on the elephant's head and waved a long lash whip in the air— merely for effect. As the table turned, different colored lights would shine on the number.

The act worked out well and was ready in time for the trip to New York for the opening of the 1937 season at Madison Square Garden. A beautiful outfit was ordered for me from Brooks Costume Company.

A little comedy was connected with this number at the dress rehearsal in winterquarters. Unbeknownst to anyone, Mr. Gumpertz had ordered dummies dressed in the same attire—as military riding maids—including one on the end dressed as I was, wearing a blonde wig and riding sidesaddle.

That was all very cute. Only, as the ponies started moving around the ring curb, the dummies started to fall apart. Arms and legs went every which way and many of the heads fell off.

Of course, all of us laughed so hard the number could not continue. Luckily this was only a dress rehearsal. By the opening all of this had been repaired.

The act turned out to be nothing more than a big production number like a spec. I was no more than a prop in the act and I was no longer interested in it. At the last minute prior to the opening of the season, my part in the act was given to another person.

In 1935 Mr. Gumpertz had hired Marie Rasputin, daughter of Russia's Mad Monk Rasputin. The Ringling management had no idea what they were going to do with her. She was placed on the Hagenbeck-Wallace-Forepaugh-Sells show that season, and it was decided to put her in a wild animal act. This had not worked out too well, as she was mauled on one occasion, and the act finally fell apart. She was still under contract in 1937, and Gumpertz was trying to find a way to use her on the Ringling show.

Pat Valdo called me to his office and said, "Dorothy, you seem to always be having ideas. Maybe you can think of something for Marie Rasputin." I did, at once. Rudy Rudynoff and his wife had joined the show, and brought with them two Great Dane dogs. Why not let Marie stand on the table with those dogs and a whip and let her direct the horse tableau number? It solved the problem of how to present her, and it got me out of an act that no longer appealed to me.

The act was display 16 in the program. It was listed as

> beautiful troupes of performing liberty horses and ponies, Presented simultaneously in all rings and stages by their trainers. In the center ring Rudy Rudynoff, ring one Adolph Delbosq, ring three

Gordon Orton, stage one Rudy Rudynoff, Jr. and stage two Paul Horompo. Concluding with Mademoiselle Marie Rasputin presenting in the center ring the most gigantic and spectacular equine assemblage in circus history, introducing sixty free-running thoroughbreds racing in concentric circles around a towering pedestal on which is mounted Mlle. Rasputin, while a flying column of tiny ponies gallop on the narrow ring curb encompassing the whole of this ineffably beautiful tableau.

It was indeed a rather impressive display with all of the show's liberty horse acts coming into the center ring after their usual numbers.

The act went over big in the Garden. The houselights were turned off and the spotlights were turned on as the table in the center revolved. In New York and at first on the road, the number was a success. Then the show began to hit bad lots, and the weight of the elephant would cause the table to sink into soft ground. In order for the elephant tub to turn, two men were beneath it turning cranks, and they were in danger of being hurt. The act was revised, with a horse on a smaller table replacing the elephant, but the effect was the same.

In mid-season some problem came up, and Marie was removed from the act, concluding her circus career. I was called back to work the act. On the horse I could not wear the beautiful long costume that had originally been made for me to use on the elephant. I wore the Indian costume that had been made for the ill-fated vaultage act that had been scratched.

Marie was listed and pictured in the program, and I am sure the audience wondered what was going on when I appeared in her place, as I had been introduced earlier in the program.

♘

The Awakening

Once more, the show was about to close. Always before I had felt a little sad as the season came to an end, but now I was anxious to get back home to my teaching and to work on my own horses. Also, I was uptight about something that had happened with Nugget. As I have explained before, in order to get the most out of a dressage horse it is necessary to ride him astride and cue him with the bit and spur. Because I had several other horses for sidesaddle at my disposal, we had broken Nugget for astride only, and he was an outstanding mount. I was very proud of him.

The show had brought over from Europe a German horse trainer and his horse, which was supposed to be one of the best horses from the Royal Stables in Holland. The trainer was a big, rather surly man, and he worked his horse hard. It wasn't long before it became lame. The show was insistent that the trainer appear in the high-school number, and they told him to select another horse to ride. He would settle for none other than Nugget, stating that Nugget was the only horse on the show that would do him justice. Mr. Valdo asked if I would consent and, although I resented the idea with my whole being, I remembered that I did not have a horse to ride when I first joined the show, so I consented.

I went back to riding Lindy until the man's horse was well again, but from then on he continued to ride Nugget whenever it suited his fancy. I never knew which horse would await me when I went to the backdoor. I boiled, but said nothing. Without Tex there to intercede for me and back me up, I was at a loss.

True, Rudynoff continued to help me with the Big Hitch and with Satan's jump over the two horses with me blindfolded, and everyone entered into the wild horse jump by standing around and cracking whips; but, as far as the high-school act, I was once more on my own.

With two people riding him Nugget became confused. I was anxious to get him home and straighten him out. Will Rogers once said, "I never met a man I didn't like." I did!

We had been hearing rumors for weeks that the show was changing hands; now it was being verified. One day Mr. Gumpertz sent word for me to come to his private railroad car after the night show. No one was there but him and his wife. He told me that they were leaving; the new people were taking over right away.

Then he told me what I had suspected for a long time—that I was worth a great deal more than I was being paid. The show had all different kinds of lithographs out on me, and I was appearing in the show eight times; I was a valuable property. I asked him why this had not come to anyone's attention long before.

"I must admit," he confessed, "our motive was a purely selfish one. Our intention was to keep you ever striving to reach greater heights. Given too much, too soon, we feared that you might become complacent and be satisfied to sit back and rest on your laurels."

While this, maybe, explained a lot of things, it didn't make me feel any better. He then advised me to say nothing at the moment, but to go home and wait until they contacted me in regard to the coming season. Naturally, they were expecting me back—where else was there for me to go?

As usual, they were sending their baggage stock to Peru, Indiana, for the winter because they could feed them much cheaper there than in Florida. I contacted the new owners and asked if I might put my horses on the train going to Peru. From there I could hire a trailer and take them home. They said it would be all right.

There was no trouble about Rex, but when I claimed Nugget, I was informed that he belonged to the show and would remain in winterquarters. It was then pointed out that I called all of the horses that I rode "my horse." Rattle-snake Bill, the ring stock boss at the time, and the only one to witness my handing over the money when I bought the horse, had caught pneumonia while we were in the Garden and had passed away. Tex, of course, knew the horse belonged to me, but he was no longer with the show, nor was the veterinarian at that time.

I tried every way I could to contact the people from whom I had bought the horse, but they had moved away and four years had now passed. I could not trace them.

My only argument was why on earth would I have spent the whole winter in Florida, at my own expense, given up playing the indoor shows, go to the winterquarters every day and work on a horse, if he were not my own? It had cost me quite a lot of money. No one bothered to listen to what I had to say.

It was now time for the train to leave for Peru. I saw that Rex was loaded and that Jimmy had plenty of food for the trip. I kissed Satan and Nugget good-bye and went home. I later took the trailer, drove to Peru, picked up Jimmy and Rex, and started my riding school again.

Ironically, years later, when it no longer mattered, I happened to be going through some of Mother's papers and among them I found the registration papers—in my name—for Nugget; they had been sent to my home in Scottsburg.

∪

I Cry My Heart Out

One of the pupils in my riding school had bought a horse that was a real handful. After he had thrown her a few times, she refused to have anything to do with him. He was a lovely bay gelding with a black mane and tail. I bought him from her and trained him for high school. Because he was a gaited horse, my teaching job was a little easier; he had good action to start with. I thought it was about time that I had a letterhead made, and one of the photos on it was of my new high-school horse, Commander. That was to be his only publicity ever. About this same time I broke Rex to do the waltz and rear.

Before going to the indoor shows, I drove over to Rochester, Indiana, to visit the Cole Bros. Circus to see if there might be anyone there I knew. Zack Terrell and Jess Adkins had teamed up as partners. Clyde Beatty and Ken Maynard, the movie star, were the big features; and Zack and Jess set about to convince me that I could be one, too, if I would just join up with them. I told them I would think it over. Now that I had my own horses, I had several other things in mind and I did not wish to commit myself just then.

The first Shrine indoor show that year was in Chicago. When we arrived at the building, Jimmy found a nice corner for my horses and, after watering and feeding them and seeing that they had plenty of bedding, Jimmy went out to eat.

An innovation that year was to be a Wild West concert, and while Jimmy was out to dinner, the cowboys and their stock arrived. One of them tied a bucking horse next to Commander, and that horse got excited about something and started kicking. He hit Commander full force on his hind leg. Commander fell—and never got back up.

I was upstairs in the dressing room when the ring stock boss came to tell me that my horse had a broken leg. I did not go to see, but I heard the shot. I went all to pieces.

Was I never to have a high-school horse of my own to ride?

It seemed I was doomed to lose every one I got. First, Dexter—through no fault of my own, I had been obliged to get rid of him; then, the Count DeGraceland—

he caught cold in New York and died; and, last but not least, I had not yet gotten over my failure to prove ownership of my beloved Nugget.

Now, once again, my horse had been taken from me. I cried my heart out. No one could say anything to lessen the hurt. Of course, the show provided a horse for me to ride, and I finished the dates. But each night I cried myself to sleep and refused to talk to almost everyone.

From Chicago we went to Cleveland; then we had a week's layoff before the next date. I went back to Rochester to talk to Mr. Adkins and Mr. Terrell. The offer they had for me was very attractive, and I was still bitter about my parting with Ringling Bros. circus. Now, without a high-school horse of my own, any other plans I may have had were shot.

I told them I would think about their offer and let them know as soon as the winter dates were over, but they said they would have to have an answer right away on account of publicity, programs, lithographs, and so forth. To clinch the deal, they took me to the ring barn and showed me a beautiful black stallion, Black Hawk. The trainer put him through his paces, then brought out a big sorrel rearing horse.

Jorgen Christiansen, the head horse trainer, assured me he would have a big hitch ready by the time I got back from the indoor shows, and I joined them in Chicago for their opening.

The first Ringling Bros. heard about the change was when they read about it the following week in the showman's newspaper, *Billboard*.

U

Cole Bros. Circus

Pat Valdo called me in Detroit at the Shrine Circus to tell me I was still under contract with Ringling Bros. for the coming season. I told him I was sure that he was mistaken.

Pat told me I was being childish and did not realize the enormity of what I had done. It was childish, I suppose, but they had made me so by treating me like one. Nevertheless, I knew I was wrong; I should have given them a chance to present their side of the story before running off half-cocked.

First one, then another of the office staff called. I explained to them that no one had asked me to come back, nor had I heard from them, other than a Christmas card. They argued that it was a foregone conclusion that I would be back; no one had ever thought otherwise. Besides, I was still under contract to them and not at liberty to go elsewhere.

When I pointed out that the three-year contract I had signed had expired, it was hastily dug out of the files. They were under the impression that it had been for five years. They still had an awfully lot of lithographs of me, and these would now have to be put on the shelf.

Upon joining Cole Bros. Circus in Chicago, I found that, true to his word, Jorgen Christiansen had put together not a ten-horse hitch, but sixteen using his palomino liberty horses for the number. He had done an excellent job.

When I reported to him for rehearsal, I found that one of his handlers for an end ring had quit just as they were leaving winterquarters, and he had no one to work that liberty horse act. He was more concerned over that than anything else at the moment.

I offered to step in and work the act if something could be found in the wardrobe department for me to wear. He was very pleased and ordered the act brought in at once so that he could teach me the cues.

Black Hawk was well trained and made a good showing. Their rearing horse, though nothing like the great Troubadour, was good, and would improve. I, of course, had my own jumper, Rex.

I had left Rex at home during the last two indoor shows, as there had not been a jumping horse number. Zack Terrell had sent a truck to my barn in Scottsburg to pick up Rex and take him to winterquarters, then on to Chicago in their train. When they went to get Rex, Mother had pointed out what a great rearing pony Barney was and had them take him along; they had already made a place for him in the show. The wardrobe department had fixed up an outfit for him. He wore a bonnet; jumped through a papercovered hoop, and came out wearing a dress; then he walked down the track on his hind legs. They called it "Aunt Jemima Goes To The Circus." In the Chicago stadium the show went over big, and everyone was sure it was going to be a winner. Then we went on the road. It rained every day, and every day the crowds were small; this went on and on. They were unable to pay anyone's salary, but most of us were trying to stick it out. A few of the acts did leave.

In the meantime, I was taking a lot of bad falls due to the muddy, slippery lots. The rearing horse fell down on me several times, and Rex would often slide and knock the hurdle down, or slip as he landed on the other side. But the big hitch was the worst. Very often one of the horses would go down, usually to scramble back up, but, when this happened, I would go from my feet to astride one of the horses on which I was standing. This was not a very desirable position because your legs would then take a beating from the harness as the horses bumped into each other.

It was at this point that Mr. Terrell and Mr. Adkins called me to their private car for a talk. They explained the situation: They were not only broke, but going deeper in debt all the time. They felt bad because they had lured me away from Ringling Bros. It was also evident that I was taking a lot of punishment on account of the lousy tracks, and they did not feel they could continue to ask me to take those kinds of chances, without pay, any longer. No one was ever more thoughtful or kinder. They suggested I take the beautiful stallion I was riding, Black Hawk, and with him and Rex I would be able to play fairs and still do all right. They made out a bill of sale on Black Hawk; then they somehow raked together the five weeks' salary due me.

I sent home for a trailer, and when it arrived there was no room for Barney, so I left him with the show. They featured him for many years in his Aunt Jemima walk-around.

∪

Horse Shows

I went back home and back to my old standby, teaching other people and their horses. I was once more making money, but I no longer enjoyed doing it. It upset me that, after working with a horse to get it perfect in its gaits, the rider would get nervous when in front of a crowd, convey this to the animal, and not have it respond properly.

I recall one time when I went with one of my pupils to an important horse show. Her husband had spent a great deal of money for her horse and I, in turn, had spent a lot of time on the horse and the rider. The horse was everything that could be desired; I can't say the same for the rider.

Before the show I took the horse into the exercise ring to limber him up. Several men were standing on the outside, and I heard them remark what a fine mount he was. When the class that my horse was entered in came into the ring, the owner became excited and miscued him several times. With the best horse in this class under her, she came out a poor third.

As we were loading to go home, one of the men who had admired the horse earlier came up and said, "Next time, why don't you let this young lady show your horse? He ought to have won first place."

"Oh, winning isn't important," she replied. "You see, the man I am married to has lots of money, but we don't know any important people, and I figure since mostly society folks come to these things I will get to meet some."

Of course, none of this was any of my business as long as she was paying me for the job I was doing.

⋃

King Kong

Meanwhile, Cole Bros. Circus had closed and was back in Rochester. I had heard that they were badly in need of money and were selling some of their stock. I phoned them and asked if the rearing horse, King Kong, was among those to be disposed of. They told me that if he were not, they would see to it that he was. Ever my friends, Mr. Terrell and Mr. Adkins saw to it that I got my horse for a fair price. With the three horses I now had, I was in good shape to go to work.

The year was 1939, and I had booked myself to play the Deutschlandhalle in Berlin, Germany. They had contacted me before, but for the first time, I had my own horses and could accept the offer. It was quite an honor, because it was the first time they had ever invited an American

A pleasing glance, 1933. *Courtesy of the John & Mable Ringling Museum of Art, Tibbals Digital Collection.*

equestrian of my type to appear in their country.

In order to present my acts, it would be necessary for them to build a track for me to work on, as they just used a ring normally. Quite a few letters were exchanged about what would be needed. When all of the arrangements were just about complete, I was warned by just about everyone not to go. I wanted to go very badly, but for once I listened. Mother and I just happened to be listening to the radio the night the news came over it that the Deutschlandhalle had just been bombed.

Ringling's, The Second Time Around

Now that I had my three horses, it was time that I put them to work. True, I would have to buy a truck to transport them, but I had a little money put aside from my teaching and was in pretty good shape.

I contacted George Hamid, the agent who had booked Dexter and me into Canada, who said he would be happy to handle my acts. The first show he booked was the Police Circus in St. Louis, and he forwarded the contracts, which I signed. More would follow. It was at this time that my mother began having heart trouble. It was necessary to send her to Cincinnati for treatments. This took quite a bit of money, and I found I would no longer be able to finance the truck for the horses.

Meanwhile, Pat Valdo had called me several times from Florida. I had been so wrapped up in my new plans I am afraid I did not listen too well; now that the wind had been taken out of my sails, it was a different story. The next time Pat called I was more amenable. He told me that the North brothers, who were now in control of Ringling

Bros., would like to talk to me in person, because over the phone we seemed to get nowhere. Would I consider coming to Sarasota for a get-together? I agreed, packed my bags, put them in the car, and started out. At that time we did not have all the nice freeways nor the high-powered cars we have today.

I made the trip there without incident. After checking into the hotel, I called Pat Valdo to let him know I had arrived and would be available the next day. I washed my hair and was in the tub when the phone rang. It was Pat and the North boys; would I please come down to the lobby. I explained my situation, as I dripped water all over the floor, and asked if we couldn't wait until morning. No. They had to talk right now. So, with a towel wrapped around my head and looking far from glamorous, I went down.

It did not take long for us to get our differences ironed out, and they had a contract with them for me to sign.

"There is one catch, however," I told them. "I have signed a contract with George Hamid to play the Police Circus in St. Louis."

They assured me that it was perfectly all right; they could fix that easily. With all of the acts they had hired through the Hamid agency, he would be glad to do them this little favor and release me from my contract. So, with my mind at rest on that score, I went to my room.

The phone was ringing off the wall. When I answered, the connection was so bad I could hardly hear. All I could gather from my mother was, "Come home! Come home! Don't do anything but come home!" I grabbed my bags, checked out, and started for home. A million things that could have happened crossed my mind.

Before long I ran into the storm that had, no doubt, caused the garbled phone connection. I had trouble keeping the car on the road. Anyone who has ever been in one of those Florida storms will know what I had to contend with—wind blowing, trees falling.

Once when I stopped for gas, an attendant begged me to wait. "Lady, you could be riding into a hurricane!" But I was so frantic I went right on.

The wind and rain stopped at last, but not I; I kept right on going. Remember, when I had arrived in Sarasota, I had not had a chance to sleep; I just turned around and headed back for home. Whenever I stopped for gas, I would grab a bite to eat or drink some coffee and continue. Of course, each time I stopped I would try to call home, but was unable to get an answer.

I knew I was weaving in the road, so when the policeman pulled me over to the side, I did not try to explain, I just sat. He told me to follow him to the station.

At the station I told them of driving through the storm and how tired I was. I could see they did not believe my story. "What hotel did you say that you were staying at in Sarasota?" asked the man behind the desk.

I told him and he left. When he returned, he said, "I made a phone call, and you did, indeed, leave when you claimed. You must have just escaped the brunt of the storm before most of the roads were blocked by falling trees and flooding. What we cannot understand is why you didn't have the sense to stop."

He then took me back to my car and handed me a couple of blankets and a pillow. "Now, you climb into the back seat and go to sleep. I know you are in a great hurry, so I will not let you sleep over long. No one will bother you; after all, you are parked in front of the police station."

After a reasonable length of time, he awakened me and took me back inside, where he saw to it that I drank plenty of hot, black coffee and then he sent me on my way. Once again, I had the police to thank for a helping hand.

I drove frantically home; each time I had the car filled with gas I tried to call home, but could get no answer. When I, at last, pulled into the driveway, Mother ran out to meet me and said, "I do hope I caught you before you signed anything. Your agent called and said he had more dates for you."

I was too tired to explain that without some sort of transportation for the horses, I would have been unable to play the dates anyway. I went to bed and stayed there for two days.

A friend of mine with a horse trailer drove my horses to Peru, Indiana, where they were loaded on the train taking the baggage horses back to Sarasota to join the show for the coming season. I bought all sorts of things for Jimmy to eat on the trip. He filled a tub with ice and soft drinks, put up his cot in the car near to the horses, and was all set for the trip.

My return to Ringling Bros. winterquarters was without fanfare. I went to the stables, saw that Jimmy was all right and that my stock had been properly housed, and then I inquired about my dear Satan. The ring stock boss told me Satan had gone sour. The preceding year one of the jumping horse riders had attempted to ride him over just the ordinary hurdles. He gave her nothing but trouble, until she refused to ride him at all. He told me that Satan would run to the hurdle as if he really meant to jump and when he reached it, he would stop suddenly and knock it down. I could picture in my mind what had happened. When the rider had reached the hurdle, she had used the reins just a little to cue him, but he had been trained to jump with no reins or cue of any kind.

I asked to see him and found him tied up with a string of horses that were used in spec. I ordered them to put him in a box stall next to my own horses. A couple of days later I started to rehearse. Of course, I would be riding Troubadour most of the time for the waltz and rear, but I would use King Kong for rough or muddy tracks, as he was so sure-footed; then, Black Hawk for the high-school act, with Lindy as an alternative.

The interest of the horse trainers and management was centered on Rex. They intended again to feature the high fire jump and were anxious to see just how good he was. He had been trained for it, and he was good—but there was no way of knowing if he had the stamina to hold up under the rigors of making that jump twice daily all season. I worked Rex for them, and they left well satisfied . . . but I was not.

I called for Satan and told Jimmy to put my saddle on him. He stood quietly when they lifted me onto him. Then he walked off, with his head hanging low. This could not be my lively, spirited Satan. I had a certain call that I was in the habit of giving him just before I was ready for the jump. I got him into a canter and gave this call. He shook his head, threw up his heels, and dashed off. I motioned for them to put up the hurdle and over we went. I was delighted! Satan and I were back together again! Now, I do not mean, in any way, to low-rate Rex. He was my own, and I loved him dearly. But it was Satan who had helped me to the top in the circus, and I owed him so much.

We took the hurdle a couple more times, and, when I jumped off him, Satan came looking for his sugar. Now, I do not recommend sugar as a rule; carrots and apples are a far better treat, but when you are on the road they are not handily available, and cubes of sugar can be carried in your trunk.

Although, on the surface, it seemed I was being welcomed back with open arms, things were not entirely compatible. They felt, and I suppose justly so, that I had played them a shabby trick by leaving them the way I did. I, in turn, felt I had been imposed on.

I agreed to ride high school, waltz and rear, the Big Hitch, the fire jump, and work liberty horses if necessary, but I flatly refused to do the ride of Mazeppa unless I was compensated for it. In case you might be inclined to think, as they did, that I was just being bull-headed and stubborn, let me relate a little incident that had occurred in connection with the act.

As I have explained, while making the ride I was

lying across the horse with my head and hands dragging. On this particular day, just as my horse and I came to the jump, one of the wild horses ahead of us tripped over the hurdle and the heavy pole came sailing toward me. I did not see it, nor could I have done anything about it if I had. It hit my head and knocked me out.

I didn't get to take a bow. When we reached the backdoor, Jimmy grabbed me off the horse and, with the help of another groom, carried me to the doctor's wagon. One eye and the side of my face were swollen and black and blue for quite a long time after.

This all went away, but then I began to have very bad earaches and, as it became worse, my whole head hurt. The show's doctor kept pouring some sort of drops into my ear and insisted I take pain pills. At night I was given a hot water bottle to put on my pillow, and some sleeping pills.

I awoke one night screaming like I was being murdered, and waking up everyone within hearing distance. The porter, who had a key to everyone's stateroom, opened the door and turned on the light. My pillow was covered with blood. The show doctor was sent for. When we arrived in town the next morning, he took me to the hospital. There they discovered that when the abscess had broken, it had broken my eardrum as well. It left me completely deaf in that ear.

I figured now that if I were to chance losing the hearing in the other ear, or maybe even an eye from another accident of that kind, I ought to be paid extra money for the act. Their argument that they had all that special paper printed that they could not use did not change my mind.

Herewith I must digress and offer an explanation. It will be necessary to change names and places, not to protect the innocent, but myself. Better that they remain anonymous; however, the events were real. Suppose, then, I just call them "he" and "they," for lack of a better way.

I clashed with one of the two new horse trainers almost at once.

The North brothers were attempting to upgrade the show and give it extra class. They had bought a string of fine gaited horses and hired two excellent horsemen. Each day they would exercise these fine show horses in the open arena alongside the ring barn.

The management had offered me Nugget to again ride in center ring during the high-school number, but I declined and I never rode him again. Jimmy had put my silver saddle and white bridle on Black Hawk, and a very pretty picture they made.

The younger of the two trainers happened to be passing by and remarked to Jimmy, "I would like to try out that saddle."

I stepped forward and said, "I do not mind you riding the saddle, but I am afraid the horse is a little flighty." For some reason, Black Hawk disliked men.

The man looked down at me like something that had been left over from an ant's picnic. After scanning my 108 pounds, he replied, "I imagine I can ride anything you can."

Black Hawk played fair—he let the man get seated and then he broke loose: He bucked and he pitched. The guy, I will give him credit, did a good job of riding the horse. And he might have had a better chance had he been mounted on a different saddle, but mine was not designed for that type of riding. I felt sorry for him when he bit the dust.

The next day, as I was walking by the stalls where the show horses were kept, the young man accosted me and said, "How would you like to take a ride on a good horse?" I declined.

"Not used to riding good horses, huh?" he taunted. "It takes a lot of time and training to be able to ride a gaited horse, you know."

As usual, I boiled.

"Just which one would you like me to ride?" I asked.

He had one of them saddled. I adjusted the stirrups and, without a word, mounted the horse and put it through its paces.

When I got off the horse, the man said, "No one ever told us you knew how to ride gaited horses."

"That is how I make my living," I replied.

The long train trip from Sarasota to New York was over, and we were once more in Madison Square Garden. I looked around my private dressing room, the same one I had occupied for so many years, and wondered who might have dressed there last year. I unpacked my trunks and hung up my costumes.

The opening was a success, as far as I was concerned, and all of my numbers went off without a hitch.

It was the third day of the show when I was called to the phone in the office. This had never happened before. If someone wished to get in touch with you, they contacted you at your hotel. I hurried to the phone; it was George Hamid. "Miss Herbert, I hope you have not forgotten that you have a contract to play the Police Circus in St. Louis."

"I thought Mr. North had fixed that with you," I gasped.

"Well, you thought wrong, and you had better get there," said he.

"I am sorry, Mr. Hamid," I replied, "but there is no way I can possibly make it; you see, my horses are here in New York."

"We anticipated such an answer from you. However, they have hired the Cole Bros. Circus animals for their show, and there are horses belonging to them that you can use. Your picture is on the cover of the program, and they also have a lot of publicity out on you. If you do not get there, they are going to sue."

I hastened to Mr. North's office and explained what had happened. He told me not to worry; he would take care of it. My mind at ease, I returned to my dressing room. Suddenly, there was a knock on the door. It was Pat Valdo. He informed me, "You are going to have to go to St. Louis."

So, I went down to the basement where the horses were kept and had Jimmy put one of my sidesaddles in a gunny sack, of all things, to take to the plane. One of the ladies from the wardrobe department found a large cardboard box and helped me to pack some of my costumes in it. I then sent Jimmy to the airport in a cab with these things, to wait for me while I went to the hotel to pack my bags and check out.

I removed my makeup and went to the paymaster with the money order that Mr. Valdo had given me to pay for the trip. I went to the hotel, packed, and checked out. Just as I turned to leave the desk, the clerk said, "Wait a moment, please. You have a phone call."

I could hear the spec music in the background; the show had begun. It was Pat Valdo on the phone, telling me to return to the Garden at once. I asked the hotel clerk please to care for my luggage and hurried back to the building, which was only a short distance from where I was staying.

When I arrived at the backdoor entrance, Pat Valdo grabbed my arm and announced, "We have it all fixed. You do not have to go to St. Louis and you can still make the high-school number. Hurry!"

I made it all right, but I only had time to get into a costume, no makeup or a chance to fix my hair. Well, at least they had squared it and I was off the hook.

As I rode out, after finishing the number, Pat again met me with the news, "We were unable to fix it, after all, and you will have to go."

I couldn't believe all this was happening. I went to my dressing room, got out of my wardrobe and into street clothes again. This time I carefully put my things into my trunks and locked them.

As I approached the backdoor entrance, the watchman stopped me. "I just had a call from the front office; they said for me to stop you. They are on their way here."

This time it was Mr. North, who said, "Get dressed for the fire jump and we will explain later."

This was getting to be like a Mack Sennett comedy.

I hurried back to the dressing room and, somehow or other, managed to make the number. No one ever did explain how they finally were able to fix it, but because I was not sued, I assume they did.

But, what about poor Jimmy? All of that time he had been sitting at the airport, waiting. I did not feel like trying to explain all of this mess to him over the phone, so I called a cab and went to the airport and picked him up. After we stopped for a bite to eat and Jimmy was back at the Garden, I went to my hotel for a much-needed rest.

It was a season of general animosity that had started in winterquarters and grew worse as the season went on. The horse show trainers felt themselves to be superior to the circus trainers, and, in turn, they considered the gaited horse riders a bunch of stuffed shirts. The new group of circus horse trainers bickered constantly. In his struggle to become the Top Banana, the German, whom they had dubbed "the Dutchman," kept everyone in an uproar.

The manege and jumping horse riders were in a constant state of unrest, not knowing which side to take. Always before, the equestrians had been a little close-knit group that hung together; now they were being drawn apart. It seemed incredible that one man could so disrupt an entire crowd. Well, maybe not so incredible at that. Hitler managed to do it.

I worked hard that season. Besides the high-school number, the waltz and rear, and the high fire jump, I also drove a hackney pony hitched to a cart in the gaited horse display and, when necessary, worked one of the liberty horse acts, plus, of course, the Big Hitch.

Then, too, while the others performers were still resting, I would be downtown at the broadcasting studio.

Sometimes in large cities, there would be two stations to go to in the morning.

Frankly, I was tired.

I cannot recall if the season was especially long, or if it just seemed that way, but now it was drawing to an end. On closing night, John Ringling North came by in the backyard where I was seated on my horse waiting for the last ride of the year. He said for me to have a nice winter and not to worry about my horses; they would see to it that they were well taken care of while I was at home with my mother. He also told me they had several new things planned for me to do in the coming season, and one of them was sensational.

I thanked him for everything they had done for me, wished him well, and I never saw him again. I had made up my mind I was not going back. There was no need for someone to dream up something new for me to do; I had only one neck to break and if I were going to break it, I would do it on my own, without anyone's help.

I took inventory: I had three horses of my own, King Kong, Rex, and Black Hawk; a stateroom full of furniture; two circus trunks filled with wardrobe; several suitcases for my street clothes; and a large trapping box full of saddles and harness—all of this with no place to go and no way to get there.

After taking my car out of storage, I asked one of the show mechanics to go with me to some used car lots in quest of a suitable truck. I learned later that no one of the show ever suspected that I would make such a move. Everyone took it for granted that now that I was back, I would stay. They felt that by now I had learned my lesson. Nevertheless, I bought a truck and had three padded stalls built into it, a good solid loading ramp, and a compartment to hold my trunks and all of the stuff from my stateroom.

While the truck was being worked on, I got in touch with Herbert Yates, who at that time owned the Republic Studios. I remembered that he had once said to me, "If you can ever come out to Hollywood, I am sure that we would be able to use you in motion pictures."

He was a very good friend of my former boss, Mr. Sam Gumpertz, who had introduced me to him in the first place; now I was about to take him at his word. When I called him on the long distance phone and asked him if the offer still stood, he said, "To be sure, come on."

♘

The Showoff

*J*left Ringling with many pleasant—and some embarrassing—memories. I think everyone likes to see a showoff put down.

It had been raining steadily for three days and three nights. The poor, hard-working big-top crew had managed to get the tent up and seats all in place. They had plodded off to the dining tent to be fed before the start of the night show. It had been impossible to present the matinee.

The track was a sea of mud. Straw had been scattered about, but did little good; nonetheless, the crowd was large. The jump, for a wonder, had been called off, and I was told to do the waltz and rear, but to take it easy. Sir Christopher, who was the most sure-footed and the slowest of my rearing horses, would have his turn today. When we had a bad, muddy track and rings like this, we always omitted the laydown from the high-school routine and we substituted the one-knee. I always wore rainy-day wardrobe in bad weather.

Now, it so happened that I had some friends whom I wished to impress in the first row, center. One of my best and showiest outfits was a long, white flowing evening dress trimmed in crystal beads, and with this I wore a headdress of long, white feathers. It was my choice for the act. My horse was perfectly trained, I'll say that for him—too perfect. When everyone else did the one-knee, he, with no cue, lay down. I, having cued him for the one-knee, was holding my whip in both hands, above my head and smiling. There was no way I could jump off in time. I went sailing, head first, into the mud and was covered from head to toe. My sense of humor kept me from making an utter ass of myself, and I started to laugh. The audience, which had at first gasped, started to laugh with me, which made me giggle all the harder. I went through the rest of the act and then rode to the backdoor where I usually changed horses, hoping that Mr. Valdo would motion me out. I looked at Pat Valdo, but he continued to look the other way, so I got on the rearing horse and finished the act. As I rode out the backdoor, I overheard Pat say to someone, "I sure wish our clowns could get that kind of laughs."

That reminds me of the time when I got the laugh on everybody. The Circus Saints and Sinners were giving a ball in New York City for all of their members and the performers from Ringling Bros. It was to be a costume affair with everyone wearing a mask. The girls in the dressing rooms were discussing which of their costumes they would wear when someone suggested switching with each other. I doubted if it would fool anyone.

It had been arranged for cars to assemble at the backdoor to take us to the ball. The only person on the show who knew what devilment I was up to (and a better conspirator you could not find anywhere) was Otto Griebling, the famous tramp clown. He worked with me several days, between shows, teaching me what to do. He was a genius in the art of pantomime.

The night of the ball he came to my dressing room the first chance he had, after his part of the show was over and he could sneak in without anyone seeing him or the bundle he was carrying. As soon as I finished my last number, which closed the show, I hastily donned one of his tramp suits as he applied clown makeup to my face. What an artist he was; my own mother would not have known me. He again cautioned me: "Whatever you do . . . DO NOT SPEAK." Otto and I hurried down the hallway and got into the car with a now inpatient driver. I handed him my suitcase and we were off.

When we reached the ball, Otto, who was dressed in an animal costume, said, "Here is where we split. Go mingle with the society people and avoid the circus folks."

The party was in full swing when we arrived. People with drinks in their hands were milling about while others crowded the dance floor. A short while later dinner was served. At the very end of the hall was a long table where the notables from the Saints and Sinners and the star performers of the circus were seated. These were the people who would be called upon to give a short speech. One seat at the table was empty.

I sat at the table where most of the show clowns had gathered. The circus clowns were sure I was a towner and the others thought I was from the show. The band continued to play during dinner, and the people were dancing between courses. I danced with a few of the town ladies and pulled some of the silly stunts Otto had taught me. Using pantomime, as Otto had told me to do, I kept pleading with one of the ladies for her handkerchief as a souvenir, and in desperation she gave it to me. In the midst of all my fun Otto gave me the high sign, meaning it was time for me to make my exit. I went to the hatcheck stand and got my suitcase, then went to the ladies room. I had a heck of a time convincing the maid that I was not only a lady but in a very big hurry. I got her to laughing at the prank I was pulling off, and she assisted me in getting the makeup and my wig off and dressed in a stunning evening gown complete with a black velvet cape lined in white.

I waited outside the door while the master of ceremonies announced each person at the head table and each one made a few remarks. Then, when the emcee came to my name, he said, "For some reason or other, Miss Dorothy Herbert has not been able to attend tonight." Otto had made arrangements for this announcement.

With that I walked to the middle of the dance floor, threw a kiss, and said, "Surprise! I have been here all of the time." Gallantly, I handed the handkerchief back to the lady who had been my dancing partner and said, "Thank you, for the dance, madame, from your humble clown."

It was absolutely amazing that no one had guessed my identity; full credit for this went to Otto. The other performers could have killed me, and I did not blame them one bit. Pat Valdo was beside himself. He had thought that the tramp clown was a towner and had instructed one of the clowns to contact him about going with the show. The next day Pat said, "If you do not stop these foolish antics, I do not know what I am going to do with you. We pay clowns to furnish comedy and we do not need any from you. Frankly, you are driving me batty."

What had I done now? This last escapade might even be too much for my friends to stomach, I thought. Maybe I had gone too far. But, much to my surprise, everyone congratulated me on the great gag I had pulled— everyone except Pat Valdo.

⋃

Uncle Tom's Cabin

Another incident from my Ringling days I fondly remember was when we chose to produce *Uncle Tom's Cabin* for the Fourth of July entertainment. I was picked to play the part of Little Eva, not because of my acting ability, I can assure you, but because (so they said) I had long, blonde hair. After we had started to rehearse, I was sure it was because of the slapstick nature of the part.

Rosie Reiffenach was cast as Topsy, and there could not have been a better choice. With her sense of humor and her German accent, she was a riot. One of the girls from an acrobatic act was Liza, and a midget took the part of her baby. All of them would work in blackface.

Between shows we would rehearse. As we went along, we added anything funny that came to us. No one had any idea what we were up to, with the exception of Merle Evans. A week or so before the great day, we got the wardrobe ladies to help us with our costumes. They carried a sewing machine in one of the wagons, which sure helped, as they would have been a great deal of work to do by hand. I recall I wore a pink dress with many ruffles and a blue sash.

We put on the play between shows. Everyone took a seat in the reserved section in the big top; even the office staff was there. Most were looking quite bored as the play opened, but not for long!

Scene One: Topsy and some other little black kids were playing hopscotch. Little Eva came skipping out and asked if she might be permitted to join them. They replied by socking her in the face with a large lemon cream pie. She fell backward into a fake drum we had made for the occasion, smashing it and supposedly infuriating the drummer, who then chased her out of the tent. This was our opening, and the rest of the play was on a par.

An example: Hunks of ice tied to ropes were dragged across the stage. The midget, also in blackface and smoking a cigar, was perched on Liza's shoulder as she attempted to jump from cake to cake of ice as it slid across the stage; Simon Legree, with a long lash whip and all of the show dogs we had been able to borrow, was not far behind.

The play ended with Little Eva going up a ladder to heaven. The ladder fell just as she was about to reach the top and there she hung, upside down, with a safety belt holding her. Topsy and her gang, plus the rest of the cast, then sang "The Man on the Flying Trapeze."

Of course, there was a lot more to it than this. I gave you just a few of the highlights. Zany, to be sure, but we had fun, as did everyone watching.

After the play we served refreshments. Later, the band played while all who cared to danced on the stage until someone hollered, "Doors," the cue that the public was about to enter.

‿

California Bound

*T*told Mr. Yates I had no idea how long it might take me to get there, but I was on my way. In those days, when the shows closed a lot of men were out of work. I had heard that Rodger Oberman was an excellent truck driver, and he offered to take that job. I explained to him that I would not be able to pay very much, as I was not quite sure what was going to happen. That was the understatement of the year!

My groom, Jimmy, was going with me, of course, and, at the last minute Jack Gibson, who also worked on ring stock, asked if he might go along. His sister lived near Hollywood, and he was planning to spend the winter with her. I figured I already had enough help, but he assured me he would pay his way by cooking for all of us.

If, perchance, you are wondering why no one inquired as to what was transpiring, I can think of only one explanation. For the first few weeks after the show closed, nearly everyone took some time off. The horse trainers were not yet back working, so there was no reason for them to go to the stables. The main offices were some distance from the barns, and the grooms did not hobnob with the office staff, anyway. Be that as it may, we loaded up and left without anyone noticing.

Thus ended all of those glorious years with The Greatest Show On Earth. I wonder if they ever did notice that I was gone.

As I write this I cannot help but think what a foolhardy thing that was to do: to start out on a trip from coast to coast in a secondhand truck, with three horses and three men, my car, and not too much money after buying and rebuilding the truck. When I was young it seems I spent most of my time taking chances of one sort or another, and usually getting into a mess.

Now, California was a lot farther from Florida than it looked on the map. It soon became evident that I was not going to be able to finance this trip. The men slept in the truck, but I, of course, went to a motel each night. Many of the fairgrounds where we stopped charged for staying over and watering; then there was the feed for the stock and all of us, plus gas for the two vehicles. I was becoming quite alarmed, but kept my worries to myself.

About this time we were passing by where a rodeo was showing, and the men wanted to stop. They got to talking to some of the rodeo hands and must have been bragging about our horses, because the promoter came over to the seats and asked if I would care to work some of his shows as a special attraction. I jumped at the chance; so now we were in the rodeo business! I was glad for the opportunity to make some money and be able to continue with what I now regarded as my cross-country tour.

That first date for him led to the rodeos and also some fairs.

Vern Elliot, who was the producer of the Fort Worth Fat Stock Show, caught my acts and booked me for that one. This was one of the big, important rodeos, quite unlike the little fly-by-nights that we were now working. We were going to make it after all.

It was in Harlingen, Texas, that bad luck caught up with us. We were playing a celebration there: the Charro Days. It was an annual event that ran for five days; riders and revelers from Texas and across the border participated. The costumes worn by the Mexican charros and their senoritas were absolutely fantastic: gold and silver braids woven into fabrics of every hue, glittering with spangles galore.

Each day a street parade was held, with much dancing and singing, and onlookers came from miles around to join in. Some of them remained the whole five days, either staying with friends or camping at a site that had been arranged for them at the edge of town.

Harlingen had a fairgrounds of sorts, and this was where the rodeo was held. It was not one of the top-rated shows on the rodeo circuit, but it was by far the noisiest and the most enthusiastically received I ever witnessed.

The Mexican charros entered into each event with no thought whatsoever for life or limb. Whether they won or lost, everyone cheered. There were two shows each day; the rodeo was set up in the infield, and I worked on the track in front of the grandstand. The high school and the waltz and rear were sandwiched in between events, with the high fire jump closing the show.

On the third day of the show the weather, which had been ideal, turned cold. By the middle of the night performance it started to drizzle, then turned to sleet. I asked the manager of the show if I might omit the fire jump. He was adamant, insisting that I go on. He pointed to the fact that I had a pay or play contract. I, in turn, drew his attention to the track, which now had small patches of ice forming on it.

I was too inexperienced to know that no person can force another to attempt a feat in which an element of danger has been added, making it almost certainly doomed to failure—such as asking a diver to jump into a pool from which the water had been removed, or a shod horse to gallop on ice.

Thinking only of the money, which we were sorely in need of, I had Jimmy saddle up Rex. Rodger lit the pole for the fire jump, but it was so sodden with water that it went out at once. Rex cleared the jump but fell when he landed on the other side. He was not harmed, but my leg was broken. Rodger picked me up in his arms and carried me to my car, while Jimmy caught Rex with the aid of a couple of cowhands; then Rodger whisked me away to a doctor.

The doctor put a cast on my leg and advised me to stay off of it for some time. We had a couple of weeks' layoff before our next date, and at the end of that time I went to another doctor and had him reinforce the cast and we went on. What else was there to do?

It so happened that the broken leg was my right one, the one I had learned to throw up in the air and still hang on to the horse. I had grown not to depend on it for either grip or balance. Had it been my left leg, which fit under the sidesaddle horn and upon which I depended almost entirely, I would not have been able to ride at all.

When we arrived in Fort Worth, Mr. Elliot was very upset when he saw me with a cast on my leg, and said that I ought not to have come. I assured him I had just finished two other shows and would be all right. The shows went off smoothly, with no mishaps. I wore long, flowing evening gowns and the cast was not noticeable.

After this engagement I felt we had enough money put aside to finish the journey to California. I had bought each of the men a new outfit, and they were in good spirits as we set off on the last lap of our trip.

It was our second day on the road after leaving Fort Worth. It was very late, and we had not yet been able to find a place to unload, water and feed the horses, and spend the night. I was overly tired and my leg was bothering me. We had started out early and had driven all day. We pulled into an all-night restaurant and filling station called the Black Cat.

As we were leaving, a group was standing outside, chatting. We had eaten our late supper in the cafe and, after filling up the truck with gas, I told the boys to go on ahead, I would service my car, pay the bill, and catch up with them down the road. My back was turned when I heard a crash and screams, then mass confusion.

I ran out onto the road where my truck and another had collided. "Rodger," I said, "I know you are tired. Tell me the truth—was it your fault?"

He assured me it was not. Just as he was pulling out of the driveway, another truck, which had been coming in the opposite direction, suddenly swerved over to his side of the road and crashed into him. Jack, who was seated next to Rodger, told me this was indeed the case.

Sure now of my grounds, I borrowed a pencil and paper from the restaurant cashier and asked all of the bystanders who had seen the accident to write down their names and where they might be reached. Because it was a moonlit night and the place was well lighted, they had been able to see everything clearly. I had already told Jack and Jimmy, who was riding in the back of the truck with the horses, to unload them and see if any of the horses had been hurt.

By now the highway patrol had arrived, and Jack came running up to tell me that they would not allow him to touch anything. I went to the officer who seemed to be in charge and informed him that I was placing a call to the Humane Society. I demanded his name and badge number. I was pretty sure they would not be open at this hour of the night . . . but the bluff worked.

The officer told me that to him, this was an unusual accident and he was not quite sure of the procedure; nevertheless, he gave his permission for us to unload. The horses were scratched; although no wounds appeared to be serious, I suspect I made quite a to-do about it.

In the meantime, the ambulance had come and gone, and I was beginning to feel faint. I went into the cafe for a glass of water, and gave the pencil back to the lady; strange that something like that could matter at a time like this. It was then I found that both the driver of the other truck and mine were under arrest, and learned for the first time how serious the accident had actually been. I was heartsick. My truck was wrecked, Rodger was under arrest, my horses were standing by the side of the road, and I had no one to turn to. It was then that the kind, warm-hearted people of this little town came to my rescue. They moved away from the corner where they had huddled, having some sort of a discussion. They came over to the table where I was seated and everyone began talking at once. There horses could stay in an old, unused hay barn down the road, and the men could sleep on their cots there, too. The owner of a small motel offered me a room at a very reduced rate. Everyone was so very kind.

A wrecker hauled my truck away to be repaired, and the men and I settled down to wait for the trial. Several days later we learned that a woman who had been in the truck had died in the hospital where she had been taken; she had been five months pregnant. I was very worried; we were strangers here, show folks to boot.

I need not have worried so. When it came time for the trial, all of those eyewitnesses described just what had happened. All of the facts came to light the first day of the interrogation. Five people had been seated in the cab of the pickup truck; the two women were on the men's laps. All of them had been drinking. The case went on until noon when everyone, except the two drivers who were still in custody, was excused for lunch.

Shortly after we returned, the second woman who had been riding in the pickup truck, and who had been unharmed except for some bruises, was called to the witness stand.

She testified that just before the crash, the driver of

the pickup had said, "Would you like to see me hit that big red truck?" He had meant only to make the women scream, then swerve out of the way in the nick of time, but he had lost control and, thus, the crash.

After her testimony, Rodger, my driver, was released. During the trial it had come out that the driver of the pickup truck had been using his boss's truck without permission.

My truck had been repaired, and we were now ready to continue on. The only trouble was that we were, again, out of money. While talking to some of the rodeo performers at shows we had played, I had picked up the name Harry Rowell. From the performers, I knew that he put on a lot of shows in California; impulsively, I phoned him.

He remembered me after I told him who I was, as he had attended the Fort Worth Fat Stock Show. When I told him I needed work, he said, "Of course, come on. I can use your acts."

I was very embarrassed to have to explain that I did not have the money to get there.

Laughingly, he said, "So, what's new? You rodeo people are usually broke. So, how much will it take to get you here?"

I can't say I liked the "you rodeo people" much, but I did like the way he operated. I named a figure and picked up the money the next morning at Western Union.

Working his shows was fun. He owned a big cattle ranch in Hayward, California. He was not a rodeo promoter; he owned all of his own stock and equipment and produced his own shows. Besides his stock trucks, he brought along to his shows a truck that was referred to as the chuck wagon, and each evening after the show was over there would be a big barbecue for all of the help. I liked his approach to show business.

By now my reader might be inclined to wonder what effect, if any, all of these delays might be having on my employer-to-be, Mr. Herbert Yates. From time to time I had been getting in touch with him to let him know how we were progressing, or not progressing, which was mostly the case.

I confided a few of our problems to him, omitting the one about the broken leg, of course; no use to worry him unduly. At first he seemed to be sympathetic, but, as time went on, I began to sense that my stories were beginning to lack credibility, because the last time I called, he asked me if, by any chance, I might be making the journey by wagon train.

So now, although we could have stayed and played some more of his shows, I thanked Mr. Rowell, and we were, once more, on our way to Hollywood—maybe not with stars in our eyes, but, at least, with a few more bucks in our pockets.

As we crossed the line into California, I could not help but feel more proud than I had ever felt before at the courage and fortitude of our pioneer ancestors; they had made this trip without even the aid of a road map. And, while we had encountered both Indians and Mexicans at the rodeos, none of them had been hostile; in fact, they had all been downright friendly.

Later, when I told this to Mr. Yates, he said, "Even with everything in your favor, the pioneers made better time than you did."

◡

Hollywood

*U*pon our arrival in California, we went directly to Burbank to the stables of a friend of mine, Sam Garret. He was a very famous trick roper and had been the world's champion several times; now he owned a boarding stable and training arena.

I rented a stall for each of the horses. Sam had a small guest house that I rented for myself. Jack left for his long-awaited visit with his sister. (He and I were to meet many times during the years to come. Being very knowledgeable about horses, he became the ring stock boss on the Cole Bros. Circus.) Rodger stayed for a few days and then got a job as a truck driver with a transportation company; our paths did not cross again. Jimmy, of course, stayed with me. He slept in the bunkhouse with the other help, and ate at a restaurant a short distance away.

After a couple of days of much needed rest I drove to the Republic Studios and reported to Mr. Yates that I was ready to go to work. He called in his production manager and told him I was to be included in the next serial that was filmed.

Mr. Yates explained to him that what he had in mind was a girl star who would do all kinds of stunts: come to the rescue, as it were (and save the old homestead, I supposed)—a sort of Gene Autry or Roy Rogers . . . minus the singing, I hoped. Mr. Yates then ordered a screen test to be made right away. Because this was on a Friday, I was told to report Monday morning, early.

On Monday, after I had finished with the makeup man and the hairdresser and was outfitted in Western garb, I was driven to location. The makeup man and the hairdresser rode in the car with me.

I did not know what I expected, but certainly not a test on a horse! There stood this big, white horse with a huge, silver-mounted, Western saddle. The wrangler who was holding him told me that he was one of the three lookalikes that belonged to the studio and were used in *The Lone Ranger* series. Silver had two doubles, each with a different function. This one was used when a scene called for a rear.

The wrangler adjusted the stirrups, which were, of

course, far too long. Another man drew a line on the ground, and the director informed me that I was to gallop up to that line and rear the horse. No one bothered to tell me what the cue was to make the horse rear, and no one was around to ask.

I cantered the horse up to the line and, upon reaching it, I pulled on the reins. The horse made what was to me, after the horses I was used to, a very half-hearted rear.

"Okay," called the director. "The next one will be a take."

Far from satisfied, I thought to myself, "I am not going to settle for this; I am going to have to make it look good."

This time, when I reached the line, I yanked on the reins and the horse reared all right—and fell over backward. I picked myself up out of the dirt and was in for another surprise.

The director was jumping up and down and shouting to the cameraman, "Did you get it? Did you get it? That will make a great stock shot."

The dirt was brushed off of me, the hairdresser cleaned my hair with something that smelled like naphtha gas, and the makeup man repaired my smudged face. The wrangler brushed off the horse, which was unharmed, and the director called for another shot, which must have suited him, because when it was over they loaded everything and we went back to the studio.

I hung around the telephone awaiting the verdict. Before leaving Florida I had been under the impression that it was a foregone conclusion that I would be featured in a motion picture. Why else would I have attempted that hectic trip? When the phone rang at last, it was Mr. Yates' secretary advising me to report to Mr. Yates' office the following morning.

When I expressed my concern to Mr. Yates the next day, he laughed.

"That is a normal procedure; everyone has a screen

test. We have to know how you are going to photograph. You photograph well. Your hair will have to be lightened some, and you need to lose about ten pounds, which you will have time to do, because the next serial to be made is Fu Manchu, and there is no way that they could write you into that one."

He told me they would send for me in a few weeks. In the long run, this was a break for me, considering the stunts I was required to do. It gave my leg, which was still bothering me, more time to heal.

Sam Garret's practice arena was large. I had Jimmy set up the hurdles for Rex to jump; I also worked Black Hawk and King Kong. I knew I would be expected to do a lot of Western riding, so I asked Sam for his assistance in locating a horse of that type. Certainly he knew of a lot of places to look, and we found one suited for what I wanted the second day. I bought it and went to work training it.

After I had been at the Garret ranch a short time, Sam told me that some of the people who were boarding their horses at his stable were very interested in having their horses trained, and also in learning to ride jumps. They wanted him to ask if I might be interested.

I welcomed the chance to earn some money while I waited around for a picture to start. We formed several classes; they were a jolly crowd, and I liked working with them.

Several times a week I would have to drive to the studio and work with the writers there in regard to the stunts I would be doing in the picture. The script was finished at last, and they gave me a copy.

It was to be a serial: *Mysterious Doctor Satan*. I was cast as the doctor's secretary and, from the looks of things, I would spend most of my time rescuing him and his daughter from all sorts of predicaments. I studied the first episode over and over. Then I found, to my dismay, that they did not start at the beginning and go through the story, but were going to shoot an episode I hadn't read yet.

The first day of shooting took place indoors on a sound stage. I had been told to report at an ungodly hour of the morning to the hairdresser and makeup man. I had already been fitted for wardrobe a few days earlier. Someone handed me a briefcase, and I was told by the director to enter a room filled with an assortment of people and, without attracting the attention of any of them, convey to a large man wearing a mask the secret formula I had in my possession, hidden in the briefcase. All of these greedy people were seeking to get their hands on this formula. This action was to take place without speaking a single word.

During the short time that I had gone to the Paramount Dramatic School in New York, I had not been coached on anything like this.

I opened the door and walked in, letting the door slam shut behind me, causing everyone in the room to look in my direction.

The director called for us to try it again, quietly.

This time, after turning around and pushing the door shut gently, I gazed up at this hunk of man, who appeared to be eight feet tall, and, with the look of a dying calf, I gave him a sickly grin and glanced down at the object I was holding in my clammy hands.

Everyone seemed surprised except the director. He was stunned.

I had a feeling I wasn't making much of a hit with the director when he inquired, "How many pictures have you appeared in?"

"None, so far."

That's when I heard him mumble, "I get them all." I guess he figured I was someone's movie-struck girlfriend who was being pushed off on him, but, because he did not know whose, he didn't say anything more.

I was taken to a far-off corner, and when my instructor felt I was ready for it, they shot the scene. Meanwhile, of course, they had been taking other shots. Nothing more was said until a couple of days later.

All of those concerned with this particular episode had been driven to another studio that had a large sound stage, with a boat and real water. I was dressed in a navy blue sailor suit trimmed in white. When I walked onto the set I noticed another girl dressed in the same sort of outfit as mine, and with the same kind of hairdo.

As I drew near, I could not help but overhear the argument she was having with one of the prop men; it had to do with the stunt she had been requested to perform. I walked over to the director and told him I was supposed to do all of my own stunt work, not use a double.

To which he quipped, "And I assume that you are going to do the horse stunts, too?"

Before the filming began I had been requested to lose a little weight, as they told me the camera adds about ten pounds to the way you look. I had managed to take the weight off, so, at that time, I weighed 105 pounds, and hardly looked like a roughneck rider. Why this man had not been informed of the work I was to do, I will never know.

One of the scriptwriters, who happened to be standing nearby and heard him, said, "That's right, Mr. Brown, she does her own stunts. That is why she is in the picture in the first place. In fact, most of these stunts were her own original suggestions, or else devised from some that she has already done."

In the scene they were about to shoot, six men were having a fight—the good guys and the bad guys. I was supposed to climb up a ladder, grab a rope with one hand, swing off, and hit a couple of the bad guys in the back, knocking them down. I was then to pick up a gun that had been dropped on the deck, and shout, "Hold it, boys!"

Now, this was not much of a stunt for an aerialist, plus the fact that I had hung up a web (a piece of rope equipment used on circuses) at Sam's and had been practicing on it. Here, however, they had a rope run through a pulley, with two men holding it. When the time came, they would

An Atwell stunt photo, sure to make the front page. With
Ringling Bros. and Barnum & Bailey, 1930. *Courtesy of Tim Tegge.*

give the rope a yank, and down I would come. I told them the way I thought it ought to be done and was informed that they had been performing such stunts since before I was born.

Came time for the shot, someone called, "Action," they yanked, the rope slipped, giving them a rope burn, and they let go; I went sailing across the deck on my backside. Now, the floor was made of rough lumber, and the shot they got (I saw it later) was me howling, "Splinters!"

I was sent to the studio doctor and, after he had removed the splinters, we tried the scene again. This time they agreed to give my way a try, and it worked fine.

Due to bad weather, until now we had been shooting all indoor scenes; now that the sun was out, we were told that the next day we would go on location. So, the next morning the actors were loaded into cars, the crew and extras were loaded into big buses, and we were driven to the mountains not too far away.

The scene, which the studio writers and I had written together, called for a horse to do a quite difficult jump. They had brought out some horses from the stable that furnished them to the studio. When I looked at the horse I was supposed to use, I said, "This horse will not do. I am sure that he has not been trained for it."

The director consulted with the head wrangler, and he agreed. They had no horse in their stable that could do the stunt as written.

"What are we supposed to do now?" asked the director. "I wish they would stop writing in things that require animals with specialized training."

I spoke up then and told him that I had the horse that had been trained to do the stunt, and that it had been written into the script at my suggestion. I do not think he quite believed me; nevertheless, he told the head wrangler to send someone to pick up the horse and bring it to the set.

I went to the phone and called Jimmy at the barn. I

told him to have Rex ready as a studio truck was on the way; also, to bring my own saddle, and for him to come along, too.   Even if the horse had been adequate, in my opinion, to take the jump, I could not have accomplished it without my own specially equipped saddle.   The director had not seen fit to discuss any of the upcoming scenes with me ahead of time, so I saw no reason to stick my neck out and offer any unsolicited suggestions.   I often wondered if he and I would ever become compatible.

When they unloaded Rex, I told Jimmy to saddle him.   It took a special know-how to saddle my horses; extra safety girths, for example, to keep the saddle from slipping.   Because Jimmy did not belong to the union, they had a stand-by wrangler to assist him.

In this scene, the doctor, for whom I worked as secretary, and his daughter were being held captive.   In order to obtain their freedom, the doctor must reveal the secret of his new formula, which he steadfastly refused to do.   I had to climb up an outside trellis and get into the shack through a small hole in the roof.   After undoing the ropes with which they were tied, I then led them out a back door where several horses were tied to a hitching rack.   As they were galloping off to safety, I spied two of the villains approaching.   In order to divert their attention, I mounted my horse and galloped off in the opposite direction.

Now, in a scene like this, where an element of danger was involved, they did not call for a rehearsal; instead, several cameras were called into play and they tried to get it on film with the first shot.

Suddenly, in my path loomed a high fence; it looked as if I were trapped.   I galloped Rex toward it, and just as he was about to jump, a shot rang out and I fell into my layback, with one leg in the air, hands dragging, as though I had been hit.   I did not know how long they would be following me with the cameras, so I remained in that position until the pickup men caught up with me.

When I rode back, the entire crew applauded.   Evidently they did not attend the circus very much, or they would have seen me perform this stunt. Then it came to me: Ringling Bros. had not played the West Coast since I had added this to the jumping number.

The director was delighted. As I jumped off of my horse, he came over and put his arm around me. "One of the writers said that you would do your own stunts, but I had not expected anything quite like this. It was great. And now I do remember seeing you ride in a circus."

"Thanks," I retorted, "and if you add, "when I was a little boy on my daddy's lap," I think that I shall slap you."

That really broke him up. I have never heard anyone laugh louder. I was twenty-eight years old.

From then on, the director and I were the best of friends. He consulted me before each stunt and used my horses for the rest of the picture. When it came time for the trick riding parts, and he found that I had had the foresight to buy a horse and train him for the special stunts, he was indeed pleased. I was happy that the director, Bunny Brown, and I were finally in accord, because some of the subsequent scenes were to call for understanding and patience.

We were at a new location, one with long, winding roads that would give them plenty of room to film long shots of the chases on the docket for that day. Everyone not working in a shot was looking for a shady spot to sit; it was so very hot, and the sun kept beating down upon us.

Now it was time for some of the trick riding. The script called for me to be galloping down the road with one of the bad guys in hot pursuit. He is madly firing his gun at me. In order not to get hit from behind, and also to be able to return his fire, I go into a fender drag, placing me facing him.

The gun was heavy and, for some reason, the horse bucked. I had practiced this stunt in Sam's arena, and had been able to do it four times in a row, which I figured was quite enough—and all that would be required. Instead, they had me do it over and over to shoot it from different angles. I repeated the drag sixteen times.

When I got off of my horse at last, I asked that someone help me to remove my boot. They could not get it off, my ankle was so swollen. They sent for the doctor, who cut off the boot and sent me home.

I figured I had blown it for sure that time.

Then the director called me at home and told me to take it easy, they were shooting scenes in which I did not take part, and to call when I felt I was ready to go back to work. Needless to say, I recovered hastily and went back to work before I actually should have. Mr. Brown sensed this and held off some of the hard scenes until he felt I was ready.

Sam Garret did a lot of stunt work in pictures, and I asked the man in charge of casting to use him whenever possible as a double for one of the villains. This worked out great, as we were able to practice and work out some of the stunts at home in Sam's arena.

There was one incident in which the doctor's daughter and I had been captured by enemies of her father. We were riding down the road ahead of the man who was taking us, at gunpoint, to his boss; ahead of us was an overhanging tree branch. I spurred my horse and he rushed forward; I grabbed the branch and swung off of my horse, hitting the villain—who was not far behind me—with both of my feet, knocking him off of his horse, which I dropped down upon astride, and the doctor's daughter and I dashed away to freedom.

Sam and I practiced this at the ranch and had the stunt ready when they called for it.

The trick riding horse worked out fine, and I used King Kong in some of the scenes in which a rearing horse was called for. They painted a star on his forehead so he would look like Rex, as I was still supposed to be riding the same horse. Black Hawk was never used at all.

The story ran on and on, with me saving either the doctor or his daughter from one danger after another. Horses were not always part of the plot; sometimes I would also use an automobile, and a couple of times even a plane. I dragged doctor and daughter out of a burning building, rescued them from a sinking boat, stopped a runaway wagon in which they were riding, and saved them from a mine that was being blown up.

When a real knockdown, drag-out action was in progress, I would call for some of the doctor's ranch hands and the masked man to come to the rescue.

Although it was not the last episode of the picture, they saved the big scene for the last day of shooting: the jump through the window with my hands tied behind me. I was locked in a barn with my hands and feet tied while a big battle was going on outside. Three men rode in, jumped off of their horses, shooed them into stalls without bothering to tether them, and ran outside to join in the gunplay. As they left, they bolted the door from the outside.

I managed to work my feet free and jump onto one of their horses; in order to get out of the barn, I was to jump the horse through the window; my hands were tied behind me and I was to hold the reins in my teeth.

The panes of the window were made of sugar and resin and put together with balsa wood. The property man told me my horse would be all right. Rex was scheduled to do the window jump, but when I saw the setup I refused to use him. In order to go through the window, the horse did not jump but rather ran down a steep ramp and crashed into it. You could not see through the glass, and I knew if I were to subject Rex to something like that it would ruin him for the reinless jump.

Production was held up while awaiting the arrival of a horse from the Hudkins Stables, which furnished the stock for Republic Studios. Before it was over I was indeed thankful that I had insisted on a change of horses.

Here I was, sitting on this strange horse with my

hands tied behind my back (we had shot the part where I had jumped onto his back from a bale of hay) and I was holding the nasty-tasting reins in my teeth. The director had told me this would be a one-time shot, no retakes. Making up another window would not only be costly but time consuming as well. Cameras would be shooting from all different angles.

I noticed that a lot of people from other sets had congregated, and then I spied the ambulance. I asked one of the property men about it, and he said, "With something like this you never can tell."

Once more the assistant director advised everyone that this was to be a one-time take. The men in the barn with me started to finger their lash whips; they meant to see that this horse went through that window.

The call, "Action," came, and all hell broke loose. Each one of those whip-happy loons seemed to think he was the only one there and getting the horse through the window was up to him alone.

Crash! Out the window we went . . . and went . . . and went. The pickup men who were to catch the horse were having trouble trying to overtake us. There was nothing I could do with my hands tied behind me, and I had long since dropped the reins I held in my mouth for fear of losing all of my teeth.

Eventually they caught up with me and dragged the horse and me back to the set, where I was congratulated for a fine job. It was then that I looked at the poor horse I had been riding. True, the candy glass did not cut, but the wood had. The horse had several long scratches. I was thankful I had not used Rex for the shot, but I was concerned about the poor studio horse. After looking it over, the head wrangler came over to tell me the horse was all right and not to worry about it.

Overhearing, Bunny Brown, the director, said, "That's right. It might have been your face. You know we were all very worried about that scene. In the picture where a stunt man doubled for the star in Jesse James, for the jump through the window he had a hat pulled down, partly covering his face."

The picture was now finished. The director was pleased with it, as was Mr. Yates. A period of waiting to see the reaction followed.

In the meantime, I was presented to an up-and-coming Western star, who had the privilege of choosing his own leading ladies. Mr. Yates thought I might be a nice addition to his cast, but the cowboy singer was not impressed; he felt I would be a distraction. He preferred weepy, clinging damsels and not, as he said after looking at some of the rushes from my recent little endeavor, "a female Tarzan of the Apes."

Mr. Yates said that he would instruct the head of casting at his studio to use me whenever possible. My future here seemed debatable, and with three horses and Jimmy to take care of I needed something more tangible than vague promises.

At this point Cole Bros. Circus came to town, and I, of course, went to visit. I was given a center front row seat, but I did not get to see much of the show. Mr. Terrell sat on one side of me, Mr. Adkins on the other. They told me the show had done very well that season. Everyone wondered where I had been hiding myself; they wanted me to come back. Before the performance was over, I had agreed to join the show for the coming season. They told me I could put my horses and equipment on their tram, with Jimmy to care for them, complete my business, and join them later. The wandering Gypsy was going home to the circus where she belonged.

◡

Back with Cole Bros. Circus

*T*sold my truck and the trick riding horse; I thanked everyone, and called Mr. Yates at the studio to tell him of my plans and to thank Mr. Brown for being so patient. He wished me luck and said he understood my wanting to go back to the circus. My car was already packed, so I lit out for home. It was quite a long trip, to be sure, but nothing like the one out to California had been.

The Cole show was in winterquarters when I arrived in the spring of 1940. My home in Scottsburg, Indiana, was not too far from their winterquarters in Rochester. I hired a truck and had my horses brought to my barn where I could work with them.

Going back to the Cole show this time was sort of like going home. My friends the Reiffenachs had left the Ringling Bros. show and were now with the Cole show. So was Jean Allen, whom I liked so well, and a host of others whom I enjoyed being with.

We no sooner had the opening over with and were out on the road than the girls asked me to form a manege club. As usual, I was handling the radio shows, so the shopping would be no problem. Without saying anything to me, they got together, held an election, and when I walked into the dressing room, they shouted, "Good morning, Madam President."

I thanked them and remarked that I thought this was a sneaky way to get their shopping done, but I was pleased as punch; I was back again and one of the gang.

I have not dwelled on what kind of a gang this one was. As a rule, we had an initiation for new members, but it never amounted to much; this time they elected to initiate the president. I was on my way to the cookhouse when a group of the members grabbed me and carried me to the elephants' watering tub, where I was dunked three times.

I was speechless, which I guess was just as well, as

they shouted "Long live our president" after just trying to drown me.

I suppose our pranks sound childish today, and maybe they were, but we had fun. We were like one big happy family. It was nothing like today in the circus business where everyone goes to her own house trailer and lives her own life in her own world, not much caring what is happening to the other person.

I remember once while I was on Ringling Bros. getting an invitation to join the Zacchinis, which was quite an event. There were so many of them they rated half a railroad car. Besides the brothers who did the cannon act were other relatives who performed different acts in the show and their wives. The food was unbelievable, at least for a midnight snack. They would begin with an antipasto—it was so good you had to watch lest you fill up on it and not have room for the spaghetti.

While the ladies were preparing all of this, the men entertained with music. Each was very talented, and if they were not playing an instrument, they joined in song. I used to imagine I was in the midst of a Gypsy caravan, and would have loved to have jumped up and danced. I never did it, of course; now I wish I had.

∪

Elephants

The year was 1940. I had taken my personal horses home with me and, after finding out that it would not be feasible to play the show I had booked in Berlin on account of the war, I then booked myself with Orrin Davenport to play all of his dates.

First came the rains, then the flood.

All of the land from Louisville up to within a few miles of my home was under water. A whole story could be written about that alone. After all of the schools and churches were full, everyone in town opened their doors and took in as many as they had room for. We had people sleeping all over the barn.

We had an old battery radio set, in fine shape, which Mother had hung onto when we had moved from the farm where there had not been electricity. Now that the lights were out everywhere, and our radio was the only one around that was working, our home became the base from which all of the rescue squads operated. Day and night we listened to calls for help. Somehow the phone was kept in order for emergencies.

Late one evening I received a call from Orrin Davenport, who had heard of the predicament we were in.

"Dorothy, somehow or other you must get here. They have put out a lot of publicity on you, and it is very important that you make it."

I told him there was no way I could possibly get my horses out. They were in no danger, but there was no transportation for people or anything else.

"All right," he said, "leave your horses, but see if there isn't some way that you can get to Peru. Maybe you can work the elephant act or find a horse there that you can ride, anything. Just get here."

There was no way out. If there were, everyone would have been going. Besides, all of the money I had on hand had long since been spent to buy food for the people who were now living in my home. There was no chance of them starving, however, as by now the Red Cross was dropping food by plane.

I went to see my good friend Mr. I. C. Morgan. He owned the Scott County Packing Company, which supplied canned goods to a chain of grocery stores. Mr. Morgan had been donating canned goods and the use of his trucks and drivers since the start of the flood, so they came and went without question. I told him my story.

"Well, now, I will tell you how we will do it," said he. "We will stack your trunk in the back with the canned goods, and you will ride in the cab with the driver. If anyone questions you, just say that you are a nurse."

Embarrassed, I added, "There is one more thing. I have no cash on hand. My money is in a Louisville bank that is under water."

Mr. Morgan reached into his pocket and pulled out a few crumpled bills. "Wait. I think I might know someone with cash: our cook. She tucks money away in all kinds of places."

Sure enough, she did lend me some money, and I was on my way.

The truck ride was long and quite scary. We went through quite a lot of deep water, and several times we had to be towed. The driver took me as far as Indianapolis, where I boarded a train for Peru.

I was wet and dirty, and my hair was in strings. People on the train were kind. They thought I was a refugee who had somehow managed to get out. I thought it might sound very odd if I told them I was on my way to join a circus, so I did not enlighten them.

I left my trunk in the baggage room at the railroad station, took my suitcase and checked into the Bearas Hotel. After a hot bath, a good meal, and a nice long sleep, I took a cab to winterquarters the next morning.

After locating Arkie Scott, the head elephant man and, in my opinion, one of the best in the business, I informed him of the reason for my visit. Now, although Arkie and I had been friends for many years, he proceeded to let me and the world in general know just what he thought of the idea—and it was plenty!

"What are they going to send me next? First, it was ballet broads, and now a horsewoman! Well, don't think for a moment that on account of our friendship I am going to go easy on you. I intend to work the act fast, like I always do, and if you miss the mounts that is your tough luck!"

I knew this tough attitude to be an act to cover up his Jimmy Stewart nature. Regardless of his ability to handle tough elephants, which was well known, he was a pussycat where women were concerned.

I countered with, "But you will at least show me how to do the mounts, won't you?"

He snapped back, "Of course, what do you think I am, some sort of a heel? But we leave for Wichita tomorrow, and you don't learn this act in one easy lesson."

It was here that my trapeze work, trick riding, and bareback training stood me in good stead. The mounts were duck soup for me, and Arkie, who was used to breaking in girls with little strength, was pleased.

"Are you sure you never worked with bulls before?" he asked.

I knew by that we would be okay together in the act.

Arkie and I, and the other performers leaving from Peru for the date, talked for quite a while on the train the next night before retiring. When we arrived in Wichita it was snowing and bitter cold. We went to our hotels, and met at the building a little after noon.

Upon arriving at the building after lunch, I found it was cold; Arkie was waiting for it to warm up a bit before bringing the elephants in. Meanwhile, the band was setting up the music for the different acts. The heat had been turned on, but the people hanging their rigging were still wearing overcoats.

I nodded to the little group chatting in the seats as I went by in search of my circus trunk. I quickly found the space allotted to me, but there was no sign of my trunk. A thorough search convinced me it had not arrived. I went to the phone and placed a call to the stationmaster in Peru, who had promised faithfully to see that my trunk was loaded on the circus train. I was told that some idiot upon seeing the rain-soaked tag attached to it and, being able to distinguish only the word "Indianapolis" on it, had returned the trunk to its original starting point. Although this explanation did not sound plausible to me, there was nothing I could do but accept it and hope that he would keep his promise to get the trunk to me as soon as possible. I will always think that he simply forgot to load it.

Returning to my friends in the seats, I found that Arkie had sent his assistant to the train to check on the elephants, but because he had been gone for an abnormal length of time, Arkie was now going to check up on him.

Arkie found his assistant pinned inside the train, one of the bulls ready to attack him if he moved a little to either side; there was no way for him to get out. Arkie jumped in and tried to beat the enraged animal away from the boy.

The elephant then turned on Arkie and proceeded to work him over. Arkie somehow managed to crawl away, and his assistant, now in the clear, ran to the nearest phone to call an ambulance. When we heard the sirens, we knew at once that something had gone wrong.

The doors to the baggage car with the elephants inside were locked until someone with expertise could be summoned. Orrin Davenport called Zack Terrell and told him what had happened. Zack, with his usual efficiency, said he would contact two elephant trainers at different places and have them come by plane. He would contact two because, the weather being what it was, one or the other might not be able to make it for the show.

Ace Donavan and Bert Pettis arrived within hours of each other, but too late to rehearse the act. They managed to get the first three elephants out of the baggage car, but the fourth one, which was causing all the trouble, would not let them get through to unchain the one behind. This all happened on the day we were to open.

Going back to the night before, with all of the excitement it was after midnight before John Smith, the horse trainer, got around to showing me the stock I was to work. Since they had been playing another indoor date when I went to Peru to practice, I had no idea at all what he might have in mind for me to do.

The Shriners' publicity department had been playing up the "just returned from Hollywood" bit big, seemingly unaware that neither my footprints nor those of my horses had been encased in cement in front of a theater. I doubt if Greta Garbo ever considered me much of a threat, or that my debut had anything to do with her early retirement.

The big black horse, which John had the groom bring out, was a doll. Because I had worked with John before, I caught her cues at once. Luckily, she did a fine act, for this, unlike most Shrine shows, was a one-ring affair, and all of the acts worked alone.

The pony drill was quite another matter. Old John was a very good trainer, but it seemed as if every time he got an act going really well, they took it away from him and gave it to someone else to work. Then he would, again, be working another green act. It was great for the show, but John got fed up with it. Now, if John liked you, he would do anything in the world for you; if not, he would act as though you did not exist.

Right now, he was taking great delight in explaining to me the cues of this pony drill, which he had broken to work on the show himself.

"Well, I'll tell you," John said, "when I broke these ponies I broke them so no one else could work them unless I wanted them to."

Such cues! Everything was backwards and contrary to the way one normally worked such an act, but once you were able to catch onto the cues they worked perfectly.

But my troubles were not yet over; my circus trunk had not yet arrived, so I was without wardrobe.

Orrin Davenport prevailed upon the wardrobe ladies to come to my rescue and, somehow or other, they managed to put together three costumes for me.

Now, for the elephant act. There would be no time for a rehearsal. Who would work the act? The two trainers flipped a coin, and Bert Pettis won—or lost—depending on how you look at it. He did not know the routine, nor did I, after just that one day's practice in winterquarters. One of the helpers came up with the fact that he knew when to set the props. I figured Bert would work the act the first time by himself, but . . . no.

He explained: "The act is going to be so weak with two of the bulls out of it that having someone in there, styling and dancing, will be a big help. I understand that Inez is a sapper [an elephant who will hit you with her trunk if she takes a dislike to you], so stay away from her. Now, every time I call out "Mount," you jump on an elephant and style; they will all hold you in their trunk."

Great . . . only when we got in the ring I didn't know Inez from anybody else! However, Bert, being the great elephant trainer that he was, made the act look good despite the fact that the odds—including the elephants and me—were against him.

In the meantime, what to do about the two elephants still on the train? The bad one was completely unmanageable. "Gone amok," they said. There was no alternative but to put her to sleep.

That might sound relatively easy, but it was far from that. First, it was necessary to obtain permission from the owners. Mr. Adkins and Mr. Terrell readily agreed, but because she was on the premises of the railroad company, it was also necessary to get permission from them. Now, it seemed that no one could make a decision without a board of directors' meeting and a lot of red tape. They finally got everything resolved—and I found myself in the ring with one more elephant.

Needless to say, I spent all of my free time visiting Arkie in the hospital. He came up with this explanation: For many years this elephant had been riding in circus trains and, to her, this was her home; however, to play the indoor shows they had rented baggage cars, which went at a much greater speed than the circus trains ever did. They also rolled and made all sorts of strange noises. Perhaps the elephant had become frightened and panicked. There was no way of ever knowing for sure.

Well, the show moved on to the next date and Arkie was left behind until he could return to winterquarters; in the spring he was able to return to the show. He and I would troop together many times in the years that followed.

After the first indoor show in Wichita, Ace Donavan returned from whence he had come, and Bert Pettis worked the elephants for the rest of the dates. We went from Wichita to Detroit, which was a three-ring show, as were the rest of the dates. Two more herds of elephants, plus numerous horses from winterquarters, joined us, and Bert took one of the elephants from another act and added it to the one we were working.

The rest of the dates went off without mishap. When they were over and I returned to my home in Scottsburg, the floodwaters had subsided and the uninvited houseguests had all departed. Things were back to normal, or as normal as they ever were.

∪

Jack Dempsey

In 1941 Mr. Terrell thought it would be a good idea if I could get Mr. Dempsey to accompany me sometimes to my broadcasts. Because Jack was working the concert on a percentage, he readily agreed.

In an effort to emulate Ringling Bros., the Cole Bros. show also had a gaited horse number that season. Mr.

Terrell had bought a beautiful gray, five-gaited horse named LeRose McAdams for his wife to ride in the show, but Mrs. Terrell had so many other duties in the office wagon that she seldom had time to appear in the number.

Mr. Terrell thought that a good way to show off the horse and introduce Mr. Dempsey to the audience the first time would be to have him ride the horse and lead the opening spec. He made his appearance in full Western regalia.

After we had made a few radio broadcasts together, we were having our breakfast in a downtown restaurant one morning when he said, "You know, Dorothy, I just don't feel right riding that horse."

Now was my chance.

"You don't look right, either. For one thing, you are not a cowboy movie star; you are riding a gaited horse with a Western saddle, and wearing an outfit that looks like you bought it at Montgomery Ward."

He burst out laughing.

"Fact of the matter, I did!"

We were playing in a large city, so when we had finished our coffee I went with him to pick out a riding habit. Riding the horse with an English saddle, he looked great.

He was fun to work with, and very big hearted. I recall one day when I had stopped at a drugstore to buy a gift for one of the girls who was having a birthday, and he went in with me. As we were getting out of the cab at the show grounds, he handed me a large box. "Here, give your friend a little gift from me." It was a box of one of the leading brands of cosmetics, and this for a girl he did not even know.

The Manege Club Weekly News

It started out rather like a joke. Somewhere down the line, in connection with my radio broadcasts, I had purchased a typewriter. The fact that I did not know how to use it in no way deterred me; I hunted and pecked, and I still do.

Anyway, the newspaper started out early in the 1941 season as a sort of report to the members. It was very dull, so I asked the members to contribute little bits of gossip that might make it more interesting. Each member was required to buy a copy, whether she wanted it or not; the price was ten cents.

They liked the idea of the gossip column, and soon other people on the show were asking to buy a copy. This posed a problem as the paper was processed in my stateroom on my typewriter; using two carbons I could print only three sheets at a time.

I called a meeting. It looked like our newspaper might be a money-making deal; however, I had neither the time nor the inclination to sit up half of the night making carbon copies. If the members agreed, we would take the money from our treasury and buy a mimeograph machine and print a real paper.

All of the members thought that was a great idea; so was born one of the few newspapers ever printed on a circus. It was a success from the start. We put a box with a slot in it on one of my trunks; anyone was at liberty to contribute any item of news, but everything was carefully screened so that no one's feelings might be hurt. We assigned two girls as reporters to interview anyone who might be of interest, and two girls to advertising.

Emmett Kelly, the clown who was later to achieve much fame, was with the show and, knowing that he had been a cartoonist with a newspaper before joining the circus, I asked him if he would do the artwork for us. We made him an honorary member of our club, and he not only drew all of our headings, but also the ads and numerous cartoons as well.

The stencils were cut all during the week, from items as they came in. The ads were set up, and then came Friday. Right after dinner in the cookhouse, we returned to the dressing room; everyone in Aisle One closed her trunk and we went to work.

As many sheets as we thought necessary were printed and placed on the first trunk; then on to page two, which was placed on the next trunk; and so on, through all of the stencils we had prepared.

As soon as the last one was finished, two girls would gather the pages up, one by one, and take them to a girl who was waiting at the end of the line with a stapler, and she would staple all of the pages together. Two girls would be waiting, as newsboys, to go around the lot selling them.

All great fun, this . . . but we hadn't counted on the circus fans and others who became interested. We soon had such a large mailing list that the girl whose job it was had to have help handling it. Even *Billboard* was one of our subscribers.

Jean Allen, one of the greatest elephant women of all times, and also a leading horse woman, was in charge of advertising; she was a go-getter and kept our pages well supplied.

Many of the issues contained a column I wrote called "Did You Know." It contained such tidbits as:

> Mrs. McFarland of the wardrobe department used to work bears, ponies, dogs and monkeys. Also used to train her own manege horses. Mitt Carl of the cookhouse was in the Army Air Corps for twenty-two months during the first world war, eighteen months were spent across the ocean. Mrs. Bigger, wife of the train master had an act of edu-

cated geese on the Ringling show. It was called the Barnyard Frolics. She trained the geese to be harnessed and pull little carts. Mr. Watts, assistant manager, was a sergeant-major of the 319th Aero Squad from 1917 to 1919. Wanda Wentz, elephant girl, was born on a steamship en route to the U. S. from Poland. Tommy Comstock, calliope player, used to play pipe organ in large theaters in Cleveland and Detroit. Harry MacFarland, equestrian director, drove a forty horse hitch, Roman standing, on the Adam Forepaugh Circus. Harry Thomas, announcer, used to do a mind reading act in vaudeville.

Our boss, Zack Terrell, was one of our strongest supporters, and he also contributed to the news. Having been a former newspaper man himself, he had a whimsical way of wording his articles. I could always tell when an item supplied by him showed up in our collection box.

Local newspapers in different towns we played thought that this was a clever idea, and we received a lot of free publicity.

The feature of the concert on the Cole Bros. Circus that year was the world-renowned Jack Dempsey. He would referee a wrestling match between one of his men and a town wrestler. They did not use a concert in the Chicago stadium, so he joined the show later under canvas.

As newspaper editor, it was my job to interview him; he gave us a nice story and offered to buy an ad as well.

◡

Equipment

*D*id I use special equipment? Yes. My sidesaddles were always made by Martin & Martin in England. Early in the game we discovered that they would have to be reinforced due to the beating they might have to take. If a horse fell over backward, or fell during the jumps, the horn would often be broken.

Martin & Martin saddles, even then, were not easy to come by and cost quite a lot of money. There was a saddle shop in New York City where we would send a newly purchased sidesaddle and they would dismantle it and replace the wooden parts with steel, which would then be recovered with leather. Because I rode barelegged, this caused a problem: The constant rubbing against the leather saddle horn would make my leg so very sore. One time it swelled up, became infected, and I had to have it lanced. This friction was finally eliminated by lining the underside of the horn with sheepskin, which was not only soft to the flesh, but stayed dry when one became hot and sweaty.

With the stunts I was doing, the girths that came with the saddles were not enough to keep them from slipping; I used an extra safety girth on each horse. In order not to discomfort the horse with the saddles perhaps moving, I had very heavy underpads made. I always used saddle covers on both the astride and the sidesaddles. They were made of a very light canvas, but the seats were of white toweling. The reason for this was that I often wore costumes made of slipper satin and when rubbing against other objects it was like sitting on a cake of soap; with the toweling, I did not slip.

At first, when wearing evening gowns to ride in, I thought it necessary to wear high-heeled shoes. Someone ought to have had my head examined. After turned ankles and other related mishaps, I learned to wear heeless slippers, and soft leather boots with a rubber sole. For both sidesaddle and astride I always taped the bottom on my stirrups with friction tape. The foot does not slip, and stays in place. When riding jumps sidesaddle, I used a breakaway stirrup, so that if the horse were to fall with me I had a chance to get away from him.

When doing dressage, I found that the pressure of the legs was of as much importance as the spur. The use of bit and spur is what makes a horse respond and bring forth whichever leg is required of him, but if a rider is able to communicate with him using the pressure of the legs only, and reserving the spur for the times that he fails to respond, he or she will have a more willing mount.

When riding astride, I like to use a small English saddle. I like to be able to feel my horse under me, so the less leather, the better I liked it.

♘

Lewis Bros. Circus

When I left Cole Bros. Circus, Mr. Zack Terrell had told me that I would be welcome back at any time, but I had made such a big to-do about making it on my own, my pride would not permit me to eat crow.

I remembered one time when Paul Lewis and his wife, Mae, were visiting on one of the indoor shows that he had remarked, "If you ever find yourself at loose ends for any reason, we would love to have you join us. We are not one of the big ones, but we run a nice, clean show, and you would be one of the family."

What better time to give it a try? In the spring of 1942 I called him on the phone, and he said, "Great! Come on!"

I told him then that I did not have a truck.

"Well, I do, and it will be on its way early in the morning. I will send Smitty, who I consider my very best driver, and, since it is such a very long way, I will let his buddy go with him to keep him awake."

Smitty, I found out later, was not only a truck driver but Lewis's elephant handler and wild animal man as well. His buddy, named Harry, was the show's mechanic. Smitty was not only big—he was on the heavy side, whereas Harry was tall and skinny. Smitty was jolly and laughing most of the time; Harry seldom, if ever, smiled. I likened them to Laurel and Hardy, which wasn't too far-fetched, as subsequent events were later to prove.

The Lewises' winterquarters was located on a large farm; later I will go into how they happened to obtain it. The main house was a large, rambling, old farmhouse with a caretaker's house off to one side and, behind it, numerous barns and outbuildings. At one time, it had been a breeding farm for horses, and the stables were well equipped. It made an ideal circus winterquarters.

They heard me coming and met me at the door. Mae showed me to my quarters at once, saying that she knew I must be exhausted after my long drive and would be wanting to freshen up before stopping to chat, which could wait until later. They dined early; dinner would be at six. That gave me a little better than an hour. The apartment was upstairs, and I found it delightful. I had never lived in a circus owner's home before, and they, in turn, had never had a live-in performer. True to their word, I was welcomed as one of the family and loved working with them.

Later on, after dinner that evening, they told me that I would need a house trailer to live in while on the road; Mae would go with me to pick out one. My horses would ride in one of their trucks, and I would pull the house trailer with my car.

I was used to a stateroom on the train, however, and I did not recall ever being inside a house trailer. Certainly I had seen them around winterquarters, and Harry

LeRoy's people had them, but I had never been invited into one. I found one that appealed to me. Because I was alone, I did not think I needed a very big one. It had a nice bed in the rear and a dinette in the front that could also be made into a bed, a tiny kitchen, and a shower. If I had had any idea how long this was to be my home, believe me, I would have bought a much larger one.

But, to get back to Paul and this big farm with barns and outbuildings enough to house a whole show . . . the story, as Paul told it to me, goes like this: His show was about to close and they had no place to winter it that year. He contacted his brother, who was a lawyer in Jackson, Michigan, and asked him to try to find a suitable place. His brother found a vacant piece of property and bought it for cash.

In due time, the show closed, retired to the new quarters, and parked itself there for the winter. Paul's brother, not being in the circus business, was unaware of the commotion an outfit like this could cause. This vacant lot was in the center of a community of upper-class residences. The residents were up in arms—this mess would have to move.

First they tried to buy out Paul, but he would not move, as he had no other place to go. Then they took him to court and pointed out that he was within the city limits. His brother, who, of course, was defending him, pointed out to the court that the zoo was also within the city limits. Paul's brother concluded his plea with the announcement that he would gladly see that they moved, if someone could come up with another place for them to stay. The landowners united and found this lovely farm, which they bought and traded him for his lot in town. They footed the bill for the difference, just to get rid of him and his roaring lions, trumpeting elephants, and yapping dogs.

The transition from a railroad show to a truck show was in no way as difficult as I had expected it would be. Pat Valdo had always said, "When you leave the big one, you are only camping out."

It was a matter of luck, however, that the Lewis show was the one that I happened to go with. Everything ran very smoothly; they had a perfect system. I did not realize this, never having been on a truck show, until much later when I traveled with other ones.

The jumps were short, and we seldom traveled at night. Very early in the morning, the concession stand would serve either doughnuts or sweet rolls and plenty of coffee to the working crew before they left for the next town. It would then pack up and follow them. The cookhouse truck always left after the evening meal and would already be there and set up. This arrangement let the equipment get there and be mostly set up before we arrived.

Later, the performers with their house trailers would start out, with Mae Lewis in the lead. Paul drove his car and brought up the rear so that he could take care of the bills after we had gassed up. Just ahead of him was the truck with the show's mechanic, Harry, and, with him, a man whose duty it was to change tires if anyone had a flat. Those who liked to eat out would usually stop somewhere along the way for breakfast.

Upon arriving at the lot you were directed to the spot that was to be yours for the stay. The show's electrician would come around and connect you to lights; it was up to you to see that your water tank was filled at the gas stations. There was a water wagon, but that was for the animals and the cookhouse.

A six-piece band was with the show. They did not have a house trailer, and preferred to stay in motels. They dressed in a small tent that was put up for them each day. They shared an automobile with a luggage trailer behind it in which they carried their instruments and personal baggage.

The show was presented in three rings, with either one act in the center or with the two end rings working in unison. The only time all three worked simultaneously was during the swing ladder and web numbers.

The track, while not too long, was adequate for me to do the waltz and rear and the high fire jump. All in all, it was a pleasing show and well received.

Mae ran the office wagon, kept the books, sold the tickets, and was paymaster. Paul ran the show and did the announcing. It was a perfect setup. The concessions were let out on a percentage basis, so they did not have to bother with them.

I have heard some horse trainers say they did not much care about working liberty horses because they were so unpredictable—with one horse you were in control; with a ring full of horses, you never could be sure what might happen.

I truly enjoyed working liberty horses. I was first taught to do so by Rudy Rudynoff on the John Robinson Circus. Then, when I joined Ringling Bros., I worked under the direction of Tex Elmlund, also a great liberty horse trainer. He would often call upon me to assist him when he was breaking new stock in winterquarters. After going with Cole Bros. Circus, I worked an act that had been trained by Jorgen Christiansen.

Now I was anxious to try my hand at breaking a liberty act. I had, by this time, trained gaited horses, dressage horses, and, of course, jumpers.

My chance came when I joined the Lewis Bros. Circus. I offered the idea to Paul Lewis, who said, "Of course, give it a try." What was there to lose?

In those days there was always a lot of help in winterquarters and they had very little to do. I owe the success of the liberty horse act to the wonderful outside help that I had, with special thanks to Smitty, the elephant trainer; and Harry, who was also an excellent animal man.

I used just six horses, but they were fast and they were good. When Mr. Lewis came to the barn and saw the act, he was very impressed and ordered beautiful trappings for them. Since there is no act like this one on the road at the present time, I would like to take a moment or two to describe it.

The horses would first circle the ring, reverse, then walk the ring curb with their front feet, after which the first horse would cut back, then the second, and so on, until they were all going the wrong way of the ring. They then would change back all at the same time, going the right way of the ring. Next, they would come up by twos, then sixes, for the wheel; after that they would go into the double waltz, and then line up.

After starting off this time, they would now come up by threes; the first three would slow down and the last three would pass them, after which they, in turn, would do the same thing. After they did this a few times they would again line up and three of them were then removed from the ring. The three that were left would then do the Ta Ra Boom Ta Ray, which is take three steps forward and rear up on the hind legs.

For the finale, one of the other horses would do a spinning rear, then run for the ring curb, place his front feet on it and shake his head up and down for a bow.

Mae Lewis had all but retired from the performance end of the business, but for one act in each show she was obliged to leave the office wagon momentarily, and that was the chow dog act. Mae, in conjunction with a man who subsequently left the show, had broken the act, and no one else was able to work it. They were a vicious lot of dogs, ready to tear each other to bits, and, because twelve chows were in the act, a number of handlers were involved. They were beautiful dogs and the act was good, so Mr. Lewis felt that it was worth the trouble it caused.

The caretaker on the Lewises' farm had five children: three boys and two girls. The lads were perfectly content to stay on the farm and help their dad till the land and raise crops, but the two girls were very anxious to try their hand at being in show business. They were rather comely girls, in a homespun sort of way, but certainly not adaptable for working in the air, and air acts were the only show-owned production numbers. They were both hard workers and would be a big asset in helping to care for the stock, but they wanted to be in the show.

This situation was resolved by letting the girls work the Angora goat act, which they called "The Farmer's Daughters and Their Pets." Never was there a goat act that received so much care and attention. Once each week the goats were bathed, and they were brushed twice daily; their hooves and horns were brilliantly gilded. The act itself was quite a pleasing number, and when it was presented at the fairs later in the season, it made a big hit with farmers who "didn't know them critters were so smart."

Smitty was one of the hardest workers I had ever encountered. True, I was not familiar with the mechanism of a small truck show; still it seemed to me that he had more to do than one man should rightly be expected to handle. He not only saw to it that the big top got up and down, spotted all of the trucks and trailers, drove a truck over the road, but also worked the lion act and the elephants, and made himself generally useful while we were under canvas in the spring.

Then came the fair season where we worked in front of the grandstand. After the poles and the riggings for the aerial acts had been raised, and the ring curbs and props were set, Smitty had little to do. They did not use the lion act on the fair unit, so he had only the elephant act to work.

His partial vacation was short-lived, however. The closing number of the Lewis Bros. Circus on the fairs was the Funny Ford, with lots of firecrackers and tomfoolery. After the first fair date, which lasted three days, the men with the comedy car left the show. Because it was a necessary part of the unit, Paul dispatched Smitty, posthaste, back to winterquarters where an old "funny car" he owned had been gathering dust for years. Harry went with Smitty, and they loaded the car on a flatbed truck and brought it back. Harry went to work on it at once and got it in working order. I doubt if either Harry or Smitty would have been in such a hurry if they had had any idea what was in store for them.

Paul went to an army surplus store where he bought a soldier uniform for Smitty that was too small and one for Harry that was several sizes too large, and informed them that they were to put on the act. Our flat-tire changer, Snakes, would be the hidden driver, lying on his belly and driving it from underneath (the car was supposedly running about by itself).

One of the three clowns with the show attempted to show Harry and Smitty how to put on makeup, while Paul coached them as to how the routine was supposed to go. But when they got in front of the grandstand, they forgot the instructions completely. Neither was quite sure where they were supposed to be at any given time. They kept bumping into each other and became quite upset about it. To top it off, it made Smitty mad to hear the people laughing at them. He shook his fist at Paul, who was doing the announcing, and told him to make them stop. Meantime, Snakes, crouched below in the car, got confused and drove the car into places where it was not supposed to be, and the whole thing was hilarious. When Smitty could stand the laughter no longer, he threw his hat on the ground and jumped up and down on it while we all roared.

Paul was pleased as punch because the act was really funny—but not to Smitty and Harry. They flatly refused to go out there and be laughed at again until Paul offered each of them a big raise. Then they didn't mind it anymore.

The aerial acts were adequate, with lovely Jean Evans, sister-in-law of the great Clyde Beatty, holding down the feature spot. The liberty horse act came up to expectations; Black Hawk, King Kong, and Rex, all seasoned veterans, held up their end, and it was a well-balanced show. For me who, up until now, had had such a hectic career, it was like a paid vacation. I went the whole season without getting hurt or going to the hospital once.

I had gone to Scottsburg to spend the Christmas holidays with my mother. On my way back to winter-quarters I had to change trains in Chicago. I had a couple of hours' layover so, on an impulse, I called one of the largest booking offices there; they asked me where I was and what I had been doing. One of their agents asked me if I could stay over and catch a later train; he would like very much to talk to me and thought it might be advantageous to all concerned. I phoned Paul, who was to meet my train when I arrived in Jackson, and told him what I was up to. He told me to stay as long as necessary and see what might be in the offing, and to keep in constant touch.

Over dinner with the agent that night, he outlined what his office would be able to do for us, and I promised to meet him the next day with an answer. Paul was waiting by the phone for my call; he was delighted and told me to go right ahead, and he thought he might have a surprise for me when I got back there.

I stayed in Chicago for several days. The agent booked us into a string of indoor shows, which were in entirely different places than those Orrin Davenport played, so all of our acts, including mine, would be new to them.

When Paul discovered that I was able to book the big indoor shows, he was very happy; help was becoming hard to get, and gas rationing was also a problem. This booking would eliminate the need for a big top and all of the extra help needed to keep a tent show going.

He made me a proposition: he would furnish all of the help, the transportation, and his stock; I would do the booking and work my acts along with his liberty horse act; and we would split the profits after expenses. As far as I was concerned, it was a very liberal deal. While they were getting things ready, I went back to Chicago and booked a string of fairs.

The indoor shows that we were now working dif-fered from the Orrin Davenport dates in that he hired all of his acts and they made a complete circuit with the show, running much the same at each date. This agency booked the acts for each show separately, so the program was different each time and you worked with a variety of people. We were working the Police Circus in St. Louis with the Lewis liberty horse act, their pony drill, Mae's dog act, and, of course, my dressage horse, Black Hawk; the waltzing and rearing horse, King Kong; and Rex, my high jumper. The elephant, seal, and goat acts had been left in winterquarters, since they were not strong enough acts to play the big indoor shows. We would pick them up when we got ready to play fairs. Paul had sold the lion act; with the shortage of help, it had become too much of a hassle putting up and taking down the steel arena.

Jinx Hogland also had his horses and riders booked for this date. Besides his "push ball" on horseback and drill team, he had several high-school horses and a number of jumping horses. His riders were to jump first, and I would finish the number with the high fire jump.

When I inspected the track I could see at once that we were in for trouble. Dirt had been packed into the rings and around the track for several feet, and then sawdust covered the entire floor. It was impossible to judge where the dirt ended and the cement started unless you were on foot.

I went to Jinx and told him what I thought. He did not wish to make a complaint, but suggested that I do so. Because he had twelve jumping horses and I had only one, I thought it was his place to point out the hazard. The result was that neither of us did anything.

Strobe light effects are obtained by materials being treated with some sort of chemical that, when the house was darkened and a special spotlight used, glowed in the dark. It was new at that time. The idea was for Jinx's riders to wear costumes made of this material and, at the finale of the quadrille, all of the lights would go out, resulting in a spectacular sight.

Riding sidesaddle with a smile, undated. With Ringling Bros. and Barnum & Bailey. *Courtesy of Tim Tegge.*

Of course, everyone was anxious to see it.

Bad luck seemed to pursue Jinx at this show: First the "push ball on horseback" number had to be eliminated. It required the removal and replacement of all of the ring curbs and many of the props, as a great deal of space was required to present the number. That took up too much time.

The costumes for the strobe light number did not get finished in time for the first show, but they went on with the quadrille anyway. A stranger sight you could not imagine: When the lights went out, you saw hats floating in the air, also gauntlets, pants, bridle reins, and the bandages on the horses' legs. That was all. Everything else was blacked out. Wow!

The high-school act, in which Jinx had six horses, along with me riding Black Hawk in the center ring, went off without mishap.

The flying act was over, the nets were dropped, and now it was time for the closing act—the jumping horses. The first show was chaos; horses slipped and fell all over the place. If they went a little too wide, they hit the loose dirt and lost their footing, or, after slipping, balked when they hit the hurdle. I could see that most of the trouble was at the corners where the horses were swinging out too far and falling.

My act called for me to go over the back jump with my hands in the air. The front hurdle would be set on fire as I pulled down the blindfold, and Rex would jump the hurdle of fire. No way would that work on this track.

Quickly I coached my groom; he would go with me to the far end of the track, leading my horse. This would keep the ever-nervous Rex quiet, having Jimmy by his head. I would NOT take the back jump. The moment they made the announcement and I saw that the fire was lit, we would go over that. I knew Rex would head straight for it and not swerve onto the concrete. Smitty, who was standing by the hurdle ready to light it, sensed my intention and lit the hurdle almost before the announcer was finished.

Backstage, they were busy rushing Jinx's injured riders to the hospital. This is how I first met Genie. She and her father were part of Jinx's troop, and her father was one of the riders who had been hurt. (Before the next show they placed extra seats all around the track and stretched a rope in front of them, giving the horses something to guide them.)

Several days later I went with Genie to the hospital to visit her dad. He had a broken arm and a broken leg; when he was released from the hospital, he was laid up for some time. He was very concerned about his daughter. Her mother had passed away, and as long as he was with her, it was fine; he did not like the idea of her traveling around without someone to look out for her. He wanted to know if there was some way I might take her with me. I told him that I would talk it over with the Lewises.

My trailer was small, but it had a bed in the back and a dinette in the front that made into a bed. I would be glad to have company while driving overland. Our next indoor date was Chicago, which Jinx was also playing; after that we would go into winterquarters for a while. Genie and I shared a hotel room while in Chicago, and we had a chance to become better acquainted. She was a beautiful girl—coal black, naturally curly hair and big brown eyes—with a disposition to match. She was a little taller and just a little heavier than I.

Because it had been my idea to hire Genie, it was up to me to find something for her to do. I had trained a couple of the horses out of the liberty horse act for manege. I could put her in that number along with another rider, and with Black Hawk, making a nice, three-ring display, but that was not much for her to do. On the larger fairs, which we were now playing, we used only the animal acts, so anything in the air was out.

Then I had an idea: If it was all right with Paul and Mae, I would put together a vaulting act, something like the one that Tex and I had trained on Ringling Bros., only this time there would be two riders. I talked it over with the Lewises, who thought the idea was great. Mae said she would gladly be the ringmaster.

We used three of the horses from the liberty act. I would enter the ring on two horses, Roman standing, Genie would jump up behind me and do several tricks with me holding her; she would step outside the ring, and I would then jump the two horses over a hurdle. These two would leave the ring and a single horse with a surcingle would come in. A surcingle is a belt or girth that passes around the belly of a horse and over the blanket, pack, saddle, and so on, and is buckled on the horse's back. Now, we completed a series where she and I were vaulting and splitting the neck, climaxing the round with Genie doing the drag . . . laying across the horse's back with her foot in a loop, she picked up flags as he ran around the ring. Then I would do a couple of stand up tricks. We would finish with the forward rollover and cartwheel, similar to May Wirth's finish, only we would alternate—first one and then the other.

What we lacked in talent we made up for in enthusiasm. This projected to the audience, who seemed to enjoy the number and responded warmly.

Playing fairs was fun. Between shows we would leave the infield and wander around the fairgrounds looking at the exhibits and the livestock, after which we would have dinner. (Breakfast and lunch we fixed in the trailer.) We soon found that the ladies from the local churches put out the best meals. Sometimes we would stop on the midway and play a few games of Bingo. Then, back to the infield for the night show, after which we would have a light snack in the trailer and go to bed. Some fairs followed the show with a fireworks display and, of course, we always stayed up to watch it.

On days when there were no shows, Mae would take Genie and me to town with her to shop and then take in a picture show, after which we would meet Paul and have dinner at a nice restaurant. It was a pleasant season for all of us.

When the season ended and we went into winterquarters, I went home to be with Mother for the Christmas holidays, and Genie left to visit her father. While there, Ringling Bros. contacted her and she joined their show. We had made plans to be together the next season, and I wish she had stayed with me a little longer as there were so many things I had hoped to teach her. As it was, they expected too much from her and she was not yet ready.

Upon my arrival back at winterquarters, Mae had a nice surprise for me; while I was gone she had had my bedroom and bath completely done over, everything in pink, white, and gold.

Mae was one of the best cooks I ever knew. It is a wonder I did not gain pounds and pounds, but, of course, I was very active. She had fixed a very special welcome-home dinner for me, and when it was over and we were having coffee in the living room, they told me the news.

In January 1944 Paul Lewis sold his trucks, stock, and equipment to Big Bob Stevens. Stevens leased the Jackson winterquarters and framed his new show there called Bailey Bros.

An agreement had been made for me to have the concert (after show) on Bailey Bros. I would continue to work for Paul Lewis doing the liberty horse act in the big show and my own acts would be the concert feature. I would receive a salary for working the liberty act, and the concert would be a percentage deal. It would be up to me to hire my own people and run the performance myself.

I knew of a family in Canada who were able to put on almost a whole show themselves. I contacted them and got them under contract. I then hired a couple I knew who called themselves "The Shooting Stars." She shot at different objects he held, and then they did an impalement act in which he threw swords around her. Here was a couple who had to get along! With my acts, we had a strong concert. The show was a success, and our concert did a big business. I was making money.

One evening, just before the night show, a taxi pulled into the back of the lot and my mother stepped out. She had an awfully lot of baggage with her, so it did not look like she was there for a short visit. We managed to cram all of her things into my car and trailer, and then I had to rush off to work the show.

When the show was over, she told me that she had come to stay as she was tired of being home by herself. She had sold the house and everything in it. I was upset because there were lots of my things that I had left there that I would like to have kept. She had also sold her car and my horse trailer.

Traveling with a truck show is quite different than with a railroad show. Mother had come to visit me at times when I was with Ringling Bros., staying for a week or so and enjoying herself immensely. On a railroad show you could retire when the show was over, wake in the next town, and expect three good meals to await you each day at the lot. On a truck show you had to get up early, have a cup of coffee, and drive to the next town. Along with working your acts and keeping your things put away, you had to find time to fix yourself some sort of meal in your trailer. Added to this was the fact that I had to check the concert ticket sellers in and out, then go to the main office and turn the money over to them and wait for it to be checked, thus making me quite late getting through at night.

I had turned my bed over to Mother; my dinette bed had to be made up before we could eat, and then made into a bed at night. Mother was used to retiring early and I would have to turn on the lights to get undressed and put things away before I could retire. No matter how quiet I tried to be, I would wake Mother up; then she would be unable to go back to sleep.

Shortly thereafter, the show started to have some

long jumps that required night driving. With the little sleep
I was able to get and as hard as I was working, I became
very tired, nervous and, I am afraid, downright nasty.

It became harder and harder for me to try to keep
up with the rest of the outfit. Sometimes I would get to the
lot just in time to make the show, so I would have to rush
to work the liberty act in the show, plus two concert an-
nouncements, and then work the after show.

They did not carry a cookhouse, so we either had
to unhook the trailer and go somewhere to eat, or fix something in the crowded little trailer. Mother was unhappy
and kept wishing she could go back to her lovely home in
Scottsburg, but, of course, this was out of the question. We
no longer owned it.

To top it all off, Mother and the Lewises did not get
along together. Because I was working for them, they expected me to carry out their orders. Mother, naturally,
thought her needs ought to come first. Arguments resulted.

Finally, I told Paul I was sorry, but I was going to
have to leave. He said he understood and wanted me to
know that we would still be friends, and we remained so. I
agreed to stay long enough to teach Mae to work the liberty horses, and the people that I had hired for the concert
would be able to continue with it.

And, now, I was worried sick, wondering where to
go, what to do. There was no turning back. I had made a
choice and must stick with it. I made arrangements to stable
my horses at the fairgrounds in the town where I left the
show, and rented an extra stall so that Jimmy would have a
place to put his cot.

Just before I left the show, Bob Stevens, who was in
partnership with Mr. Lewis, came to talk to me; he told me
he would be taking out a show by himself the coming season. As long as I was working for Mr. Lewis, he could not
try to hire me, but now that I was leaving he would make
me a proposition.

He was in contact with a man who had agreed to

break a liberty horse act and a couple of high-school horses for him. He wanted me to go to Texas and help the man select the horses and, when they were trained, to work the liberty act on his show, along with my own horses. I agreed to think it over.

I went to say good-bye to Paul and Mae. We parted, still good friends. I cried as I drove away from the lot, and in the rearview mirror I could see Mae wiping her eyes.

Mother and I went to a trailer camp, where we stayed for a few days. I caught up with the laundry, cleaned up the trailer, and rested. Of course, I went to the fairgrounds each day to see that Jimmy and the horses had everything they needed.

Well, I was going to have to do something; I could not just sit there. I found out where Dailey Bros. Circus was playing and managed to get Mr. Davenport on the phone. I told him I had no place to go and asked if I might send my horses to his winterquarters. He said that it would be all right, so I hired a truck, loaded my horses, trunks, saddles, and Jimmy, and sent them on to Gonzales, Texas. They would be secure there until I could find out where I was going to light.

Where to now? I had a little money put away as I had been doing very well with the concert . . . but I had no gas coupons. The show had arranged to fill up all of the trucks and carried all of the stamps. I am sure that they would have given me some if I had thought to ask, but I was so upset when I left I had forgotten to mention it.

I explained my position to a few of the people around the fairgrounds and the trailer park and, one way or another, I was able to buy some coupons on the black market, but they were not cheap.

It did not matter where we went, so I settled for Houston. I figured that if I could get in touch with some of the Shriners, someone would remember me from playing their indoor shows and help me get gas stamps.

I pulled into a trailer camp on the outskirts of town,

freshened up, unhooked the trailer, and went into town to make some contacts. It took quite some time to find someone who was able to help me, so it was late when I got back to the trailer, and Mother was already asleep. I, too, was tired, but before going to bed I went to the phone and called Gonzales to see if the horses and Jimmy had arrived and were all right. The night watchman assured me they were all okay, so I went to bed for some much-needed rest.

My Show

Frankly and truthfully, I do not know quite what was the matter with me. I had had a nice season with the Bailey Bros. Circus until leaving and I had enjoyed myself; this ought to have been enough. But I had a feeling that I was not getting ahead. Ahead of what, I wonder?

It had been drilled into my head for so many years when I was with Ringling Bros. that each year I must have a new act and something far more sensational than the last. I firmly believed this to be true. Nothing else mattered so much as this; it was the only way to stay on top, so they had told me. On top of what?

Here I had spent a whole season on Cole Bros. doing high school, waltz and rear, high fire jump, and the Big Hitch, but nothing new. What a fool I was! Many performers do the same acts year after year and manage to keep right on going. All of the coaching I had been subjected to had made a very deep impression on me, I am sorry to say. I must get ahead!

When the season ended, Mr. Terrell invited me to return for the coming season. I thanked him for all past favors and told him I thought it was time for me to try something else. I was sure I could play fairs and rodeos.

I had my horses sent home to Scottsburg and tried to break the new act I had devised. Perhaps with different horses it would have been feasible, but with mine, and only Jimmy for a ringmaster, it was a total disaster. For the benefit of anyone who, by chance, might be looking for an unusual act to attempt, I will briefly outline how the routine was supposed to go.

A trapeze is hung over one side of the ring, just high enough so that a rider, standing on a horse, can grab it when going under it; she then performs a trick on the trapeze. Meanwhile, the horse continues to canter around the ring, she drops to the horse as he passes under her and does a stunt on him; back to her feet and up again to the trapeze, off and on, up and down. It was wild, it was hectic, and I damn near killed myself!

I cannot help but wonder if things might not have been a great deal different if I had had someone to advise me. I was always so busy breaking and presenting that I never had time to learn the business end of show business.

Faced with the realization that my inspiration had been a failure, and the fact that people and animals were depending on me to feed them, I was going to have to use what resources I had on hand to do so.

I called Orrin Davenport and asked if there was still time to fit me into the indoor shows. I am sure he considered me a pain in the neck, but was too much of a gentleman to say so. He did ask why I hadn't waited until the first overture was playing before contacting him. Anyway, I was welcome.

But after the indoor shows, what? I would cross that bridge when I came to it . . . unless someone blew it up before I got to it. I was at loose ends and could not make up my mind what I would do.

Why, I did not know, but in my life so many things just seemed to happen for no reason. While I was in this frame of mind, Harry LeRoy approached me during the

Cleveland Shrine show. He may have been what they call a "high pitch-man," an expression I was to learn about later. He spun a grand tale: We could put out our own show; with the publicity I had obtained and his expertise, we could make a lot of money. Lest you think me gullible, please keep in mind that until then I had never seen a "mud show"; I had been too busy with my own affairs. He read off a list of figures from some of his past enterprises, and the profits from the concessions alone were staggering.

All right, you say, then why did he need me? I asked the same thing.

"In order to have concessions, you need to have a show." That made sense. "Also," he said, "you have to have a title. With your name and my know-how, we can make a real go of it."

I took the bait.

We had arranged that he would send a truck to pick up my horses and trunks at the closing date, which was in Detroit. I had a friend bring my car from Scottsburg; I would drive it and follow the truck to Texas.

Harry had told me that he intended to buy the equipment from a large truck show that was converting to a railroad circus. I assumed he must have quite a sum of money to do this. He had a show of his own on the road, but it was small and, at present, playing in schoolhouses. I was to meet him in Gonzales, Texas, where the trucks he was buying were stored.

Harry's truck arrived a day late, and I was far from impressed when it did. The driver explained that he had had engine trouble. I wondered not only how it would stand the trip back to Texas but how it had even gotten this far. I was glad that the rest of the acts had left so no one was around to note my departure.

Because Harry had told me that he had to get back to his show, I could only assume that all of his good motor equipment was being used at those dates and this was an old truck he had stored away in case of emergency.

When I drove into the winterquarters of Dailey Bros. Circus in Gonzales, one of the first persons I met was Ben Davenport, the owner. I told him why I was there.

"So you are Harry LeRoy's new partner," said he. "My condolences. Harry and I were once partners, a long time ago." He did not elaborate. Then with true Texas hospitality, he invited me to have my stock unloaded and stay there for a few days.

It was his understanding that Harry had rented an empty field somewhere down the road but, as no tents or anything else had yet been put on it, there would be no place to keep my horses except tied to the side of the truck. And if old Harry was running true to form, it was doubtful if water or anything else had been arranged for. In the meantime, he would like me to meet his wife, and I could check into the hotel in town later. I found his wife, Eva, to be a delightful person, and she made me feel welcome at once, which I sorely needed at that point.

Two days later, Harry came trotting in, with his mincing little steps and lame excuses, to which no one listened, why he had been delayed. With his arrival, we moved to our own winterquarters, which was merely an old hay field where he had some worn-out tents erected.

There was little I could do there at the moment, so I spent a great deal of time with Eva Davenport. She attempted to teach me the ins and outs of running a small tent show in a few easy lessons, knowledge that had taken her a lifetime to learn. I was very grateful, and she knew it.

Now it was time to look over the trucks and equipment that Harry had been negotiating to buy. I was pleasantly surprised; all of it was nice and clean and in good shape. The truck's light plant and so on had all been gone over and was in running order. The tent and seats, while not new, could be repaired with little trouble. For the first time, I became encouraged and enthusiastic: This show could be a winner after all.

I did not have any doubts until it came to signing

the contracts for the equipment, trucks, tents, and so on. I learned, for the first time, that everything was being bought on the cuff, with me as cosigner of the note, thus making us both liable for the payments.

When Harry had talked to me in Cleveland, he had stated that he was buying a truck show. He needed someone to run it and put on the performance and furnish some of the acts while he went ahead and handled the advance. He had suggested a partnership, but nothing had ever been said about a joint ownership.

Our agreement had been that we would use my name and my stock and we would split any profits there might be after all of the expenses and the salaries had been paid. It did not include buying a circus on time. I had no interest at all in owning a show, either alone or with someone else.

I went to Mr. Davenport. "I am afraid," I confided. "I have my home and my horses, and I do not wish to take a chance of maybe losing them for a deal like this."

"Very well, then," he advised, "tell him to assume ownership of the show and to pay you a percentage of the take, with no partnership involved, and be sure that you do not sign anything whatsoever."

Harry reminded me of a bantam rooster; he was always in a hurry. When he breezed in, I always had a million questions I wanted to ask him, but he was too busy to ever listen, or answer, if he heard. He did have a lot of followers, "drifters" he called them.

A cook tent was set up, then the paint started to fly. Things were beginning to look a little more promising.

It had been agreed that I would manage the show and Harry would run the advance, his job on the various shows he had been with. He was the most nervous person I had ever been around. I do not recall ever seeing him sit down, except to eat, and then he would gulp down his food in a hurry and start pacing again.

One day, Mr. Davenport arrived at our makeshift

winterquarters and presented me with a half truckload of "paper"—lithographs, window plaques, and so on. All you do is cross-line them, put your title on, and you have your advertising. This was a really big help, as those things cost quite a bit of money.

We were all set to go: Acts had been hired, the sideshow was ready, and we would move to the opening spot just fifty miles away a day ahead of time to get things set up.

I had stayed behind to make sure that nothing was left, making me much later than the rest, so when I arrived in the town where we were to have our grand opening, I expected the natives to be aware of our coming. No one I asked could tell me where the show was setting up, as they had heard nothing about it at all. In desperation, I called the police station.

The officer in charge told me about a commotion on the outskirts of town, where some people were trying to set up tents in a farmer's field. When they failed to remove their trucks after he ordered them off of his property, he had called the police. As I drove up, a heated argument was still in progress.

"Yes," the farmer agreed, some feller had been by to see him and offered to rent the south end of the field, but he had also agreed to pay the rent on it in advance, and he had not been by to do so. He had also said he would send some men to clear off the knee-high weeds so a tent could be erected, but he had not done that, either.

Thereupon, one of the policemen who had been standing by informed me that no street parking was allowed and, as no one had rented space or made arrangements for cars to be parked, the likelihood of people walking for many blocks to see a show was remote.

I was beside myself and then, to add to my frustration, I was informed that no license had been issued, or even applied for. To top it all off, not one piece of paper had been posted anywhere.

Just then Harry drove up. The back of his truck was loaded with pre-popped popcorn and a couple of dirty kids, who were to have the job of sacking and selling it. The concession man had not showed up. I blew my top!

Harry explained he had been unable to get a sponsor, so he was going to play the town cold for a tryout. I told him that was where he was going to be—out in the cold. I had had enough.

Although he had been gone for more than a week, he had not had time to put up any paper or arrange for the spot for the tents. He chose this time to inform me that he was out of money, hence no license; I would have to come up with the money to get the show open.

"But, don't worry," he hastened to add, "I have been working on this guy and I think I have him about to buy a half interest in my new show. I showed him the equipment and he was very impressed. I will be able to collect a nice hunk of cash from him; everything will be just great and we will make a lot of dough. In the meantime, how about some pocket money for me?"

The newly repaired and freshly painted trucks and equipment did look good, and I did not doubt that he was about to rope in a sucker to buy a half interest in "my new show." Only it wasn't his to start with; so far the only thing that he had put down on it was conversation.

I went to the nearest telephone and called Ben Davenport. I hated to do so, knowing that he must be having troubles of his own just opening up a railroad show. But, of course, he had all of his old experienced people with him. He told me to sit tight, that he would be there. He had several men with him when he arrived. He took complete charge.

Harry's dogs, ponies, props, and so on were still loaded in his original animal truck, which was parked behind a filling station with one of its tires flat. My horses and paraphernalia were in one of the Dailey Bros. freshly painted horse semi trucks, proclaiming to the world that the great Dorothy Herbert & Harry LeRoy Bros. Circus had arrived, or that it was passing through their city. It was parked on the "No Parking Allowed" street, along with the truck containing the single elephant leased from the Davenports (rather than the large herd depicted on its sides) right behind.

A policeman kept pacing back and forth, trying to decide if he ought to give everyone a ticket or forgo ticketing, as they seemed to be in enough hot water as it was. The other six trucks—ticket wagon, canvas truck, seat truck, concession wagon, light plant, and prop truck—were in a row behind the elephant truck.

Harry's cookhouse truck, which belonged to him personally, had pulled onto the lot, and the cook, who was one of Harry's regulars and no doubt used to his eccentricities, was calmly handing out twice-perked coffee to the roustabouts hanging around to see what might transpire.

So far, the only acts, other than mine, that had been engaged were those that normally worked for Harry; we had planned to start out small and add to the show later. Ben disposed of them first: As they had been working schoolhouse shows to start with, it would be advisable for them to continue to do so.

That left the working crew. Ben called these men together and told them he had jobs for them on his show. Nothing had been unloaded yet, so he would have the truck drivers take the equipment back to Gonzales. He had two extra drivers with him in case they were needed. He invited me to take my horses and equipment to his winterquarters and stay there until I could make my arrangements as to where I would go.

I was sorry we had not been able to give even a few shows, just to see how we would have gone over, but Ben assured me it was a lost cause and would never have made it. He spoke from experience where Harry was concerned.

I sat around the almost deserted winterquarters for a few days, trying to make up my mind what to do next.

Frank Walters

*F*rank Walters was born with money, lots of it, and more was always coming in. He had inherited it from his father, who first struck it rich in the oil business and then, being a very smart businessman, had invested his money in various other enterprises, including buying lots of real estate.

Frank, after finishing college, was at loose ends. Never one to sit around, he amused himself by collecting artifacts. He traveled far and wide. Before his enthusiasm waned he had established a small museum of his own. Some of the jewelry in it was fantastic, all handmade, all authentic. Tiring of that, he then went in for art, and some of the Western scenes he painted were beautiful.

He then married. His wife was very horse minded and, although he did not care for riding himself, he indulged her. It was while riding at a horse show that she first met A. W. Kennard. He was showing horses for another lady, and Lucia Walters persuaded him to train her gaited horses. This, of course, was just a part-time deal, for A. W. was employed as sales manager by Raymond Pierson, who had the Ford dealership in Houston. Frank and A. W. became close friends; they both belonged to the Shrine, and Frank was very interested in the circus that they put on each year. One evening, over a glass of beer, A. W. happened to mention that he had spent some time with the Christy Bros. Circus. He also mentioned that he had been taught to train animals by that noted trainer, Merrit Blue. Frank questioned him as to what kinds of animals he was able to break.

That was all Frank needed to set him off on a new hobby. Whatever Frank did, he did in a big way. Frank was an exceptionally big man. He seldom smiled, and had an air about him that demanded attention wherever he went. As he owned property all over Houston, he chose a lovely spot just at the edge of town for his winterquarters. The spot had lofty trees loaded down with birds, and small wildlife.

First he had his barns and stables built. His plan was to have a complete circus in miniature—a special show for the kiddies. He and his wife then traveled all over the United States buying up small circus wagons. When it became evident that he was not going to be able to purchase very many, nor the kinds that he wanted, he located an old wagon builder and moved him, bag and baggage, to Houston.

I do not know how long this project took, but I do know that he ended up with a complete circus parade. This necessitated ponies to pull them, and also harness. Meanwhile, his training barn had been completed and acts were in the process of being trained.

His ring barn was unique. You came up a long driveway and stopped before what looked like a beautiful home; in the front was a parking space for many cars. You entered into a huge room rather like the lobby of a hotel; couches, seats, and small tables were everywhere. The walls were lined with glass cases containing all sorts of silver and turquoise bridles, belts, and necklaces; in the center was a long table where, if they were entertaining guests, a meal could be served. Off to one side were the restrooms for ladies and gentlemen and, at the far end, was the kitchen. At that same end was a long flight of stairs, which led to the Walterses' bedroom in case they didn't wish to drive home; next to that was a guest room and bath.

Back to the lounge room. When you pressed a button, the two walls on one side slid back and you were looking into the training arena, which contained the ring curb and various props. The steel arena for training wild animals was outdoors in the open. Frank bought a regular circus tent, complete with seats. The only things missing were a ticket wagon and ticket boxes—all of the seats were free.

When Frank had it all completed and the animals he bought were trained, he took the show around to different towns in Texas and put on shows for underprivileged children beginning with a street parade in town. At each location the local merchants would donate all of the ice cream, soda pop, peanuts, and popcorn.

Each year the show became larger as he added to it and more people became involved. Many circus people who wintered in and around Houston would donate their acts. The Shriners, their wives, and youngsters worked most of Frank's animal acts.

A. W. broke a liberty horse act for Frank's wife to work, as well as a number of manege horses that were ridden by her friends. Merrit Blue, who was retired and living in Houston, broke a couple of pony drills and two dog acts; they also had a goat act.

As for Frank, he insisted on a lion act for himself. He persuaded Terrell Jacobs and his wife, Dolly, to winter at his quarters one year and, while there, Terrell trained a lion act for him. Just six lions, but Frank was a handsome man, the act was good, and the kids loved it.

Frank was a very good friend of Clyde Beatty and, after Clyde took out his own show, would often travel with it. It was rumored that his interest was more than just as a bystander. During the off-season he and Clyde would take trips together, usually to some foreign country. Once they went on a safari with Frank Buck.

Whenever any circus came to Houston, Frank would invite some of the performers out to his training barn for a buffet supper after the night show. After supper he would have some of his trained animals and handlers put on a show for us in the training ring. That was where I met A.W. for the first time; later on, he often came with Frank to visit different shows I happened to be on. Because this was the man who Big Bob Stevens had told me he was going to have train his stock for him, I thought I might look him up. I had not made up my mind if I was going to take

Mr. Stevens' offer, but, as I had nothing else in mind at the moment, it was worth looking into.

I phoned Frank Walters, who was surprised to hear I was in town. I told him that I was trying to locate Mr. Kennard. Frank said he was no longer with the Ford Motor Company, but he had gone into business for himself, running a used-car lot. Frank said that if I would meet him that evening at his ring barn he would arrange for A. W. to be there.

After I explained to A. W. what my connection with Mr. Stevens was, he said he would appreciate any advice I might offer in helping choose the horses for the liberty act he was to break.

Finding the horses could be difficult. Mr. Stevens wanted a six-horse act: a black, a white, and a black-and-white; the same act that Rudynoff had had on the Sells-Floto Circus. Trying to find the horses in and around Houston was a lost cause. People there had money and were interested only in high-class show horses. Run-of-the-mill horses, such as were used for a circus act, were not available. We would have to look elsewhere.

I mentioned knowing Jack Sellers in San Antonio, who had bragged about knowing the whereabouts of just about all of the horses in Texas. A. W. told me to call him to see if he knew where we could find what we were looking for. He said that indeed he did, and we arranged a meeting for a few days later.

A. W. assigned one of his salesmen to handle his used-car lot, and Mother offered to go to his office to answer the phone and take messages. So, early one morning we drove to San Antonio.

Jack had not been just bragging; he knew where to look for most any kind of horse. The trouble was that ranches in Texas were so large and far apart, it would take more time than any of us had to spare to run them down one at a time. He did know one man who had not only more kinds but more horses than anyone else, period. In spite of being eccentric to an unbelievable degree, he might be just the man we were looking for.

It looked as if we were going to have to stay overnight, so Jack began calling hotels and motels, but all of them were filled. We would have to leave shortly to return to Houston, but decided to talk with the man Jack had spoken of before going back. Jack piloted us out to his place and took us in to meet the one and only Mr. Glasscock.

He and his wife lived in a three-room shack that looked as though it belonged to a sharecropper. The old man greeted us warmly and invited us in to sit a spell. The living-sitting-dining room was unbelievable. A large, bare wooden table dominated the center of the floor, with wooden crates serving as chairs. The place was devoid of any decorations whatsoever. The one jarring note was the most beautiful piano I had ever seen; it sat off to one side by itself, and on top of it were assorted frames with photos of boys and girls who looked to be of all different nationalities.

Mr. Glasscock, himself, was a sight to behold. He wore a pair of once-blue coveralls with about a five-inch tear down one knee, exposing the fact that he was wearing long underwear in the heat of summer. His white hair hung down to his shoulders. His beard touched his chest, its whiteness marred by tobacco stains from the wad he seemed to chew constantly.

After Jack explained the reason for our visit, the old man said he was sure he had what we were looking for, but it was a long way out to the ranch and an early morning start would be advisable. A. W. told him we would have to return to Houston right away, as no accommodations were available in the area.

The old man asked what we needed, and A. W. told him two single rooms. Mr. Glasscock went to the phone, and when he came back he said it was all arranged. We were to stay at the largest hotel in San Antonio, and he would meet us there in the morning.

At the hotel we were given the red carpet treatment, the clerk ignoring the fact that we had no luggage, not having planned to stay over. We said goodnight, and A. W. retired to his room while I went to the drugstore to buy a few necessary items.

The next morning, Jack met us for an early breakfast. The dining room was quite elegant, with the waitresses all decked out in pretty, starched uniforms. We were seated quite far back; I heard Jack, who always looked like a fashion plate, gasp.

I turned just as old man Glasscock, who had not seen fit to change clothes since yesterday, waved and called out, "Hi there, girlie." Many heads turned and stared. He came over and sat down; we hurried through the rest of our repast and then headed for the front door. Mr. Glasscock offered me his arm as if we were about to enter a ballroom for a dance.

Jack and A. W. got into a controversy over the bill, only to find that Mr. Glasscock had already paid for the meal. I did not feel very good about that, as I figured the old man could ill afford it.

When we got to the car, no one asked me if I had my "druthers." I was ushered into the back seat with Mr. Glasscock while Jack sat in front with A. W. They engaged in men talk, while the old boy figured it was up to him to keep me entertained. I had heard all of my life that Texans were prone to brag and exaggerate (or maybe even stretch the truth to make an impression), but this old man didn't only take the cake, he took the whole bakery!

As we passed a building, he would point it out and say, "I had that building built," or "See that library there; I gave that to the city." He even professed to own the largest department store in town. No doubt about it, the old coot was stark raving mad, and I wondered how long this ride was going to last; forever, it seemed. Once in a while he would lean over the front seat and give A. W. instructions as to where to turn.

After a time, A. W. began to worry and asked how much longer it would be before we reached our destination.

"Ain't but a hop, skip, and a holler," the old man replied.

"With the gas rationing and all, I am wondering if I am going to be able to go much farther and also get back," A. W. returned.

"Don't give her a thought, sonny," said Mr. Glasscock, "just pull into the next gas station."

We did, and the attendant filled up the car, refusing either stamps or money.

Some time later, Mr. Glasscock directed A. W. to pull off onto a private road, which seemed to go on for miles. On either side, lined up like deserted tract houses, were oil wells, most of them merrily pumping away. For some reason, each of them had a name and even a birth date, which the old man rattled off as we drove by.

We came, at last, to a large ranch house with numerous small bunkhouses in a row down one side; a mess hall and kitchen were at the far end. It looked like we were expected, as an ample supply of cowpokes came out to greet us. It transpired that the old man had called ahead the night before, and they had rounded up several herds of wild horses and penned them in corrals awaiting inspection.

The head wrangler was the tallest, most handsome Indian I had ever seen. He seemed to tower over everyone else. He was a wizard with the rope, and, as the horses circled the corral, he would catch whichever horse was pointed out to him. He spoke not one word of English, but Mr. Glasscock seemed to have complete command of whatever language he did speak.

Thinking out loud, I noted what a remarkable man I thought the Indian to be.

"You ought to see his son. I'm sending him to college," Mr. Glasscock replied. Oh, brother!

We picked out the most desirable of the candidates, and Mr. Glasscock said he would have them delivered to Jack's stables, which he had offered the use of, within a few days.

We then ate with the cowboys in the mess hall. Huge bowls were piled high with potatoes, brown beans, rice, stewed canned tomatoes, corn, homemade bread, and steaks the size of a pot roast.

There was complete silence at the table, with everyone intent on their food, with the exception of Mr. Glasscock, who now attempted to impress me with tall tales of his gold and zircon mines in Mexico. He said he would like to fly me there in his airplane some day . . . and there was still the long road back to San Antonio to look forward to!

When we got back to the hotel, I excused myself and left them to finish up their business. I was hoping Mr. Glasscock would make himself a nice profit on the deal. Not wishing to run into them in the dining room, I ordered some food sent up to my room.

A. W. phoned me early the next morning, saying that he would like to get started back to Houston as soon as possible. When we went to the desk to check out, the clerk said that there was no charge. Not understanding, A. W. asked for an explanation.

"Gee, I thought you knew," said the clerk. "Mr. Glasscock owns this hotel, as well as many other businesses in this city. He even donated the grounds and a great deal of money towards our college. You see, he himself never had a chance to get an education and he thinks that is the most important thing on earth. I understand he has in his home a piano, and on it photos of kids he adopted and put through school. He bought the piano for one of his protégés who he took into his home as a barefoot, hungry, little boy and who is now a famous musician."

When we got back to Houston, A. W. rented a ranch on the outskirts of town, with a barn for the stock. He then asked me to go with him to help pick out the two horses he was to break for manege. While looking for these horses, we happened upon some beautiful, matched black-and-white spotted ponies. I called Mr. Stevens, who was now in his own winterquarters putting his new show together, and asked if I were to buy the ponies, would he have a place for them on his show? He said he certainly would. I had in mind that if I were to help Mr. Kennard break the liberty horse drill, he would, in turn, help me break my pony drill; this he agreed to do.

A. W. told me where I might hire a truck, and I sent it to Gonzales to pick up my horses and Jimmy. I then took my trailer to the ranch, and that is where Mother and I stayed. There was a house on the ranch, but we did not have any furniture. We did take advantage of the bathroom in the house, and it was nice to have a tub bath after all that time of having to shower in the tiny trailer.

In the meantime, A. W. went with a truck back to San Antonio, bought two palomino stallions from Jack Sellers to break for manege, and picked up his horses for the liberty act. As soon as he returned, he had a ring curb made and then went to work on the horses. He continued to live in town while running his used-car business, and came out each day to work the horses. Mother and I felt safe with Jimmy there with us.

Several months of hard work followed. Then came the rains, and it was impossible to do anything as the ring was outdoors. Frank Walters had been spending a lot of time at the ranch, watching the training and offering advice. Now he suggested that we load everything and take it to his winterquarters and work the horses there. Due to the war, gas shortage, and the scarcity of help, Frank's show was no longer in operation and he had plenty of room. We were glad to accept his kind offer.

Frank and his wife had recently separated, so he spent most of his time at his barn. He was a very likeable person once you got to know him. We spent many pleasant evenings in his clubroom after the day's training was over.

Then came the time for the deal to be consummated. I, of course, had not been aware of the agreement between them. I did know that A. W. kept close watch and retained all of the bills he paid; how much he had paid for the horses, I did not know. Although I had gone with him to pick them out, I did not stay around when the deals were made. One thing I was sure of, though: The trappings for the horses had cost a great deal, as I had the harnesses for the ponies made at the same place, and they did not come cheap.

I was never told just what transpired; all I ever knew was that A. W. and Mr. Stevens got into an argument and that their deal fell through. I assumed it had something to do with the amount of money involved. All of the money spent had been A. W.'s, so he was now in possession of a liberty horse act, something he certainly did not want.

This left me in a predicament also. I not only did not have a job, I had spent all of my savings on a pony drill for which I now had no use. I had to come up with something in a hurry.

I called Orrin Davenport and asked if he might be able to use me on the indoor shows.

"Yes. And where have you been, and what are you doing in Texas?"

I told him that I had gone there in the first place looking for gas stamps and had been detained, which didn't make much sense at all.

He told me to catch a train and get back there. They were using the Cole show stock and somebody would be able to come up with something for me to do.

That somebody was John Smith. I was given the same black high-school horse I had ridden at the Wichita date a long time before. They had a gaited horse number, and I rode Mrs. Terrell's personal horse, LeRose McAdams, a sweetheart; it brought back memories of Jack Dempsey. Once more I worked John Smith's pony drill.

For the jumping number, they brought forth a very large horse called Pale Face. Without my own personally trained horses, I was expected to do only the regular jump like the other riders. We rehearsed, and all went well.

Then came time for the first show—the pony drill was early in the program. I ran into the ring and gave a hitch kick and turned to face the ponies, to discover that they were NUDE, no trappings at all. The surprise was that they worked; John wanted to show everyone how well-trained they were.

My gaited horse worked fine, as did the high-school horse later in the show. They did not have a rearing horse, though I am sure John would have managed to come up with one quickly if anyone had asked him.

The last number in the show, before the cannon act, was the jumps. I was not doing anything special in the number, so I was not being featured. I figured out later that this was more than John could stand. For seemingly no reason, except maybe to quiet the horse, which I must say was fidgety, John came and stood by his head. He let all the other riders jump first, then he motioned for the jump to be raised so high I thought he must be out of his mind.

Satan and I had jumped six feet, twice a day, but we were a team, trained together; the same with Rex. Now here I was, on a strange horse, jumping a hurdle so high I was petrified. As a final gesture, John stepped forward with much élan and removed the bridle from the horse. With no reins to hold on to, what was there to do but throw my arms over my head.

The horse, as John had known he would, cleared the hurdle with room to spare. This is the only time I can recall ever having an announcement after an act: "And there, ladies and gentlemen, is the one and only Dorothy Herbert."

I did not know it at the time, but John, at the instigation of Mr. Terrell, was setting the stage for me to go back with his show.

With all of the complications I now had and they were unaware of, it would have been impossible. First and foremost, there was my mother, who, having no place to go, I would have to keep with me . . . and railroad shows do not permit mothers to travel with their grown daughters. Next, there was the pony drill in which I had so much invested, and which they would have no use for since they had their own.

I contemplated a question arising in the minds of my readers: What had become of the money from the sale of the house and ring barn? Located right off the main highway, it must have fetched a tidy sum. This, Mother considered HER nest egg, and it was not to be touched, in any case.

Working the indoor shows that year was fun. I hadn't realized how much I had missed all of my friends. We had so many things to talk about and catch up on, the time was all too short.

When I returned to Houston after the indoor dates, I was halfway engaged to a wild animal trainer. When I say halfway, he had asked me to marry him and I told him I would let him know right after I got back to Houston; I felt that I owed it to my mother to talk over such a step with her.

The name of the man is of no importance to this story. Suffice to say I had known him for a long time and had never dreamed of his interest toward me until we renewed our acquaintance on the indoor shows. He felt, and I agreed with him, that together we could do a lot of great things in show business. He was of the opinion that if I were to work his wild animal act it might enhance its value, but we never had a chance to find out.

Mother and A. W. met me at the train. I was very tired from the long trip. We drove out to Guido's, a very exclusive restaurant. I had little to say. A. W. and Mother did all of the talking, and they were full of news about what had happened while I was gone. Frank and A. W. had kept

Mother entertained while I was away. Since they both dined out, they had seen to it that she was included. She had been to several rodeos and horse shows, and had not had time to be lonesome.

On the way home to the little trailer, Mother was on the front seat next to A. W., and I was in the back. I was sleepy and had just started to doze off when I heard A. W. say, "Mrs. Herbert, would you mind if I married your daughter?"

Mother replied, "It would make me very happy indeed. I do not have long to live, and I would die happy if I knew she had someone like you to look after her."

We were married in Frank Walters' home. Just a few people, Frank and his mother, my mother, and a few of A. W.'s friends, were guests. Our honeymoon was short; we went to Galveston for two days. While there, we made our plans: A. W. would sell his used-car business and buy a semi to transport the horses; I would go to Chicago and book some fairs.

I was a little leery starting out with all of this green stock, but what else was there to do? At least I was sure of Black Hawk, King Kong, and Rex. I booked just a few fairs to start with. If our unit was successful, more would come later.

When I returned to Houston, Jimmy was gone; he had left without saying a word to anyone. I was sure that someone had done something to make him go. I found out much later what had happened. He had been injured in the war, and now he was hurting again. He had not wanted to bother anyone with his troubles, so he went to the veteran's hospital, where they removed another piece of shrapnel. They kept him there for quite some time, and when he was well again, he rejoined me. I never knew how he managed to find out where I was—one day he just reappeared. But, for now, he was gone.

( )

Typical publicity shot, to an unidentified admirer.

Another Life To Live—Fairs

D uring the winter of 1944–1945, my husband and I watched the building of the Austin Bros. Circus in the Gonzales winterquarters of the Dailey show. Ben Davenport had taken Harry Hammel as partner, and they were framing a new ten-car railroad show for the 1945 season. When the show opened in Austin, Texas, on April 30, A. W. and I were with it.

I worked my dog act and high-jumping horse and rode manege with Elizabeth Kitchen. We left the show after about a month.

A. W. bought a large semi, and he hired a young couple he knew who were very anxious to break into show business. Harold was a tall, lanky guy who chattered constantly, asking a million questions and then not waiting for an answer. He grinned far too much, and was so nervous he made others feel that way. His wife was a petite gal and everyone called her "Tiny"; she must have had another name, but that is all I ever heard her called. She had a whiny little voice, was prone to complaining, and she expected Harold to drop whatever he was doing and fetch for her. Harold had fixed a little compartment in the front of the truck for them to live in.

They were supposed to care for the stock and ride the two manege horses. I had misgivings, but they were A. W.'s friends and this was his ballgame. There we were . . . starting out with green stock and green people.

So that is how we began our life together, A. W. and I—he driving the truck with Harold and Tiny in the front seat with him, plus Tiny's two dogs; me driving my car with Mother by my side and, behind me, the little trailer.

I had thought the trailer small before, but now, with three of us living in it, it seemed to have shrunk. Plus, as the truck had no running water, Harold and his wife had to wash up in the trailer. The dinette-bed in the front of the trailer, where A. W. and I tried to sleep, was small, and I found out he was a very restless sleeper. The only place where I could get some rest was sleeping in the front seat of the car.

The journey to the first stand was not bad, with everyone in a jovial mood. Mother loved to travel and see new sights, A. W. was reliving his boyhood days on a circus, and Tiny was dreaming of being a big star. If Harold had a thought of any kind, it was in a strange place. I was the only one who was depressed, but then, I was the only one who knew wherefore I worried.

We planned it so that we would get to our first stand several days in advance of the show, so as to acclimate the green stock to working in new surroundings. It was a good thing we did as we had our first lesson when it came time to load the truck in Houston. The horses, although trained to do a liberty act, had a whole lot more to learn with regard to being loaded into a truck.

Now, the training of the horses and ponies had begun out in the open. Then, because of the heavy Texas rains, we had later moved to Frank Walters' ring barn, with the security of four walls. Now we were out in the open again, with all kinds of new sounds and different smells. Remember, we were working with untrained Texas broncs. We had brought along the electric fence to be placed around the outside of the ring, and a good thing, as we really needed it. I was sure glad that I had had the foresight to book small fairs to start.

We took the horses one by one into the ring, then kept adding one as they gained confidence and settled down. At the end of a couple of days they were still nervous, but working.

It was when we got ready to practice the manege high-school act that we ran into real trouble. Things had already begun to live up to my worst expectations. Tiny refused to have anything to do with the big horses, and would only go near the ponies. Harold had assured A. W.

that Tiny was an accomplished horsewoman; I could not help but wonder why A. W. had not bothered to find out if this was true.

The two palomino stallions, I will admit, were a little peppy, but not all that bad. Tiny hit the dirt about the second waltz—seems she had ridden on a Western saddle, but never had been on an English saddle before. She picked herself up and announced that she had had it. So, A. W. rode one horse and Harold the other.

A. W. was then obliged to hire another man to help take care of the stock. This posed another problem. The new man had to have a place to ride. The back of my car was filled to the rooftop with Mother's and A. W.'s things, so there was no room there. Mother refused to have him sit next to her on the front seat, ditto Tiny and her two dogs. Tiny ended up riding with us, the new man holding the dogs on his lap.

When booking this new unit for the first time, I had been unable to limit the number of miles we would travel in any given time, and some of the distances were long. Tempers grew short, and, the weather was unbearably hot. There was no such thing as air conditioning in trailers at that time. With it shining all day, right out in the infield, it was like walking into an oven. One day Mother could stand it no longer and she packed up and went to visit relatives in Cincinnati.

Surprisingly, the green stock worked well and we received more bookings. The season, though not too pleasant, was not a total loss, but I was glad to see it draw to a close.

Frank Walters had invited us to spend the winter at his place, and a bit of a rest was welcome. Mother joined us as soon as we got back to Houston. Frank offered her the guest rooms in his training barn, saying that A. W. and I ought to have some time to get acquainted, as we had been too busy while on the road; so A. W. and I had the little trailer to ourselves.

As a rule, two people who are in the business of training animals have many conflicts. Whenever working with a new horse trainer, I made it a point to try to do things his way, and learn all I could from him in the process. One thing that I had never liked to do was argue. After I was married, I started to wonder how I ought to handle it if I did not always agree with A. W.'s methods of training.

A. W. had received his basic training from Merrit Blue on the Christy Bros. Circus; Merrit had served his apprenticeship with Ray Thompson. I considered Ray a wonder trainer who turned out well-trained horses without straining them to the breaking point, whereas others I worked with might not have achieved the same spectacular results in as short a period of time.

I wondered how I might best impart to A. W. some of the things I had learned from other trainers without hurting his ego. I hit upon a method that worked out beautifully: I never made a comment in the ring barn. I would wait until after dinner, when we were alone and relaxed, and then I would go into a long drawn-out tale about how so-and-so had trained a certain horse to do a trick; I never suggested that he do likewise. Before long, I found that he was asking how different trainers handled each situation. Without ever having to ask me what I would do, he had the answers. The acts he turned out were first rate. He did, however, have one drawback: He was not good at presenting a number. He was so intent on seeing that the animals worked perfectly that he paid no attention to the audience whatsoever.

This worked out all right in the long run. Ham that I was, I delighted in working all of the acts and taking the bows. A. W., in turn, liked to train animals but was not too happy about presenting them. He was not the only one to which this applied. I have found that a great many trainers are so intent on keeping their animals working that the audience is of secondary importance. Now, this is great up to a certain point, but bear in mind that the people watching the show are the ones who are paying the tab, and they deserve something for their money. At least that was my attitude, and I tried to do my best for them at each performance, whether the crowd was large or small.

If one of the animals I was working made a mistake, I just laughed it off and corrected it at the next performance. In the event it happened twice, we would have a refresher course between shows.

As a wedding present, A. W. had given me a beautiful white stallion. Most girls, at some time in their life, get a diamond ring. There had not been time to train the horse before taking off on our first jaunt, so we had left him with Frank Walters.

I had been quite taken with Dr. Ostermaier's horse when he first came to this country, so A. W. broke the stallion for that act—dressage on the long reins. We had rhinestones on white leather trappings made for the horse, and a lovely white wardrobe for me, with turquoise ostrich plumes galore on both of us.

A convention is held each year in Chicago, and it is there that agents, acts, and fair personnel congregate and deals are made for the forthcoming season. While there, I found that units like ours were much in demand and I could get us work that would not entail such long jumps. But it was the agent, Boyle Woolfolk, who set me off on the right track.

"Dorothy," he said, "if you could somehow get hold of a dog act, we would book you into all of our fairs without having to hire any other animal people for that date. We would, of course, raise your salary to make it worth your while."

When I got back to Houston, I told A. W. about the conversation with Boyle. (And, if you are still with me, Dear Reader, this is when I went to the dogs.)

Merrit Blue, who was acquainted with all of the animal people in Houston, told us of this little old lady who had a dog act that he thought might be bought. Her husband had passed away and, as she did not know what else to do with them, she had just kept them.

We obtained her address and paid a visit. A worse looking bunch of mutts I had never seen, but they did quite a good act.

A. W., ever the optimist, said, "All of the necessary props are here. I will go to the dog pound, pick up some more prospects, train them, add to these, and we will have a dog act."

After the original dogs were bathed and clipped, they did not look too bad. A. W. bought a rhesus monkey, and, at the same time he was adding to the dog act, he broke a riding dog and monkey act. When we got to the first fair, I understood what the agent had meant: We could be every other act. With some aerial acts and a few on the ground, no other acts were necessary. With gas rationing being what it was, this was a boon for everyone concerned.

Our second season on the road, we started out by playing a series of fairs in Minnesota. The farms there were lovely, everything so neat and clean. The houses and barns all looked as though they had just been newly painted, without a scrap of rubbish anywhere. I could not help but wonder where they put their trash. Everywhere we went, the people were so very friendly. The fair was a big event to them each year. This was before the invasion of television, and they really enjoyed the grandstand shows.

The townsfolk got a big kick out of watching us load and unload the semi. Everywhere we went, people were amazed at the amount of stuff we carried on the one truck. Often we were asked when the rest of our outfit was going to arrive.

This one semi carried eighteen head of horses and ponies, consisting of the six-horse liberty act, six-pony drill, two palomino manege horses, King, Rex, Black Hawk, and the white stallion. Underneath the truck on one side were boxes, each containing a dog or a monkey, sixteen in all. Each animal had his or her own cage, with plenty of room.

On the other side were stored the ring curb and all of the props used in the different numbers; hay and grain were loaded on an overhead rack above the cab; and just behind the cab we had a large tank for water.

A. W. had hired two men to look after the stock, and A. W. and I moved into the little compartment Harold and Tiny had occupied, thus leaving the trailer to Mother.

We had a good unit, but it was hard on me. The acts we presented, with a few aerial and ground acts in between, ran as follows:

> Riding Dogs and Monkeys—I worked
> White Stallion on the Long Reins—I worked
> Dog Act—I worked
> Pony Drill—I worked
> Dressage—A. W. and another man
> Dressage (Black Hawk)—I worked
> Waltz and Rear (Rex)—I worked
> Liberty Horse Act—I worked
> Fire Jump (Rex)—I worked

Each act I worked required a complete change of wardrobe. I had worked just as hard with a circus, but there when I was finished I could go to the train and relax. Now, besides the acts, there was the packing up, loading, and driving the house trailer overland. True, I had driven overland with the Lewis show, but I had not had all the extra work to do. Quite often, when the others went to eat, I would just lie down and rest.

Upon our return to Houston after the fairs, we learned that a real catastrophe had occurred just a few days before we arrived: Frank Walters' winterquarters had burned to the ground. The help who lived on the premises had managed to save the livestock, but the ring barn and the long barn, which had housed his little parade wagons, had all been lost before the fire trucks could get there. Frank gave some of his stock to Clyde Beatty, and the lions to

Terrell Jacobs, and that was the end of his show.

A. W. finally found an old ramshackle barn on the outskirts of town for the horses, and there we would spend the winter months. Not a pleasant prospect, at best. It wasn't too bad on sunny days when we could go outside; but on cold, rainy days, when we had to sit huddled in the little trailer, it was murder. It was also difficult to prepare meals in such a small area; on the road, we mostly ate out. Mother felt she would be more comfortable elsewhere, so she went to Cincinnati.

∪

The Montgomery Circus

We did not linger long in Houston. Now that our acts had proven themselves, we did not have to seek out the agents; they contacted us. We spent the greater part of the winter months playing the big indoor shows. I was very enthusiastic, and we were off and running.

If A. W. had faults, and we all do, the one that annoyed me the most was his habit of making decisions without consulting me first. It seems that in the part of the country from which he hailed the menfolk did all of the thinking and, right or wrong, the women just tagged along. If he had been right even half of the time, I would not have taken exception.

We were playing the Police Circus in St. Louis, and, at dinner between shows, he broke the news to me: He had just signed a contract to go with the C. R. Montgomery Circus for the 1946 season.

Now that our acts were A-number one, it was time to cash in on all of the big fairs; instead, he had committed himself to an unknown would-be showman. I was appalled.

People go into the circus business in many different ways and for as many reasons. C. R. Montgomery owned a mink farm or ranch, whichever you care to call it. These little animals eat meat. Even though you have a great number of them, they are small, and, when you butcher a horse or cow, there is always plenty of meat to spare. So Mr. Montgomery bought first one wild animal, then another, and still another, to feed them the meat that was left over.

So, what now? He hired an animal trainer and, thus, he had an act. An animal act belongs on a circus, so he bought some secondhand equipment and put on a show. He was able to hire a number of other gullible performers and so . . . we opened.

We wandered in and out of towns with hardly any effect on the citizens, except the few that had never been to a zoo and came to the back lot to look at the elephants. The elephants were there on lease and, after the first three payless paydays, the owner came after them and took them home, along with their trainer.

When city officials came by to talk over some sort of business with the show owner, they were always a little abashed to find him butchering and cutting up some sort of carcass to feed to his wild animals and usually declined shaking hands.

The putting up and taking down of the big top was like an unscheduled army drill: great exercise, but serving little purpose. I am sure the original intention had been for people to enter said tent and attend the performance. Whether they did not get the message, or chose to ignore it, the fact remains that very few of them elected to go inside after the tent was up. This lack of interest had an adverse effect on the box office, which carried over into the backyard as they were unable to pay anyone a salary. All work and no pay makes a sad "Jolly," and the clowns, who hadn't been too funny to start with, ran Pagliacci a close second when it came to vocalizing their laments. The finance companies, with whom most everyone seemed to have an affiliation, were disinclined to forgive and forget either the debts or their debtors.

Not seeing a chance for things to improve in the foreseeable future, like the Arabs in the story, we quietly folded our tents and crept away. We went back to winterquarters, where we sat around waiting for Mr. Montgomery to raise the money to pay us off.

While we were waiting there, A. W. had a phone call from George Christy of the Christy Bros. Circus located in Houston. He wished to know if we would be interested in taking our unit to Hawaii for a winter date in 1947. He had been authorized to intercede on behalf of E. K. Fernandez. A. W. thought this might be interesting and quoted him a price, which was agreeable.

∪

Garden Bros. Circus

It was obvious that with the number of animals we had and the expenses connected with them, we were not going to be able to work just during the fair season and then lay off all winter.

I did not feel that our acts at that time were of the right caliber to try to book on the big indoor shows. Therefore, I contacted Boyle Woolfolk, our agent, and instructed him to try to place us on the Garden Bros. indoor show in 1947, a comparatively new unit that I understood was having difficulty hiring animal acts due to the restriction on taking them into Canada. We offered just what Garden Bros. was looking for. The only animal that could not be used was Rex; he would go along just for the ride. Garden Bros. Circus also had an elephant act, Professor Keller with his wild animal act, and Ira Watkins' famous chimps.

Upon hearing the news about our new contract, Frank Walters again stepped into the picture. He pointed out that we were going into cold country in the wintertime and, although the animals would be housed in a warm building, our little house trailer, with its oil burning stove, was far from adequate for us to live in.

Frank knew of someone who had a Sparton Manor trailer for sale and took us to look at it. After the down payment was made, the papers signed, and it was fully insured, I moved everything into our new home. Compared to the little trailer, the size of a camper, it was a palace. We left the little trailer in Harold's back yard.

A. W. hired a couple of men to travel with us to take care of the stock. One of them was a truck driver. A. W. figured with the jumps we were going to have he would require someone to one help him with the driving.

It so happened that A. W. was not the one to need help; it was me. We all ate breakfast at a roadside restaurant, but did not order the same things. Just before going into Detroit, I became very ill. I was in the lead, so the first chance I had I pulled over to the side, parked, and flagged down A. W.

He told the truck driver to take over my outfit and I got in the back seat of my car and lay down. It wasn't more than a half hour later that we had a smashup. Hit by a huge truck, the car was not damaged, but the trailer was a total wreck. A wrecker towed the house trailer into a garage where we unloaded it, more or less, by just throwing everything on the back seat and floor of my car; we were running late and had to get to the border and into Canada.

A. W. and I were very thankful that it was my rig and not the horse trailer that the man had been driving— the house trailer could be replaced. From that time on, no matter what, A. W. always drove his truck himself.

The first few days on the Garden Bros. Circus we stayed in a motel, and, after the insurance company settled the claim, we bought another house trailer.

Everyone on the Garden Bros. show was congenial. All of our acts worked well and were now acclimated to working either indoors or outdoors with equal ease.

∪

Honolulu

Just as we were loading the truck preparatory to leaving for Houston, whom did I spy coming toward us but Jimmy. He told me where he had been all this time—in the hospital. He didn't ask if he could have a job, but he knew he didn't have to.

Mr. Christy had contacted E. K. Fernandez and arranged the deal. Mr. Christy's interest was related to the fact that he was leasing his tent, sidewalls, and seats for this venture. He turned over the business of getting same to its destination to A. W.

The various performers and animals would all congregate in San Francisco, where they would debark on two ships. The animals and their handlers would leave on a cargo ship several days before the passenger ship carrying the performers. Most acts would, of course, make the trip to San Francisco in their own motor equipment.

Our stock would travel in the baggage car hired to transport the big top, poles, and seats. Sharing the animal section of the car would be the stock belonging to Merrit Blue, who, besides his act, had been hired as equestrian director, a position he had held on Christy Bros.

Merrit Blue had retired, and, now that he was no

longer employed, he had broken an act of his own. I am of the opinion, knowing his reputation as a trainer, that if he had had a little more money he would have broken something more impressive. As it was, his act consisted of a pony, a dog, a goat, and a monkey.

Merrit and A. W. would go ahead to Hawaii, set up everything for the arrival of the stock, and help to arrange the program.

Someone had to travel with the stock on the train to San Francisco. Since there was no one else, that left me. Merrit's wife would go by plane to San Francisco to board the ship there. Merrit did not have a groom, so no one else was in the baggage car but Jimmy. George Christy's men had loaded all of his paraphernalia the night before. As soon as they saw that the livestock was loaded, Merrit and A. W. took a taxi to the airport and from there they would go to Hawaii.

I had no premonition whatsoever of what might transpire on this journey. All expenses to San Francisco had been paid, which had included first-class accommodations with a lower berth on the train for me.

The war had just ended, and everywhere was bedlam. They switched the baggage car with the stock back and forth from one train to another. Because it was booked to go passenger class rather than freight, there was a big mix-up. When they finally got the car hooked up behind an engine, my reservation was no good on that train . . . it was for one that had left three hours earlier.

I found myself in a coach so crowded with servicemen that no seats were available at all. I sat on my suitcase, and was slightly more than uncomfortable. I wondered if it was going to be like this all the way to San Francisco.

They gave the call for dinner and I got in line, along with a few other civilians, only to be informed that meals were being served to servicemen only. The man in charge said that when we got to the next station, we could get off to buy sandwiches and coffee.

I did not mind so much for myself, but what about poor Jimmy up ahead in the stock car with nothing to eat. We had loaded that morning at five o'clock, and it was now after dark.

After all of the servicemen had been fed and the diner was closed, I walked up and knocked. When a man opened the door, I explained that I did not wish to eat for myself, but that I had a man ahead in a car just behind the engine who would be needing food.

"Lady," he replied, "the only man who would be riding in a baggage car up ahead would be a stiff, and he would not be needing any food."

I told him that the man was riding in the car with some horses. I was sure from the way that he looked at me that he thought I was "cracked." Horses on a passenger train? He did, however, tell me to sit in a corner of the diner. At least now I had a seat, which was far better than my perch on my suitcase.

At the next stop, about an hour later, he came over to where I was seated. "Now, young lady, let's you and me go and visit your mysterious stranger up ahead. It will be interesting to hear what he has to say."

The moment he flashed his light into the baggage car, Jimmy rose up and said, "Miss Herbert, I am awfully hungry."

We went back to the diner and the steward told one of his men to see that the man up ahead with the horses had plenty to eat. When I asked him what I owed, he said, "It's on the house." I thanked him, and picking up my suitcase, I started to leave.

"One question before we part," he said. "I would like to know how long it has been since you have last eaten."

He told me to sit down and went back and talked to his chef. A little while later I was wolfing down a delicious meal.

I again offered to pay, but he would not hear of it.

He was eager to hear all about the circus business and wondered why we would be on a train traveling like this. We sat up most of the night talking and drinking coffee, and when I fell asleep in the easy chair in which I was sitting, he did not disturb me.

When we arrived in San Francisco, the passenger train pulled into the station and everyone started getting off. As I was standing on the platform with my suitcase, I saw that they had uncoupled the coaches from the baggage car and the engineer was about to go elsewhere. I grabbed my suitcase and ran as fast as I could to ask him where he was going. He told me that he was going to the stock pen with the animals aboard so they could be unloaded.

"But how will I get there?" I asked. "I have to go along."

"No way, lady, it ain't allowed," he replied.

I began to cry. "The man in the car with all that stock will not be able to handle the situation by himself."

He climbed down from the engine and went to the baggage car and had a few words with Jimmy. That was enough to convince him that Jimmy would not have the faintest idea of what to do when he got there unless someone was there to tell him.

When he came back, he said, "Okay, come on up here," and I rode in style to the stockyards in the cab of the train.

Once there, Jimmy and I unloaded. While he fed and watered the stock and dogs, I went to the phone to find out about the ship. I was informed that the elephants and the rest of the livestock had already been loaded; we were the last to arrive. A truck was waiting and would pick up the big top, props, and dog cages, but I would have to make my own arrangement to get the horses and ponies there. I asked them to have the other horse people there send along a couple of their men on the truck to help me ride and lead horses.

It was a long way from the stockyards to the freighter loading docks, and I was glad there was plenty of help because Jimmy and I were both exhausted. As soon as everything was loaded and Jimmy safely aboard, I took a cab to the hotel to await the ship that would take the performers.

Mr. Fernandez had hired an impressive array of talent: the Wallendas' high-wire act; three rings of liberty horse acts; the Flying LaForms; Dolly Jacobs' elephants; Landon's Midgets; Manuel Verlarde and Phil Escalante on the wires; three rings of foot jugglers; three rings of trampoline acts; aerial ballet featuring Marilyn Rich and a number of girls on the webs; Escalante brothers; Frank Doyle, heel and toe catch without a net; three rings of ponies; three rings of trained dogs; a monkey act; a host of clowns; and many, many more. As some of these troops were quite large, it meant many people had to be accommodated.

When one thinks of going to Hawaii, one envisions a trip to remember always. I assure you, this was one that will be remembered not only by me, but by everyone else who made that fateful voyage.

This trip took place after the bombing of Pearl Harbor and the subsequent war that resulted. Peace had now been declared. The people on the islands had been without entertainment for a long time. E. K. Fernandez was anxious to supply them with amusement, posthaste.

The ship on which passage had been booked to carry the performers had been used, until now, as an army transport ship. There had not yet been time to convert it back to a passenger liner, so it was completely devoid of any of the things one might expect when taking a pleasure cruise. One section had been designated for ladies, and another for the men. Married couples would be together during the day, but not at night. Steel cots, three high, with wire springs (and mattresses so thin you could feel each one of them) were covered with sheets and two army blankets each.

Small tables and chairs were grouped around in the lounge rooms and decks of cards were supplied. No other entertainment was offered.

There were a few other travelers besides our troop but, for the most part, the rest of the passengers consisted of a band of Gypsies who had fled to the States for safety and, now that the war was over, were returning to the islands where they had formed some sort of settlement.

Each of us had been given a key and issued a locker in which to place our belongings, along with a warning to keep everything we owned put away and locked. It was a warning best heeded.

The Gypsies were housed on another deck and had been told that our deck was off limits to them. They were served their meals at a different time than we were.

Each morning after our bunks had been made up, a towel and a small cake of soap would be placed at the foot of it. During the time we were having breakfast, the Gypsies would send their youngsters to our deck to pick up anything that wasn't nailed down. Because this was mostly the decks of cards and the cakes of soap, the captain found it necessary to lock up the playing cards until someone asked for them, and we were handed a cake of soap as we left the dining room.

As luck would have it, we ran into bad weather most all of the way over and, as the ship did not have the proper ballast, we had a rather rough time of it. Many of the women became ill and spent most of the trip in their uncomfortable bunks.

Of all who made the trip, Dolly Jacobs perhaps saw the worst of it. Punch and Judy, her twins, came down with the measles, contracted from the Gypsy kids. One of the ship's officers was rousted from his compartment, and there she was confined, with the twins, throughout the trip.

Upon our arrival we were given a royal Hawaiian welcome. Everywhere we went the people were friendly and jolly. We opened in Honolulu, and then went on to the smaller islands. Since this was the first circus to play there since the war, the people were hungry for entertainment. We found it necessary to give three shows a day.

The only way that we could be reached by phone was at night in our hotel; thus, one night we were awakened by a phone call from Clyde Beatty.

He now had his own show and wanted to know if we would join him; he and A. W. talked for quite some time. There was one drawback: He could not use the liberty horse act; he had three liberty horse acts of his own, which he had just bought, along with the other show equipment. He had room for the ponies and the rest of our stock, including the dog act. A. W. told him he would let him know as soon as possible what might be worked out.

The prospect of again being with a railroad show was enticing; no more all-night drives overland, and then work all day. As fate would have it, things worked out much faster than we had any idea they would. The very next day, A. W. was talking to Dale Petroff in the men's dressing room about Clyde's call.

Dale turned to him and asked, "I don't suppose there is any chance that you would consider selling the liberty act, is there? I would sure like to own it."

A. W. talked it over with me, I agreed, and he quoted Dale a price. That night, after the show, he returned Clyde's call and they made a deal for the coming season. As soon as the Hawaii dates were over, A. W. would have to take a plane to Shreveport, Louisiana, and practice the liberty act he would be working and, along with Johnny Cline, get the girl riders in shape for the manege act.

I would stay with our stock and turn over the liberty horse act to Dale Petroff when we landed stateside. A baggage car would be ordered to take the rest of our stock and the dogs to Shreveport.

◡

A Slight Delay

Sounds easy, huh? Only it didn't work out that way. The show in Hawaii did close, A. W. did get on a plane, and he did arrive in Shreveport. Period!

We had played all of the smaller islands and were now back in Honolulu waiting for the freighter that would take the livestock back to the mainland. As soon as everything was loaded and on its way, other than the men who were making the trip with the animals, the rest of us would make the return journey by plane. The boat arrived on time, but they would not let the livestock on it. They accepted the tent and all of the props, trunks, and the rigging belonging to the performers; but they were transporting sugar, and it was against the law to carry animals at the same time they were transporting foodstuff. The next boat would sail from there two weeks later.

Everyone was worried because we would now be short of feed for the horses and elephants. We had just enough for the boat trip home; none was available on the islands, but Mr. Fernandez assured us he would have some flown in from the mainland.

Now, about the dogs, which were sitting in their cages on the docks. When in Hawaii, the dogs were kept in quarantine the whole time, except when they were performing. Now they had to be sent back to the kennels.

Mr. Fernandez had rented a building for the livestock, and, after seeing that all of the animals were taken care of, all of us went back to town and checked into the hotel.

At long last the freighter arrived. The place where all of the stock was being kept was quite some distance from the docks. The stock would have to be either ridden or led to the loading place, and it made quite a display going down the road. The horses, ponies, and Kitchens' mules in the lead, and Dolly Jacobs' elephants close behind.

About midway to the docks, one of the little railroad cars they use over there came passing by; the engineer gave a friendly little "toot, toot" with his whistle, and that was all she wrote: Off dashed Dolly Jacobs' elephants, trunks and tails in the air. They were captured after a merry chase, and, so, onward to the docks.

Now, another fine kettle of fish. This boat was not equipped with a loading ramp; the animals were to be put in crates and hoisted aboard. Some of the horses would walk into the crates, but others would not. Blue, Kitchen, Petroff, and the grooms got the job done at last. The elephants were put in slings of some sort and hoisted aboard. The final blow . . . no dogs were allowed on board.

The following day Mr. Fernandez made arrangements for the dogs and monkeys to be put in crates and be returned home in the baggage compartment of the plane. I was advised that it would be very cold there, so I took a cab to an army surplus store and bought a lot of blankets to cover the dogs.

We arrived in San Francisco a week ahead of the freighter. I said good-bye to those who had been on the same plane with me and checked my baggage. I then hired a truck and loaded up the dog crates, hired a cab to follow it, and had the dogs taken to the railroad yards, expecting to house them in a railroad car that was to take them to Shreveport. Of course, I should have known better, but I just wasn't thinking straight. When this proved to be impossible, I just did not know what to do.

I went from one person to another, pleading. The driver of the truck started to raise Cain; he wanted to unload and leave. I do not know who or how, but some kind soul arranged for me to rent an empty storeroom for the dogs.

After seeing to all of their needs, I checked into a nearby hotel, then took a taxi back to the airport and picked up my baggage. By the time I returned to the hotel, I was very tired and retired to a fitful sleep. I spent most of the next week taking care of the dogs.

By this time, it was too late to join the Beatty show in Shreveport. I was advised by phone to go to San Diego and wait for the show there. The boat carrying the stock finally arrived, and I was waiting at the docks to meet them. I turned the liberty horses and their trappings over to Dale Petroff, and hired a truck to take the rest of our trunks and props to the freight yards. We then had to lead the horses and ponies from the docks to the freight yards, which was no small chore in a city like San Francisco, especially as Jimmy and I were the only ones around to do it. I was sure glad that Mr. Petroff had taken over the liberty horses at the docks.

After arriving at the freight yard, I went in to make the necessary arrangements. The baggage car had been hired to take the stock to Shreveport, and I could not seem to make anyone understand that I did not wish to go there. Also, since we had not taken occupancy of the baggage car when it was ordered, demurrage was now due on it. I asked why they had made me hire a building for the dogs if a baggage car was being paid for? No one bothered to answer that one.

The Beatty show was contacted and the railway agent had several long discussions with Mr. Beatty's manager. Other phone calls were made, and, after what seemed like a very long interval, I was told that the baggage car would now go to San Diego. Jimmy and I got everything loaded at last, quite a job in itself, considering the dogs, the props, and the horses were in two different places. I breathed a sigh of relief. It was short-lived, however, for when I went back to the railroad office to check on the time of departure, I found that this time the baggage car would not be hooked to a passenger train, but to a freight train scheduled to leave in two hours.

There was no passenger train out of there to San Diego until noon the next day, so now the stock would arrive in a strange town, and poor Jimmy would have no idea at all of what to do, where to go, or how to make any arrangements.

I told Jimmy to not move from the stock car for anything. I gave him the money to pay for the hay I had ordered, and I hailed a cab and dashed to the hotel and checked out. On the return trip, I had the driver wait while I ran into a grocery store and bought a lot of food and assorted drinks.

Upon arriving back at the train, I handed Jimmy all of the foodstuff and then, after making certain that no one was about, I gave Jimmy my suitcases and told him to hide them, after which I climbed into the car and disappeared behind the stacked-up hay. I felt like a lady hobo, and I won't say I wasn't scared. I had no idea what might happen if the brakeman were to discover my presence.

It was a godsend that I went along because, when we got to San Diego, we had no idea where to go or how to get there, but I, at least, would be able to ask questions. In any given situation, Jimmy would have just sat there and waited until someone came along and told him what to do.

I had figured there would be some sort of stock pen where we would unload, but, no, the motorman just shunted us off onto a sidetrack, uncoupled his engine, and left us. Luckily, there was a little settlement within walking distance. I told Jimmy to sit tight, and headed for the settlement. I asked around and was told that I might be able to rent some stalls at the polo grounds. I phoned them, and they said they could put us up. I then asked if they knew someone who I could get to haul the stock and also transport the dog cages, trunks, and props. After what seemed like hours (and it probably was), I got the animals and Jimmy settled at the polo grounds, and I took a cab to the hotel.

A hot bath and a couple of cups of coffee made me feel a little better. I then called the police station in the town where I knew the Beatty show was playing that day, and asked if they would see that a message got to the show grounds informing them of where I was staying, in case they might wish to get in touch with me.

A. W. called late that night. "We will be there day after tomorrow," he said. "Be sure to have everything cleaned up and looking right, as I would like to make a good impression."

I told him everything was filthy dirty, and nothing had been groomed for days. With just Jimmy and me, that was an impossible job.

"Well, get somebody to help."

I wondered how, way out there on the polo field.

I took a cab to the polo grounds early in the morning and Jimmy and I started bathing the horses. I could see we were never going to get the whole job done. About that time, a group of youngsters came by and were admiring the ponies.

I asked one of the biggest boys if he would like to bathe one of them and he said, "Gee, sure."

Another boy asked if he might wash one. The girls thought this looked like it might be fun and asked if they might join in. I told them that it was men's work, but, if they liked, they could help me with the dogs. I turned the boys over to Jimmy for instructions, and the girls and I went to work bathing the dogs.

All of the youngsters had bikes so, at noontime, I sent a couple of them to pick up some sandwiches and cold drinks, and we had a party of sorts. There was no time to do any painting, but we did get the props washed off and by evening everything was shipshape—except me. I was bushed.

The show arrived the next day and A. W. took charge. When I began to tell him my long tale of woe, he laughed before I could get started and said, "I don't know why it is, but you always seem to have so many little troubles."

Somehow I thought that was an understatement.

I told him to see to it that all of the kids who had

helped me got in to see the show. I need not have bothered. They went right along to the show grounds with the animals and were part of the show itself—helping with the trappings, feeding, and so on. A. W. took them to the cookhouse for dinner between shows, and they got a big kick out of that.

When I fell into bed that night after giving two shows, I thought, now I can sleep until noon tomorrow. Just as I was about to doze off, A. W. said, "Oh, I forgot to tell you, you have an eight o'clock broadcast tomorrow morning." I was back with the circus again.

○

Clyde Beatty Circus

Some of my girlfriends from both the Cole Bros. Circus and the Ringling show were on the Clyde Beatty Circus in 1948. After we had been on the road for a few weeks, they asked me to form another club, as it had been so much fun in the past. But all of that was over, I could not do it; I just did not have the time.

While in Shreveport, Clyde and A. W. had figured out that a pony ride would be an asset to the show, and a means of making extra money. A. W. had a sweep made and had bought saddles. Our ponies were broken to ride, and when I would arrive on the lot after the morning broadcast, we would open up.

This meant quite a lot of extra work, because either A. W. or I had to be there at all times, along with a groom. A. W. would go to the cookhouse first, and upon his return, I would go. There was no time left for extra activities and, as I had to get to the lot as quickly as possible after my daily broadcast, I would not have had time to do the shopping for club members anyway.

I did nothing out of the ordinary that first year, the 1948 season. I worked my ponies in their drill; drove the white stallion on the long reins as a special display in center ring; rode my palomino stallion in the high-school number, and ended it riding King Kong for the waltz and rear; and, of course, did the high fire jump with Rex.

I worked my dog act, and if A. W. was busy elsewhere, I would sometimes jump in and work the riding dog and monkey act, which, along with another act in the other end ring, was used to kill time and entertain the people while Clyde's steel arena was being taken down.

And with the radio show each morning and the pony ride before and after the show, I managed to keep busy.

When the season was over, the show went into El Monte, California, for the winter. We rented an apartment, and I looked forward to having a little time off with nothing to do but rest.

Suddenly, there was a wave of excitement over winterquarters—Clyde had booked all of his acts to play the dates for E. K. Fernandez in Hawaii; only this time the performers were to make the trip on the luxury liner *Lurline*. What a thrill!

Just a week before we were due to leave, A. W. came into the apartment and said, "I'm afraid that I have a little disappointment for you; you will not be going to the islands with us."

I began to cry. I had been packing for days. "But, why? Why am I being left behind?"

A. W. said they had been discussing the Beatty program for the coming season, and they had decided that I ought to have a bigger dog act. I had nine dogs in the act, but Clyde thought I should have a more impressive display, say fifteen or so.

Tearfully, I went to watch the show leave for Hawaii on that beautiful boat. The next day I paid a visit to the local dog pound, picked out a batch of mutts, and went to work.

Upon their return from Hawaii, everyone was bubbling over with stories about the great times they had had. Because Clyde refused to work his act more than twice in any given day, all performances had been limited to two a day. There had been all sorts of parties and entertainment for them. I turned a deaf ear; I did not want to hear about it. I now had a big dog act, and it was good. Clyde and A. W. were both very pleased, but the results left me cold.

Some of the performers on this newly formed circus had formerly been with truck shows and, being accustomed to the extra luxuries of a home on wheels, had disdained riding the circus train. Now that gas coupons were no longer necessary, they made the tour with their house trailers.

Our one big problem had been with the dogs.

They were transported in a cage wagon, each having his or her own compartment, and this was loaded on the flat cars. On mornings when the train arrived in town early, there was no difficulty; as soon as the wagon was unloaded the dogs were allowed to "go out." At other times, when the train was late getting into town, since it took quite some time to get the flats unloaded, it was necessary to climb up onto the flats and lift the dogs down to the ground so they could answer the call of nature, and then we had to put them back up.

One man was assigned to feed, water, and care for the dogs, but it was quite impossible for one person to jump up and down from the train with each dog, so we would be called upon to help.

Johnny and Molungia Cline, who also had a dog act, bought a truck and house trailer and were going to travel overland. With as many dogs as we had, A. W. thought that that was an excellent idea; so he took a plane to Houston, where our house trailer was in storage, bought a truck in which the dogs would be transported, attached the trailer, and drove back to winterquarters.

We stuck close to the Clines while traveling over-land, stopped at the same roadside restaurants so that we could dine together, and formed a close friendship that lasted throughout the years.

Nothing untoward happened all season, yet I was looking forward to a few days leisure when the season came to an end—not, however, as many as were in the cards.

∪

Big Cats

We must go back to the time that I was with Ringling Bros. in order to understand what led up to the events that were now to happen.

The executives of the Ringling Bros. circus and Clyde Beatty, who was working for them at the time, were having some sort of disagreement. Just before the show closed, I was informed that I was to remain in winter-quarters at the end of the season and learn to work a wild animal act. John Herriott was given the thankless job of teaching me. He was a wonderful teacher, but I was not very keen on the idea and I am afraid I was not a very good pupil.

Noted for being willing to try most anything, my bosses could not understand why I was not enthusiastic about this idea, which they thought was so sensational.

Sam Gumpertz was negotiating with someone in Europe to buy an animal act he had seen on his last trip there. He offered to send me there to look the act over, but I declined. In the first place, I was doing so many numbers in the show I felt that was all I could handle. Then, too, I knew I was being used as a threat against someone I greatly admired and respected.

One day, the animal trainer mentioned to one of the bosses that, due to the fact that I worked so much with horses I was bound to carry the scent on me and, as wild animals eat horsemeat, it would be especially dangerous for me to work with them. Whether this was true or not, or just a ploy to get rid of me, I do not know. Personally, I doubted it; anyway, it worked.

When told about it, I drew a breath of relief. I was in the show six different times, plus, by now, I was handling all of the radio work as well.

Before A. W. left to go on the tour, we arranged with the caretaker on Gene Autry's ranch that one evening each week I would go to his cottage at a certain time and A. W. would phone me there. One day the caretaker's wife came by to tell me that I had just had a call, and the party would call back in an hour. I imagined all sorts of things, else why would I be called at this hour?

When the phone rang, I picked it up with a shaky hand. It was Clyde Beatty. Harriett Beatty had passed away just before the closing of the show. Clyde, grief stricken, had gone back to their home in Florida for the winter; now it was spring and time to get back to the business of living. He was desperately in need of someone to work her act; it was very important that it be in the show. It followed a couple of acts after the opening lighting the fire, so it would be all set for the spec, there would be two more numbers in each end ring, after which they would announce Clyde Beatty himself.

I didn't say I would think it over; from experience I knew one did not do business with Clyde that way. Rather, I said, "I have animals here for which arrangements will have to be made. It will be necessary to find someone to take care of them."

Clyde agreed, and advised he would be willing to compensate someone to do so. Next day, I made a deal with the caretaker's son, who always seemed to be having

Striking a stylish pose. With Clyde Beatty Circus in Los Angeles, 1940. *Courtesy of David Reddy.*

trouble making ends meet, to care for the dogs, see that no one walked off with the trailer, and give the ponies and Rex their little treats.

Then I called A. W. at the hotel in Boston, where I knew he was staying, and told him I was running away to join a circus. He asked which one, but forgot to ask what I was going to do when I got there.

I was glad for the chance to get away for a while. I packed what I thought I would need, and hired the caretaker's son to drive me to Los Angeles. When we arrived, I found that there would only be time for one rehearsal before the matinee.

In this modern age, when a hoop of fire is used, it is a round loop with perforations, a long hose connected to a butane tank is attached to it, and it can be turned on and off just like a stove. In the period of which I am speaking, they wrapped the fire hoop with sacks soaked in gasoline; the fire was put out by dousing it with water. Clyde told me we would practice the act without lighting the fire, so it would be all set for the first show.

The act consisted of two Bengal tigers riding and performing on the back of an Indian elephant. They did a number of tricks, finishing with Prema, a huge tiger, jumping onto and off of the elephant through a hoop of fire.

In all of the years his wife worked this act, Clyde had always stood just outside the cage; he would now do the same for me. He was a few seconds late during the first show, so I did not see him until I was already inside the arena. I noticed that, instead of standing outside, he was in the safety cage, gripping the bars with both hands. I began to get nervous. When I picked up the match to light the fire hoop, I looked up and Prema's eyes were like two big, green flashlights.

It suddenly occurred to me that my horses, Rex and Satan, always jumped the moment they saw the fire and I wondered if this cat would do the same. I did not know which way to jump. She just sat and looked, and I looked back at her; then I heard Clyde yell, "Light the fire and get behind her." Then I remembered the cue.

When I left the cage, Clyde grabbed me in his arms, I thought, to congratulate me. Instead, he shook me and said, "Don't you ever wear feathers in that arena again." I had worn what I thought was one of my best-looking costumes, complete with a fancy feather headdress.

"Cats," said Clyde, "catch birds, you know, whether they are house cats or big ones."

When I had talked to Clyde on the phone, I had thought that I would be with them for the Los Angeles engagement only, until they could find someone else.

George Smith, who had been the assistant manager when I was with the Ringling Bros. show, and whom I had revered from afar, was now Clyde's manager. It took very little persuasion from him to convince me I was wasting my life sitting on a hilltop and working as a dog boy.

I had never, ever, had such an easy season. Other than Harriett's act, all I had to do was the radio show each morning. Television was now becoming quite the thing. Clyde thought it would be good publicity for me to carry a wild animal with me. He bought an ocelot for me to take to the TV shows. We called her Maria Christina; why, I don't know.

By the time that his year contract with Gene Autry was up, A. W. was ready to join me the following season on the Clyde Beatty show. I do not know what he was hunting for when he went to work for Gene Autry; whatever it was, he never found it.

While still at the Autry ranch, A. W. had bought a pretty, white stallion to replace the one that had died. In the evenings, after he was finished training Gene's horses, he broke it to work on the long reins. He also brought with him, of course, the ponies, dogs, monkeys, and Rex.

Things were going well, I thought; I was working Harriett's tiger and elephant act, my white stallion on the long reins during the high-school number, the dog act, and

Rex in the high jump closing the show. The pony ride was doing well, we were saving money, and we were having a little fun.

Several of the other performers were traveling overland with their house trailers. Johnny and Molungia Cline, Con and Winnie Colleano, and A. W. and I always traveled together and stopped and had our meals together at the same restaurants.

I recall our trip through Canada. We were booked to play Victoria Island for ten days; everything would be loaded onto boats for the crossing. We were permitted to take our trucks or cars, but the trailers would have to be left behind.

After the boat trip, while the rest of us were busy with our stock, Winnie Colleano, the wife of the forever-famous wire walker, made the rounds. She came back with word that the rates in the hotels, this being tourist season, were out of the question. She had inquired around and found that here, the same as in her native England, some of the people took in paying guests. This idea would never have occurred to any of the rest of us, mainly because we had never heard of it.

Because Johnny and A. W. were rather tied down, their trucks being loaded with dogs, Winnie suggested that she, with a car, would find lodgings for all of us. We were very grateful. After the animals were all taken care of that night, Winnie drove us to a private home.

Hilda, a real cockney from the word go, met us at the door. A hostess such as she very few have ever met, unless it was our boys in uniform, whom, she told me, she had made it her business to entertain while back home in Dear Old England.

When we came in each evening after the night show, she would have a nice lunch waiting for us. But, best of all, she would entertain us while we were dining by singing funny songs and telling jokes. We were sorry when it came time to leave.

The season came to an end.

I was looking forward to a little time off before starting to get things in order for the following year. I had all kinds of plans for new wardrobe. Clyde had told me that I would be working the riding tiger act with him that winter on all of the big indoor shows—nothing else, just the one act. Another paid vacation.

U

King Bros. Circus

For the 1954 season A. W. and I cast our lot with Floyd King's truck show. This turned out to be an interesting experience.

Floyd and Howard King each had a predominant passion. With Floyd, the most important thing in the world seemed to be getting the street parade underway on time. On a truck show, this was a hazardous undertaking no matter how you looked at it. The odds of all of the trucks and equipment getting to town, unloaded, hitched up, and ready to roll by 10 A.M. were all against it. It had been too big a hassle for the railroad shows, which arrived in a town all at the same time; that is why they abolished street parades in the first place.

Now, here is this man, with his equipment strung from one town to the next, valiantly striving to renew one of the glorious traditions of the past and, by cracky, doing it, one way or another.

Of course, it was not always the same parade in each town—something or other would often be missing— but a parade there was, rain or shine. Giving a street parade daily did not endear him to the performers, of course. Upon returning to the lot and eating a hasty meal in the dining tent, it was usually time for the matinee.

Howard King was engrossed with only one thing— his "Ding Show." (I had never heard of one, so I will assume that some of my readers may not have either.)

A tent was erected at the most advantageous spot on the midway and, unlike the sideshow, which was usually across from it, would open up to the public as soon as the displays were set up in it, rather than waiting until the townspeople began to assemble. Once it opened, it continued to run until it came time for teardown. The banners across the front proclaimed, "Wonders From All Over The World." At the entrance was a sign, "All Free, Everyone Welcome."

Cages set on platforms lined each side, with various small animals enclosed and signs explaining what they were and where they were from. A canvas sidewall ran down the center and almost to the far end where you turned and walked down the other side, again lined with cages.

As you came to the exit, an elderly man attired in a veteran's uniform explained, with a constant flow of patter, that the exhibit was wholly dependent for its existence on the contributions made by kindhearted animal lovers. So eloquent was his spiel that few passed by without giving a donation. It was a moneymaking proposition, which required just about all of Howard King's attention. It was always the first thing up and the last thing down on the lot.

So, with Floyd's attention focused on the parade, and Howard's on the Ding Show, the big top show pretty much ran itself, with one exception—Floyd always showed up for the closing number, the races. The finish race consisted of Shetland ponies on which were tied an assortment of monkeys, holding on for dear life and usually screaming at the top of their lungs. Floyd rang a large bell alongside the bandstand all of the time the race was on.

The parade had not concerned me as I was, as usual, doing the radio broadcasts for the show each morning in town. But they knew A. W. was able to drive most any kind of team, and he was constantly being called upon to do so. After driving his truck and seeing that our stock was attended to, this was a bit too much. Consequently, when asked to return for another season, he declined.

Frank Walters had located a nice barn for us in Houston, so that is where we planned to winter. We had all new wardrobe made; painted all of our props; and broke one of the palomino stallions, which had been doing manege, to the bit and spur and put a few more tricks on him. He was very adaptable and responded quickly.

Black Hawk had been getting out of hand. A mean stallion to start with, as he got older he became cranky and constantly caused trouble around other horses—kicking and biting and rearing when he was not supposed to. On fairs, it hadn't made too much difference, as we worked alone. But on a show with other riders in the same number, we had to warn them lest they might be kicked.

We decided to sell Black Hawk to a breeder, and I rode Golden Arrow.

Monkeys

Why I should write a chapter about monkeys I'll never know, because they are something I know very little about; but, they were there off and on, and I guess I owe it to my readers to share my limited experiences with them.

The first one I ever met in person as I was standing at the back door of the circus tent with my long rein horse waiting to go on. The act I was to follow consisted of an assortment of monkeys. One of them got loose from the trainer and, espying the feathers on my headdress, proceeded to attack it, including my hair and scalp. I ended up covered with my own blood and was sent to the hospital where, in order to put in the necessary stitches, they shaved off part of my hair. That event did not endear the little creatures to me one bit.

A little later on, we acquired a dog act, and A. W. broke a riding dog and monkey act. We did have a monkey of our own, a tiny cinnamon capuchin who didn't know he was a monkey and loved everybody. We called him Cocoa.

My next encounter was while I was appearing with the Garden Bros. Circus in Canada. I had the misfortune again to follow a monkey act with my white driving horse. As they were going out the backdoor, one of these chimps jumped at me and landed in my arms. Ira Watkins shouted, "Freeze! Don't move!" He needn't have bothered; I was petrified. The chimp looked into my eyes, reached up, and kissed me on the cheek.

"He likes you," said Mr. Watkins, for which I was thankful. The chimp's name was Taboo, and I got into the habit of having a little goody for him each time he passed by, and the chimp and I became good friends.

One day Mr. Watkins asked me if I would come over to his trailer. He had a baby chimp, and it was a doll, but he was having trouble getting it to take its food. His wife, who no longer went on the road, had been raising it while he had been at home and now, for some reason, it was refusing to eat. He thought that perhaps it missed his wife. He gave me a blanket to put across my knees, and a short time later the chimp had crawled up on my lap. It looked me over, and I guess I passed inspection. Mr. Watkins handed me a can of baby food and a spoon, and I dug out a spoonful and presented it to the chimp, which promptly turned its head away.

I paid no attention to it, nor did I again offer it anything to eat; rather, I pretended I was eating the food. I put the spoon from the can to my mouth and made noises I hoped would sound like enjoyment to a chimp. I licked my chops and started the spoon going faster, as if I intended to eat the whole can of food. The chimp started hollering as if someone were sticking it with pins and, after grabbing the can of food from me, started to scoop the contents into its mouth—without the aid of a spoon. Not the best of table manners, but at least it was eating. From then on I visited with them every day. Sometimes Mr. Watkins would let Taboo come in and join us.

Mr. Watkins and his two sons traveled in two units. One boy drove the big truck with the chimps and the props, the other son drove the car that pulled the house trailer in which they lived. Mr. Watkins rode in the car with him.

One day we had an unusually long trip. Buddy, with the truck containing the chimps and the props, got to the building in time for the show, but the other brother and the father did not make it, having had to stop and change a flat tire on the trailer.

The house was packed, and several of the other acts had not yet arrived. The show was about to start when Buddy appeared and asked me for help. The management was asking him to put on the chimp act, but there was no way he could do it alone. He could leave out a couple of the chimps and still put on an act, but he needed a few seconds between tricks to take off the roller skates, and so on. Would I please help?

"But I know nothing whatsoever about chimps."

"Well," Buddy said, "here is my idea. We both know that Taboo likes you; take him in and place him on his seat. I will bring in two more that I work, the rest we will leave out. There is no time to practice anything, so I will work my chimps as I always do; when I turn my back, you take out Taboo. If we are lucky, he will go to the prop that is his, either the scooter or bicycle, and do his trick. This will give me the time I need to get ready for the next part of the act."

When we entered the ring, Buddy placed his chimps on their seats and I, holding Taboo's hand in mine, led him to his. Just as we reached it, he grabbed me around the neck, causing me to stumble and fall backwards, landing on the seat with dear Taboo on top of me. I scrambled to my feet and stood behind the seats trying to look as though I had some business being there.

Buddy did a couple of tricks with his chimps, then shouted, "The scooter—put Taboo on the scooter."

I did, and as he went around and around I kept calling out encouragement to him. I guess he liked this, because he just kept going on and on. I couldn't stop him. Buddy finally grabbed him as he went sailing by and, after handing him to me, went on with the act.

One of the webs from an aerial act was tied off quite close to the stage where we were supposed to be putting on the act. Taboo spied it and took this opportunity to show off . . . up the web he climbed; without thinking, I started to climb up the web after him. Suddenly it dawned on me that the people were laughing, not at Taboo's antics, but at me.

Buddy managed to finish the act and leave the stage with his two chimps, closely followed by me, dragging Taboo by one hand, while in his other he was clinching for dear life a box of Cracker Jack, which he had managed to

grab from a passing candy butcher. We came face to face
with Ira Watkins who was laughing his head off. Mr.
Watkins tried several times to get me to appear again in
the act, but once was enough . . . as far as I was concerned,
that act was TABOO!

My next experience with a monkey turned out
badly. He was a very big rhesus that A. W. had trained
with two dogs and a pony to do a riding act. We had had a
similar act when we were playing fairs. This one he broke
while with the Clyde Beatty Circus. It was just a fill-in act,
but it went over well with the youngsters. It worked early
in the show, and sometimes if A. W. was late getting back
from the pony ride and did not have time to change into
wardrobe, it would be my lot to work the act.

One day, while in the middle of the act, I caught
this monkey staring at me with a strange look on his face.
After you have worked with animals for many years, you
develop a sort of sixth sense that warns you when something is amiss. By this time, A. W. had entered the tent and
was standing outside the ring. I called to him to come in
and take over. Thinking I was ill or something, he finished
the act. Later, when I explained my misgivings, A. W. pooh-
poohed the idea. Jocko would not hurt anyone; nevertheless, I refused to work the act any more.

Less than a week later, Jocko bit A. W. on the arm
as he was putting the monkey in his cage. A. W. excused
Jocko, saying it was just an accident. Two days later at the
matinee, during the riding dog act, Jocko left his seat and
jumped on A. W., for no apparent reason, tearing his dress
suit pant leg to bits and chewing on his leg from the knee
to the ankle.

Jocko then left the ring and, dragging his lead rope,
headed for his cage in the backyard, seeking safety, only to
find the door closed. His eyes were red as fire as he sat
there glaring at everyone. One of the cowboy ropers from
the concert threw a rope and it landed around Jocko's neck.
Someone else quickly grabbed the rope Jocko was drag-

ging, and now they had him between them, but where he could not grab them. A policeman, who seemed to have taken charge, told them to follow him into a little grove of trees behind the tent. I heard a shot, and they came back and handed me Jocko's lead rope and collar. They said that if Jocko had attacked a child in the same manner, he could have killed it.

While all of this was going on, I had quickly changed out of my scanty costume into street clothes so I could go to the hospital. It was a long time before I was permitted to see A. W. When I did get to see him, he told me to carry on, and I did. He would have to remain there for several weeks, and when he did return to the show, he never asked what had happened to Jocko, and I never told him.

∪

Gene Autry

Near the end of the season, A. W. told me he was going to work for Gene Autry, the cowboy movie star. Now, this move made absolutely no sense to me. A. W. was not movie struck and had no aspirations of going into pictures. I was at a complete loss to understand why he made such a deal. The salary he was to make was not that terrific.

I was well satisfied where we were. We had our own acts, what I considered pleasant associations, an adequate salary, plus we were making quite a nice sum on the pony ride.

I was concerned as to what was going to happen to my horses and ponies and our dog act. A. W. assured me that there was plenty of room for everything at the ranch where we were to live, and Mr. Autry had said they would all be welcome.

Johnny Agee, who had been one of the leading horse trainers in his day, was now well along in years. At one time he had had his famous brewery act on the fair circuit advertising a well-known beer, much the same as Anheuser-Busch is advertising its beer today, using a team of Clydesdale horses in many of the leading parades.

I had seen Johnny's act once when I was very young, and I had never forgotten it: Four large draft horses came down the track pulling a long flatbed wagon, on which were mounted three barrels large enough for a horse to be standing in each of them. The wagon would stop behind the circus ring; the three lovely, matched bay American saddle bred horses would jump down, enter the ring, and go through their liberty act. At the finish of the act, the three would jump back into their respective barrels and be carried down the track to a resounding round of applause.

John had joined Gene Autry when Gene was first starting out and had worked for him for many years, training the first "Champion" and all of the rest that followed. He still went to the ranch each day, but was no longer able to work. Gene was in need of someone to break some new horses for him. John had advised him to hire A. W., which he did.

So, once more, I said good-bye to the circus. Luckily, my old friend Jack Gibson, who had made the never-to-be forgotten trip from Florida to California, was now on the Beatty show as the ring stock boss. I had been told that the horses and my ponies would be put in pasture at the ranch, and I would not need a groom. I asked Jack not only to give Jimmy a job, but to look after him as well. Jack promised he would do so and he kept his word. With tears in my eyes, I told Jimmy that if I ever had a job for him, I would let Jack know about it and send for him.

So, the house trailer was placed behind Gene Autry's ring barn, and I was on the famous Melody Ranch, which sounded delightful in the movie magazines, but in reality it was far from it. Located way out in the San Fernando Valley, high up in the mountains, with rock and huge stones, it was hot as Hades, and full of rattlesnakes. I wasn't quite sure what I had done wicked in my life that I had been sent to the bad place, but I was convinced this was hell. I spent most of my waking hours huddled in the house trailer except when I was watering, feeding, and taking care of the dogs.

Most of the time, the horses that went to the studio were loaded up early in the morning and they would return really late. A. W. would go straight to bed, so I seldom had a chance to talk to him.

On the days they were not working at the studio, the cowboys and wranglers would gather around and swap tales, but it was evident from the first that there was no place for me there. I cramped their style.

It had been bad enough when they were working at the studios, but then it came time for them to go on the road for several months on a personal appearance tour with an indoor rodeo. Of course, I was left behind. Just before they left, A. W. bought me a television set, the first I ever had.

After everyone left to go with the rodeo, the only people I ever saw were the caretaker when he came twice a day to feed the horses that had been left behind, and once in a while his wife if she happened to be out taking a walk.

Other than a trip once a week to the grocery store, there was no place else to go. The nights, too, were frightening. The caretaker's house was quite a distance from where the house trailer was parked; besides that, after the others had left for the rodeo circuit, and after the horses were fed in the evening, the caretaker and his wife usually went to visit their son who lived not far away and played cards most of the night. So the days dragged on and on.

I had plenty of time to reminisce. About a month prior to the closing of the Beatty show, my lovely white stallion—my beautiful wedding present—was walking down the ramp from the train when it broke with him on it. They tried to save him, but he was hurt so badly it was not possible. Before moving to the Autry ranch, A. W. sold the two palomino stallions.

Each day I would go to the pasture where my ponies were kept with a treat for them, then I would visit with King Kong and Rex. The pasture extended a long way into the hills, and other horses belonging to Mr. Autry also roamed there, but somehow King and Rex knew about when I was due and would be at the gate waiting for me. Then, one day, Rex alone awaited me. I went for the caretaker; we saddled up two horses and went to look for my dear King Kong. He had died in his sleep. He was still fat and beautiful; the years were just against him.

♘

Bird Wonderland

Circus fans are a big part of any show and a great help. Some of them even join up and spend their vacations with the show. One was C. B. Glick. He would come on the show and help out by collecting tickets at the front door; that was how A. W. became acquainted with him.

Mr. Glick was an importer of birds and small animals, such as monkeys. He had a bird farm and pet shop in Encino, California, and he also furnished birds and other animals to the motion picture industry and television studios. What stories he had told A. W., of course, I did not know. All I know is that while we were in Clyde's winterquarters, Mr. Glick would call A. W. to take studio calls, in preference to the men who were working for him. I was busy breaking in three new dogs for the dog act and didn't pay much attention to what A. W. was doing. I did know that animal handlers' pay was good, and that A. W. was impressed and liked the work. Before I had any idea of what was happening, Mr. Glick had talked A. W. into buying a half interest in his business.

I was aghast. A. W. assured me we were very lucky to have connected with such a man, and he would do far better than in show business.

The hardest thing I ever had to do was say, "Sorry, I'm going away," to my friends at winterquarters. Somehow I had an idea that I was saying good-bye forever to the circus world, which I so dearly loved, and I was. I had a feeling I would never have another chance to run away and join a circus again, and I never did.

Now came the most unhappy years of my life. I had a premonition the moment I set foot in the place. Mr. Glick lost no time in telling me what I had to do: My part in the business would be to run the store, handle the books, answer the mail, clean all of the cages in the front part of the store before opening in the morning, wait on the customers, and take phone calls.

It was far from easy. I had never made out my own income tax, so a bookkeeper was called in to teach me how to "post" (I had always thought that was a way to sit on a horse). It took time, but I did learn to keep the books.

Living in the house trailer, which was parked at the far end of the bird farm, was far from pleasant. The bird farm was smelly, and I am sure not a very healthy environment in which to be confined both day and night. The ponies were in a corral and posed no problem, but the dogs were housed in runs that had formerly been used to keep monkeys. Because they could see each other through the wire, they barked at each other endlessly. Sixteen dogs can make enough racket to disturb one's slumber, and waking hours, too.

When Mother learned that we were in business and

no longer on the road, she again came to live with us. She was surprised when she saw the conditions under which we were living.

I had saved my money diligently during the season when I had been on the Beatty show by myself. It looked as though we were going to be stuck here for quite some time, so I went in search of a house. I found what I was looking for in a surprisingly short time.

It wasn't just a house; it was quite adorable. Situated on a little over an acre of ground, it was a cozy two-bedroom ranch style house, with a two-car garage, a barn in the rear, and another building that, with very little work, could be converted into a nice home for the dogs. All this was on one side of the driveway. The other half-acre was fruit trees, with the exception of an open space that had been used as a tennis court, and was later used by my circus friends as a parking space for their trailers.

It was only a short distance from the bird farm, and I figured it would be easy to commute back and forth. I bought the place and was quite pleased with the deal I made.

A. W. was away on a studio location job, where Mr. Glick had sent him at the time, and he was furious when he found out what I had done. I had bought a house without telling him about it, forgetting he hadn't asked my opinion when he took all of our money and bought the bird farm without consulting me.

The house trailer and the animals were moved to their new home and, strangely enough, in their new environment we again had peace and quiet, away from all the squawking birds.

The store was open every day, seven days a week, from eight in the morning until six in the evening. But it took an hour before opening to get the place cleaned up.

Because this was, for the most part, a mail-order business, I found myself staying up until all hours of the night trying to get the mail answered. Many a day I did not have time for lunch.

Each day I grew to hate it more and more. After all of those years I had spent working with horses and other animals, I was now training parakeets to sit on my finger. I was, of course, learning a lot about birds, but I was sure that it was useless knowledge for me.

A. W., on the other hand, was enjoying his job very much. Going to the studios was fun, and it was easy work. Bird Wonderland . . . the wonder is that I lasted as long as I did.

The studio was filming the life story of Pancho Villa. Rita Hayworth was cast in the role of his sweetheart, a Mexican girl who followed him from place to place, taking her pet parrot perched on her shoulder everywhere she went, even when she was riding horseback. A. W. went with them on location for four months to New Mexico, caring for the parrot that worked with Rita.

I had never gotten along very well with Mr. Glick, but as long as A. W. was around I had little to do with him. As a rule, he acted as though I did not exist, unless he found something I had done that did not please him. Then he would tell A. W. about it, always referring to me as "that woman" or "her"—tell "her" to do such and such. He never spoke my name.

Where before he had been in the store only part-time, now he was there every day and figuring out so many things for me to do, I never could find time to answer the mail on time, even though I worked until all hours after he left at six o'clock.

He nailed up a blackboard in the office and each day he would write out all of the things I was supposed to do, eliminating the need to talk to me. Nothing I did ever seemed to please him, so I did what I was able to and forgot about the rest.

When A. W. returned from location after the picture was finished, Mr. Glick told him I would have to be replaced. My feelings were not hurt one bit. I had wasted three years working day after day, with never so much as a thank-you. After I left, they hired a young couple to take my place.

The smog was starting to get so bad that Mother was becoming quite ill from it. The doctor told her if she intended to remain in California, she would have to find some place out of town to live.

As I now had time on my hands, I started looking around for another house. I found a place, way out in a small town called Thousand Oaks. It had been a dog kennel, so there was plenty of room for all of the animals. There were two houses on the property, so I promptly rented out one of them to help make the payments.

I was able to get quite a bit of work with the dog act on television shows and other spot dates. Then I bought a little one-horse trailer and was also able to put on a little riding dog and monkey act. I did not use the ponies, as A. W. had retained the truck, but it didn't matter—I would not have been able to drive it anyway.

I had put up the house in Encino against the payment on the one in Thousand Oaks. As soon as the deal was completed, Mother and I moved there. A. W. had taken the house trailer, in which he lived, back to the bird farm. I assumed he was busy because I heard very little from him; when I did hear, the news was not good.

After I had left, Mr. Glick had talked A. W. into buying out his half interest in the bird farm. A. W. had signed a promissory note, which was now due. In order to meet it, it was necessary to sell the ponies, the dog act, the truck and trailer, and just about all of the stock he had on hand, including some of the animals used for studio rentals. He had already drawn out all of the money he had in the bank to swing the deal, but he was now the sole owner of Bird Wonderland. It was rumored that Mr. Glick had made a fortune from the business, and A. W. expected to do the same.

About a week after the ponies and dogs had left, A.

W. called me on the phone and asked me to come back. He would have to let the couple go, as he could no longer afford to pay them.

I was truly dismayed. I thought back over all those years of hard work, of skimping, and doing without things I would like to have had, and now to give it all to this old man whom I hate. For what? I thought about the many youngsters I had lifted on and off of ponies on the pony ride, how my back had ached; about the days when I was not feeling well, but worked just the same, always saving for the future, and now this was it!

Of course, I went back to the bird farm. What else was there to do? And now, just what did I have to look forward to? Feeding and cleaning up after the animals in the outside cages was now part of my job, because there was not enough money to pay for extra help. Paul, the old Mexican who did the heavy outdoor work, was retained. I, who had always been so careful of my appearance both off stage and on, just let myself go. I wore blue jeans and shirts all of the time; my nails were broken and usually dirty.

Work was no stranger to me. All of my life I had worked hard . . . but some work is fun. Other work is labor. There is a difference. My work was no longer a pleasure; it was a serious business. All of my exuberance was gone, and there was nothing to look forward to.

I had never been around when the deals with Mr. Glick had been made, so I was in the dark as to what their agreement had been. A. W. had told me that when he bought out Mr. Glick's final interest in the business, Mr. Glick had assured him that he would continue to rent the property to him for the same amount he had been paying, unless property taxes increased; that increase he would have to pass along. On the face of it, the agreement seemed fair enough. Leasing the property was a separate deal from the partnership in the business. A. W.'s first lease was for five years; the second was to be for five more. Unfortunately, A. W. did not have this part of the deal in writing.

After I had been back at the bird farm about a month, I discovered that Mr. Glick was filling bird orders from his home, and taking studio calls. He had kept certain birds and animals when he sold out to A. W., claiming they were pets and he could not part with them. For years some of the studios had been in the habit of contacting him at home in reference to animal and bird jobs, as he usually had someone else running the pet shop.

Of course, this had not been the agreement; he had sold the business and everything that went with it. A. W. took him to court. The final bill of sale stated that the name "Bird Wonderland," inventory, goodwill, and future business were sold to A. W. Kennard for X dollars. The judge ruled that all future business meant just that. A. W. won the battle, but lost the war.

The first lease still had few months to go at the time of the trial and, as soon as it was up, Mr. Glick sold the property and we had to move. We moved everything that was left, which, by that time, was very little, to the place that I had bought in Thousand Oaks.

A. W. never quite recovered from the blow Mr. Glick had dealt him. He kept blaming himself for the loss of everything we had worked so hard to get those many years. From that time on, he was a changed man. He kept telling me how happy he was that I had had the foresight to buy a piece of property.

Things grew steadily worse as time went on. Shortly after we moved to Thousand Oaks, the bottom started to fall out of the bird market. Two factors contributed to this: First, they stopped the exportation of all birds from Australia. Mr. Glick had had advance notice of this, which was why he had wanted out of the business. Finches were a big item. The more colorful ones, which went for high prices, were imported from Australia. The second reason was the swift drop in prices of birds that were being raised locally: parakeets, lovebirds, and cockatiels. The prices on them dropped to almost nothing when so many people began raising them in their back yards.

Studio calls were few and far between. If they called Mr. Glick, he told them we were out of business, and if they called the old bird farm in Encino, they reached a disconnected number. I sent each of the studios a card with our new phone number, and one of them paid off.

We were contacted in regard to a picture that would go into production later, but would require a great deal of preliminary work. After an interview, we were awarded the contract to furnish and train the birds.

Shortly after the picture went into production, we were asked by *All Pets* magazine if we would keep them posted as to how the picture was progressing, as they were very interested in it. The following chapters contain the material I forwarded to them and they printed in three issues.

∪

The Bird Man of Alcatraz From Inside the Cage

In 1961 when we were contacted in regard to training the birds for Harold Hecht's movie *The Bird Man of Alcatraz*, my first reaction was one of thankfulness that the life story of this great bird doctor would at last reach the public through the medium of motion pictures.

Frankly, when I found that Burt Lancaster was to play the part of Robert Stroud, I was surprised. He did not seem quite the type. But, after two days on the set, I not only changed my opinion, but was convinced that no one else would have been able to play the part as well.

All actors try to assume the character of the person

they are portraying, but this man actually lived the life of the "Bird Man" day by day. Throughout the many weeks of filming the scenes in the prison, a feeling of sadness and tension conveyed itself to every member of the crew. The usual laughter and kidding that goes on between takes was missing.

Unlike most pictures, which skip from one part of the script to another, this one was taken step-by-step through the story. This was necessary because of the makeup problems involved, as the actors went through the years in this story; thus, the crew was aware of everything that happened to this man as the story went along.

So strong was the sense of reality that, when they filmed the scene where Stroud was transferred to Alcatraz prison and the guards from there came to get him, as he said good-bye to Ransom, the man who had guarded him those many years in Leavenworth, all over the set you could see men blowing their noses and wiping their eyes. This was quite a testimonial from seasoned stagehands used to witnessing every kind of emotional scene and never batting an eye.

We were flattered, of course, to be selected to train the birds for this picture, but, upon receiving the script for it, had doubts as to whether we would be able to do it. Some of the things called for seemed to be almost impossible, and we told them so. Where Stroud had raised his birds from the nest and handled them every day, we were asked to take wild birds and try to tame them. Everyone was very considerate, telling us to take our time and do the best we could.

Since no baby sparrows were obtainable at that time of the year, we were obliged to trap wild ones. We placed them in a large outdoor aviary to get them used to being close to people. We spent weeks, first one and then another of us, just sitting in there with them before placing them in smaller cages.

We imported hundreds of canaries from both Holland and Japan, in order to have all different kinds available. Then we partitioned off part of a bedroom in the house, the same size as the cell Stroud occupied. We knew that either one or two sides would have to be open for the cameraman to take the shots, so we enclosed two sides with plastic glass to accustom the birds to staying in a certain place. We put cages containing four birds apiece in this enclosure, and allowed the birds in each cage to come out every day, with some person sitting in there either reading a book or typing.

Feed, water, lettuce, and their bathing dish were placed on the floor and table. The more aggressive birds were soon flying around and landing all over us. These were the ones chosen to work in the picture.

The first scene with the birds was one of the most difficult to film. In it Stroud finds the babies in a nest, and the mother bird keeps flying around him. As this takes place during a thunderstorm, with lights flashing, leaves flying, and a strong wind machine blowing, it was a very hard shot for the cameraman to get, and they spent most of the day on this one scene.

The sparrow had six understudies, and each one (after making his bid for stardom as an actor) was dried off and placed in a nice, warm cage. Burt Lancaster, however, remained soaking wet through the entire thing with all that cold air blowing on him, and I was thoroughly convinced that by the next day he would be in bed with pneumonia and we would be out of a job.

In order to get a number of canaries to fly to you and light on you of their own accord, we used a well-trained bird we called "the teacher." Unlike the parakeet and cockatiel, on which you clip the wing feathers in order to finger train them, we were obliged to leave the canaries with their entire wings, as they had to fly all over the cell. We started them flying low to the ground with the teacher coming to you first, and two or three of the others following. They soon learned to have no fear of people and would come to you from any point in the cell. Of course, each time they were rewarded with a treat.

Percy and Runty, the featured sparrows, were selected from more than fifty birds. Both were not only very smart, but seemed to take a great delight in performing; a little on the devilish side, they would pull on Burt's eyebrows while sitting on his glasses.

Our macaws, parrots, and trained cockatoos would work for anyone, but we were worried as to how these little birds would react to a stranger. We needn't have worried; in no time they found out who had the treats, especially the mealy worms at the end of the day. You will notice in the picture how they watch him, and react as if he were the one who had raised them. We found Mr. Lancaster to be a man of great patience, ready to devote a lot of time to winning the confidence of his little friends.

The set dressers came into their share of hard work and research on this picture, more than in most period pictures where records are available on most every subject, and the equipment available. In this one they ran into things like having special medicine bottles made, as there were no screw cap bottles in those days.

A word of thanks is due the Pet Dealers Supply Co. of California for the time and assistance they so kindly gave us; also to the property men and electricians, who cooperated in so many ways above and beyond the call of duty, such as helping to catch birds and furnishing us with lights when it was after time to go home. Everyone was wonderful; otherwise this would not have been such a pleasant experience.

This was the picture they said would never be made. It probably would not have if it were not for the persistence of the producer, Harold Hecht. In someone else's hands, this might have been just a run-of-the-mill picture, shot in a few weeks' time at the least possible expense. *The Bird Man of Alcatraz* cost as much in money and time as a lavish production would have. You have no doubt read of the pressure applied to suppress this picture; however, I was sure Mr. Hecht would put it through, for here was a man who, busy as he was, always found time to take care of the smallest detail.

For example: Runty and Percy were trained in a cell just like the one used in the picture, except for the two sides partitioned off with plastic glass. We began with Percy first, as he seemed the least frightened of the two. We kept him in a small cage for several weeks after taking him from the large outdoor aviary where we kept all of the wild, trapped birds. Each day I fed Percy and the others with little, special treats. Then, for three days he and Runty had just the regular bird feed.

I turned Percy loose and let him fly around the cell. Meanwhile, I sat on the floor with a dish in my lap, filled with all the things he liked to eat. He flew all around and, after seeing there was no way out, he finally got tired and lit in a corner. I placed the training stick in front of him and, after he jumped on and off a few times, he finally concluded it was almost like a perch and decided to stay there. Getting him to my lap took a lot longer, and he stayed only long enough to grab a mealy worm from the dish before flying away.

I then turned Runty loose and he, at once, made a dive for Percy's worm. He then flew all over the place trying to find a way out, and then started to look around. Seeing the worms, he zoomed right over and grabbed one. Having gained this much, I then caught both birds and put them back in their cages. We continued this for a couple of weeks, three times a day, until it finally became a game with them and they would fly right to me as soon as their cage was opened.

The first day on the set, the producer explained that Percy and Runty were to be in many scenes where they would be free in the cell, but they were not to fly around all over the place, so could we suggest where they might be inclined to stay? Not knowing where they might care to perch during the many days ahead, we turned them loose in the cell and let them fly around until they found a place to their liking. Of all places, they chose the old-fashioned shaving mug that was on the shelf, and for the rest of the picture, when either bird was not working or in his cage, that was his perch.

It is the custom of a company like this to have an urn of hot coffee and doughnuts or sweet rolls set out each morning for the crew when they arrive, as a little pick-me-up for them after the long drive most of them had to make to the studio. Paper cups are handy to the coffee and everyone helps himself.

This happened to be one of those days when things were running late. The director called for Percy and Runty, and we turned them loose in the cell. They flew to their usual perch, but their cup was gone and they flew all over the place. The director called me, and I put them back in their cage. The prop men hunted for the shaving mug, but it could not be found. Someone suggested using a tin cup that Stroud might have placed there after having his meal, but the birds would have none of it. They stayed there only a couple of seconds and then flew away.

Just then, in walked Mr. Hecht and, with everyone all "up in the air," he calmly said, "You know, I think that someone in this company doesn't like his coffee out of a paper cup. I suggest that instead of wasting all this time hunting, you get on the loud speaker and announce, "Will the mug that has that mug please stop acting like an ostrich and bring it back?" A very sheepish newcomer to the crew then brought it back.

I would like to be able to say that we encountered no mishaps in making *The Bird Man of Alcatraz*, but that would not be true.

John Frankenheimer, the young director of this picture, was a perfectionist if there ever was one and, although he demanded the almost impossible, you could not help but admire the results he achieved. For a scene requiring

Mr. Lancaster (as Stroud) to treat a sick bird, the director would settle for nothing but a sick bird. Because we tried to keep all of our birds healthy, it was several days before we came upon one that was a little puffed up. We took it to the studio so that they could get the shot, and Frankenheimer at once wanted to know what medication could be given to it from an eye dropper. We had no medicine with us, so we suggested a drop of brandy mixed with water. Lancaster gave this concoction to the bird, the scene was shot, and we placed the bird in a heated cage. So much for that; everything was fine.

We got ready for the next take and looked around for Percy and Runty. Percy was right there on the job, but Runty was gone. Everyone became excited, as we thought he had flown off somewhere. He then came out from under the cell bed, but something was wrong. He walked a few steps and then fell over. We could not understand it, as he had been all right less than an hour before.

We placed him on the shelf with the water dish, thinking the lights might have made him too hot, but he staggered past the water to the container from which Mr. Lancaster had filled the eye dropper and had himself another drink of brandy. Runty was drunk! I'll bet this was the first time a bird's hangover ever held up a movie production.

When it rains, it pours. That night a beautiful red factor canary got loose. He flew out of sight and it was impossible to get him back.

Next day was Christmas Eve, and the plan called for us to finish early, in order to attend a party to be given by the producer, Harold Hecht, for everyone connected with the picture. Stroud's cell was full of male canaries. In filming a picture like this it was necessary to have a female bird as a double for every male, so that when there was dialogue, a male would not burst out in song and ruin a scene. The rest of the time they use the males, so their singing can be heard throughout the picture. The cages were swiftly changed and the female canaries put in; however, in doing this, one of the prop men let the bottom fall out of the cage and a European goldfinch and a Dutch frill canary escaped. One of the prop men climbed high up on the catwalk and put out feed and water where he thought the birds might find it; but, with the heat off in the studio over the long holiday, we were all worried about what might happen to them.

For some reason, the last scene of the day did not seem to run right and it required several retakes. It was a close-up, so all of the lights were out except those on the two actors.

Suddenly, the director called out, "Something is wrong here. One of the female canaries is singing. Get it out of here."

We rushed in and there, sitting on top of the cages, were not only the Dutch frill and the goldfinch but also the red factor canary we had lost the day before. Needless to say, production stopped while we caught the runaways.

At the Christmas party a little while later, where everything from ham to turkey with all of the fixings was served, our host also served a drink before we dined. The toast was given by the prop man who had accidentally let the birds loose.

"I am thankful," said he, "that tonight I will be able to have a very merry Christmas with my wife and children, which I am sure I would not have had if I had to worry about those little birds that got loose."

After their one bid for stardom, Percy and Runty retired—Central Casting doesn't have too many calls for educated sparrows. One of the members of the cast did make it big, however. He shaved off his hair, picked up a lollipop, and became an overnight sensation—Telly Savalas.

♘

The San Francisco Zoo

When A. W. received the offer to work for the San Francisco Zoo, he thought he might like it for a while. He was still brooding over the dirty deal Mr. Glick had pulled on him, and after finishing *The Bird Man of Alcatraz* he needed to get away somewhere and think things out for himself. He blamed himself for everything that had happened. I understood and did not try to dissuade him. He liked it there so well that he stayed with the zoo for five years. He was put in charge of the Children's Zoo where all of the animals were let free to mingle with the kiddies, who were permitted to feed and play with them. I do not know who enjoyed it the most, the kids or the animals.

A. W. had been there close to a year when I went to visit him. They were in the process of putting in a nursery when I arrived, and the director asked if I might like to be in charge of it. After all of the hard work I had put in at the bird farm, I could think of nothing I might like less; however, I said I would give it a try. I was never sorry.

But, first, I had to return to Thousand Oaks and put my affairs in order there. I was assured that I had plenty of time as the building was just getting under way.

The commercial property in Thousand Oaks, which had been necessary in order to run a business, was far too expensive to keep up just as a residence. I bought a small house for Mother to live in, sold off the few birds that were left there, and put the place up for sale.

After getting Mother settled in her new home and finding someone to stay with her, I hired a truck and sent my white stallion and Wango, the gibbon ape, to the zoo. The rest of our equipment I stored in one side of the garage, and my personal things in a spare bedroom.

The Children's Zoo employed young college students as guides. Their duties were to acquaint the kiddies with the different species and show them the proper way to caress and play with them.

One of the main reasons for building the nursery had been to accommodate baby animals from the big zoo whose mothers, for some reason or other, had abandoned them.

This happens, at times, when animals are born in captivity. Many of these young animals had to be hand fed. I thought it might be a nice idea to have the guides handle the bottles and allow the children to assist in the feeding. The idea proved to be a big success, and the children vied with each other to see who would get to hold the baby bottles.

The most popular of all was the baby elephant. The kids got such a kick out of giving her the bottle that I continued to allow them to do so even after she was eating solid foods. Each year the big zoo would buy us a new baby elephant, and the older one would join the big herd there.

I often noticed how people would crowd around the monkey cages, observing their antics. Everyone seemed to be looking for entertainment. It seemed a shame that someone couldn't come up with an idea to help them while away their Saturday or Sunday afternoons.

The girls who were helping me in the nursery were very interested in my horse, Cimmaron. When they learned that he had been with a circus, they kept asking me what he had done, so one Sunday afternoon I put a saddle on him and worked his act for them. Our guests also seemed to enjoy the act. It got so I would ride him each Saturday and Sunday for the entertainment of the visitors. People started to ask what time the show was going to be.

Now, just one trained horse is hardly a show; I pointed that out to the directors. I told them that, with their permission, we could perhaps furnish a little entertainment. One thing led to another, and the zoo directors agreed to allow us to put on a little show. They had no

Offering a patriotic salute. Cole. Bros. Circus, 1941.
Courtesy of Tim Tegge.

idea what they were letting themselves in for. Once we got the green light, there was no stopping our gang.

A. W. and one of his helpers made a quick trip back to Thousand Oaks with a truck and picked up the props we had there and brought them back to San Francisco. Since he could not take the time to sort them out, he just loaded them all. There were quite a few of them, and that gave our young folks a lot to think about. They kept asking questions: What was this and that used for?

The Children's Zoo was maintained mostly by donations. One kindhearted lady had spent a great deal of money to have an auditorium built where young people could produce and put on plays, but for some reason, no one did. Now we could put it to good use. Although some of the animals had to be trained outdoors, we could also do a lot of work inside.

Everyone employed seemed to want to be part of the show. We had a number of young men caretakers who, after their chores were done, had little to do until feeding time in the evening, except to keep order in the yard. When they learned that the people in the show were to train the animals themselves, under supervision, we had an ample supply of volunteers. Because our superiors seldom if ever visited the baby zoo, as long as things were running smoothly and there were no complaints, it was months before they had an inkling of just how far the mania had progressed.

A. W. made several trips to the dog pound and bought an assortment of canines for a dog act. With all of the enthusiastic help at his disposal, it was only a matter of sitting back and giving instructions. An excellent dog act was soon in the offing.

We still had Wango, the ape who had worked in a riding dog and monkey act. This act would require a pony, so we bought one. Why not add a few more and have a pony drill?

Aerial acts had not been on the original agenda.

Some of the students were well into gymnastics, and when they discovered all of the riggings, they were anxious to try the stunts they had seen the circus stars perform. They were willing to come in after working hours, on their own time, if I would teach them. Knowing that this would interfere with the little leisure time I had (with all the baby animals, there was always a late bedtime feeding for them) the students offered to take turns handling that chore, leaving me available to hold an aerial class in the auditorium.

The cockatoo-breaking props were among the other things, and one of the girls was very interested in working a bird act. Of course, cockatoos were out of the question, but I told her that, if she liked, we could break a fantail pigeon act.

The college kids worked a five-day week, and the show would be put on for seven, so it would be necessary to break two people to work each act. We would put on two shows each Saturday and Sunday, and one on weekdays after school was out for the day.

Several students were anxious to learn to ride, so I told them we would have a tryout for a bareback act. First I taught them how to groom and harness the horse. I used an extra-heavy felt pad (which would later be dispensed with) under the surcingle, to protect not only the horse, but the riders as well. Each one was given several turns learning the correct way to sit, holding onto the hand grips at first, then turning each hand loose, then both at the same time. After attaining balance, there would be no need to use the handholds, except when executing a trick.

Not wishing to impose any hardship on Cimarron with a bunch of amateur riders, I had the kids rig up a dummy horse with equipment borrowed from the gymnasium. This I used to first teach them how to vault, both astride and side seat. Later we used it to teach them to jump from the ground to the back of the horse. This might sound like a long way around to accomplish an objective, but Cimarron was getting along in years, as horses go, and he had worked hard and deserved to be allowed to take it easy.

One of the boys, besides becoming a good rider, was also a natural as a clown. We copied some of the old Poodles Hanneford stunts, and he did them well.

It was soon evident that the bareback act would be the feature of our show. I wondered how we would cope with the fact that the students worked a five-day week. There were substitutes for all of the other acts, but to break two sets of bareback riders was impossible.

With the fortitude of youth, the youngsters worked it out for themselves. In order to keep up with their classes and still hold down their job at the zoo, they had been in the habit of exchanging working hours with each other, so, in one way or another, they worked it out and the act was always in the show.

The auditorium was open and anyone who wished to do so could come in, sit down, and watch our practice session. It was surprising how interested people became in what we were doing. They kept returning, watching, and often bringing others with them.

The aerial acts were working great . . . indoors, that is. In the auditorium were plenty of girders from which to hang rigging. We had single traps, double traps, swinging ladders, and webs, but the show was to be presented outdoors. Everyone involved became more concerned as we went along, but no one had a solution.

I was never able to get over the interest and enthusiasm people displayed. This might have been understandable in some small town, but in a city like San Francisco, it was quite unbelievable. We had our first demonstration of this during a practice session when we were discussing our big problem.

Overhearing our conversation, a rather elderly gentleman entered into the debate.

"I am wondering," he said, "why telephone poles wouldn't do the trick. How about it, young lady?"

"That would be great," I replied, "but where in the world would we get them?"

"Why, the phone company, of course. I will arrange it."

The men that brought the poles a few days later and not only delivered them, but, after asking where they were to be placed, erected them in the air.

The second display of someone's benevolence came to us through the mail. The girls had expected to make their own wardrobe for the show, and the costumes for the boys, as well. Suddenly, we were told that a kind lady had been watching us train and was donating the money for all of the wardrobe. She had consulted with a costume maker in town, and he had agreed to donate his services if she would shoulder the expense of the material. The lady wished to remain anonymous, but I thought she gave herself away when she closed her letter by saying how happy she was to see the auditorium finally serving a good purpose.

The board of directors, who had to put their okay on everything, including the purchase of a can of flea powder, requested a preview of this little entertainment. Our dress rehearsal would be a private showing for them.

They strolled in like reluctant fathers forced to witness Junior's rendition of "The Charge of the Light Brigade," or little Susie's singing "On The Good Ship Lollipop." To say that they were amazed would be putting it mildly. The results were just as amazing. A board of directors' meeting was hastily called, and they all agreed that with such an entertainment in the offing, an admission should be charged. The fee was small, and no one objected to paying it.

Soon we were having large crowds, especially on Saturdays and Sundays.

Families would bring their lunch and eat in the park, and between shows the kids could play with the baby animals. At first we had only a fence and a railing around the outside of the ring, and people watched the same as they did the cages in the big zoo. This did not last long, though; someone donated bleachers. So many people congregated in the Children's Zoo that they put in first one concession stand, and then another.

We had known all along that the show would have to close for a few weeks during the rainy season, but everyone was sorry when that day came.

At our last show of the season, we were surprised to see all of the members of the board of directors present. They had gotten into the habit of dropping by from time to time, but this was the first time since the opening that they had attended as a body. The crowd was huge for our final performance. Just before the show I was called aside and told that at the end of the last act I was to have the cast remain in wardrobe and line up for a final bow. Both sets of students were appearing in this last show.

When they lined up, each girl was given a corsage and each boy a flower for his lapel. I was so proud of them I could have cried. Then the audience rose to their feet and began to applaud. The zoo director came into the ring and asked me to come forward and take a bow. He then explained that it was impossible to offer me a key to the city, but he did have at his disposal the key to the auditorium and would like to offer that. In one accord, we were all urged toward it and, after fitting the key into the lock, the door opened, revealing a sumptuous catered party.

During the off-season, we again worked out in the auditorium and added new things to our repertoire. The big zoo sent down a couple of macaws and three cockatoos, which we incorporated into the bird act.

The girls were having all sorts of ideas for new costumes and looking forward to our next season, and so I entered into my second year at the zoo.

♘

Penguins

*D*own around Fisherman's Wharf in San Francisco is a place called The Cannery. It consists of many shops, boutiques, and restaurants. As an attraction, the owners had built an amphitheater and hired a man to break a penguin act for them. Two shows were presented there each day. As time went on the parking lots became overcrowded, and they needed more space for the customers who patronized the shops. The penguin show took up a great deal of space, so they were going to abolish it.

They told the zoo officials that they would donate the birds and props if someone at the zoo could handle the act. Our director sent me out to look over the act, and when I told him it would be a good addition, the board of directors agreed to accept it.

It was no small project transferring all of the paraphernalia. In the first place, quite a large pond with a large island in the center of it had to be installed before the props could be erected. When it was completed, the penguin act was adorable.

The first act consisted of a penguin working on a skateboard. An attendant would then place a surfboard in the water, and one of the birds would swim up and place his head and neck through a loop that was attached to the board. Five or six penguins would climb on the board and away the underwater penguin would swim, faster and faster; one by one the penguins on the board would lose their balance and fall off into the water.

On the far side of the pond was a high ladder that the birds would climb. On the other side of the ladder was a slide they would scoot down, landing in the water with a splash.

They seemed to enjoy this trick.

Then, back to the platform, where one of the penguins would play a toy piano. No tune, of course, but don't knock it. I can't play one either, leastwise not with my nose. Let's give credit where credit is due.

At this point, a little boat appeared on the scene. On the upper deck the captain pulled a string, causing a bell to ring madly. Penguins on either side scrambled aboard. I never did find out why. Nonetheless, they would start out for a ride. A cork in the bottom of the boat was attached to an invisible wire, the same as magicians use. An unseen attendant pulled the wire, releasing the cork. Water would then run in and the boat would begin to sink. One by one the birds would jump off, except the gallant captain who went down with his ship, still ringing the bell.

For the finish trick, there was an elevator. Seven or eight of the penguins would walk into it, the door would close, and it would be cranked up high into the air. At the top was a platform. The birds would walk out onto it and, one by one, jump off into the water below.

Since none of them had had a swimming or a diving lesson, each devised its own method of landing in the water. A swan dive or a back flip, with a belly landing, seemed to be the top choices. A clown penguin by the name of George would chicken out and refuse to dive at all.

This was where the kids in the audience got a chance to exercise their lungs. They were invited to help in calling him down.

"Come on, George, come on down. Don't be chicken."

Very often the older children and the parents would get caught up in the fun and join in. When George could stand the racket no longer (and the trainer cued him), he would jump off, amid cheers and a big hand. However, all that interested him was his extra helping of fish. Humans are the only animals that live for applause.

We now had this exhibition in addition to the "Zoocus," which was the that title we gave our show. You take a ZOO . . . you add a cirCUS . . . and you have a Zoocus.

○

Zoocus

The program for the Zoocus the first season was as follows: riding dogs and monkey, single traps, pigeon act, swinging ladder, dog act, web, six-pony drill, double traps, and bareback riding act.

We would have liked to add a few clowns, but the zoo directors did not think that would be dignified. We had to settle for the boy who clowned in the bareback act to furnish all of the comedy, and I noticed that the zoo directors laughed at him just as hard as everybody else did.

The show continued to improve each year, and we were allowed to buy all new wardrobe for each opening. We added new things to it as we went along.

One of the girl riders was exceptionally adaptable, and I taught her a lady principal act (a solo act standing on a horse and doing ballet positions, and so on). We were presented with a well-trained pick-out horse. Things were going great, and we were drawing big crowds.

It happened quite suddenly and unexpectedly, just as our third season was drawing to a close. Someone in the office, while going through the records, happened to notice A. W.'s birth date—he would reach retirement age on his next birthday. They sent for him to come to the office. There was nothing they could do; it was a civil service job, and that meant retirement at age sixty-five. Everyone was very upset. Without the animals, which belonged to us, there would be no more show.

Shortly after we left two months later, the penguins were sent up to the big zoo; the Children's Zoo was closed; and the nursery was turned into a hospital for animals from the big zoo.

♄

Making News

News media were always of interest to me, and I have an idea that if it had not been for my great love of horses I might have tried to enter the field of journalism. I probably would not have been very successful at it, but it might have been fun to try. The one time I did, I had a ball.

We were playing the Police Indoor Show in Des Moines, Iowa. Their publicity staff had placed numerous ads in the local newspapers, but had been unable to obtain any write-ups, which are always a great help to any show.

I happened to be in on a conversation when they were discussing the cooperation they were not receiving and asked if I might offer a suggestion; there was a chance I could break the ice and make the press. I had noticed while in town that they were in the process of installing parking meters—an innovation in that city. With some help, I might be able to attract some attention and get the interest of a reporter or two.

I dressed up in a flashy Western outfit, a throwback to the time when I was playing rodeos and needed something to wear in the grand entry. Now, the palomino stallion, Arrow, was quite well behaved as long as he was with the rest of the horses, but take him any distance away, by himself, and he became very nervous. He displayed this trait by dancing around and letting out a loud whinny every so often.

Just across from the newspaper office, which was located on the second floor, was a very swanky restaurant with waitresses attired in cute little Dutch girl costumes. I rode up to the front of the cafe, dismounted, and tied Arrow to the parking meter. The customers who were having breakfast stared, but I paid no attention and seated myself at the counter where they could get a good look. I ordered a cup of coffee from the astonished waitress, and by the time she brought it, quite a crowd had gathered on the sidewalk outside.

At that point, a motorcycle officer (who was my partner in this little caper) arrived. He strode into the restaurant, looked all around, and, in a loud voice, demanded to know who owned the horse that was tethered to the parking meter. My Western outfit and big, white Stetson hat did not seem to offer him a clue, so he yelled out again.

By now, most everyone there was pointing in my direction. I arose from my seat and asked what was bothering him. He took my arm and escorted me to the door. Once outside, we got into a heated argument. I pointed out that a hitching post was the proper place to tie a horse. Finally, in desperation, he wrote me out a parking ticket, which I promptly tore to bits. By this time, we had gained the attention of the newspaper personnel, who were leaning out of the upstairs window of the building across the street.

Mission accomplished, he ordered me to get on my horse and follow him to the police station. Once there, we tied up Arrow in the backyard and went inside. We did not have long to wait as several newsmen soon arrived. The chief hid me in his office and told them only that I would be brought to trial shortly. Officer Tony Mihalovich and I stayed in the private office, where he regaled me with stories of some of his escapades, until noontime, when lunch was sent in to us.

Around one o'clock, I called the personnel director at the building where we were showing and told him this little escapade was going to take longer than I had anticipated, and I might be late for the matinee. He said it did not matter, we had already had a picture in the morning paper with only a sketchy explanation, which was sure to have a follow-up story on it; take as long as necessary to complete the stunt.

Shortly thereafter I was escorted to a police car, which took me to the courthouse. Officer Mihalovich was whisked away in another car. Arrow had been picked up by a groom and returned to the building where we were showing, which could have been construed as concealing evidence, I suppose, but no one noticed the discrepancy. Upon arrival we went directly to the judge's chambers. Of course, he was also in on the deal, but it suddenly occurred to him that it would be a great gag to call in another judge who knew nothing about the conspiracy, and see what his reaction might be. He would fake a sudden illness, then hide where he could witness the action, unseen.

I quote now the news story as it appeared in the *Des Moines Register* on Friday, October 3, 1947:

Can A Horse Use Parking Meters Too?

A blond lady and a lanky cop glared at each other Thursday in municipal court. Then, Dorothy Herbert of Houston, Texas, took the witness stand next to Judge Ralph Moore's bench. The judge peered at her solemnly as she related:

"All I was doing was going in for a cup of coffee, and I tied my horse up to a hitching post, and he came along and told me I couldn't."

"It wasn't a hitching post—it was a parking meter," put in Tony Mihalovich, a Des Moines patrolman. He was silenced by City Prosecuter Anthony T. Renda.

"Was it a parking meter?" Judge Moore asked Miss Herbert. "You mean that hitching post there?" she countered. "Do you know what a parking meter is?" asked the judge. "No, we don't have them in Texas. We tie our horses to anything there."

Mihalovich later told his side of the story:

"I came down Locust Street and saw a big crowd. A horse was dancing around on the sidewalk across the street from the Register and Tribune building. I followed this lady into the coffee shop and told her she couldn't park her horse there—it wasn't a hitching post and, since she hadn't put a nickel in she was parking overtime and, besides, the horse was illegally parked on the sidewalk. Then she knocked Des Moines and asked what kind of a town was this where you couldn't hitch a horse, so I gave her a summons. She mounted up and tore the ticket in half. I picked it up and told her to come to the station; we would see a judge. She rode over and I followed her on my motorcycle at about a mile and a half an hour.

Mahalovich lowered his voice, "But she didn't have a chance to drink the coffee, Judge, I'd like to be a gentleman and pay for it." He dug for a nickel.

"I owe the city a nickel," said Miss Herbert, "we're even."

"You can't do that," snapped Renda. "The city would be out a nickel."

Frank McKeon, deputy court clerk, who had overheard the argument, was called as a witness. "Miss Herbert seemed to sort of lose control of her horse," he said.

"I never lost control of a horse in my life!" she shouted.

At this point a light began to dawn. A smile lit up the judge's face.

"Aren't you in on this gag?" Judge Moore asked McKeon, "and isn't Miss Herbert part of the circus playing in town?"

"Matter of fact, Judge, I think she really thought it was a hitching post," said McKeon.

"We rest, Your Honor," said Renda.

Judge Moore cleared his throat. "I happen to know Patrolman Mihalovich has a special interest in some crippled children," he said. "I'm going to dismiss the charges on condition that these children be admitted free to the circus."

Miss Herbert smiled approval. She and the patrolman grinned at each other; Renda and McKeon appeared puzzled—they hadn't known the arrest was a pre-arranged publicity stunt either.

⋃

Cockatoos

At one time there was a bird trainer by the name of Proskie who, like many other circus people, used to spend his winters at George Christy's winterquarters in Houston. As a boy, A. W. had spent many hours watching him train his birds.

Mr. Proskie had three daughters, and he broke a cockatoo act for each of them just before he retired. This was, of course, in the days before the ban against the importation of parrot-like birds. As eight birds were in each act, plus a few spares, it must have been quite a sight to watch him at work.

He made all of his own props for the acts. He also taught his girls how to train the birds, so that they might break replacements from time to time. Each of the girls traveled around the country for many years with their acts and then, one by one, quit the business.

While we were still at the bird farm in Reseda, we had a phone call from one of his daughters. She was retiring and leaving the road, and she asked if we might be interested in buying her act. We went to see it and liked it, so we bought it. I then worked it a number of times on television.

Shortly after completing the motion picture *The Bird Man of Alcatraz*, I worked the bird act on a nationally televised show. The next day we received a call from August Busch, the owner of the Budweiser brewery. He invited us to St. Louis for an interview. He requested that we bring the birds and props with us; he would pay all expenses.

We were met on arrival in St. Louis with a car for us and an enclosed van to transport the birds. We drove directly to Mr. Busch's zoo and, after the birds were situated, drove to the hotel where reservations had been made for us.

The next day we worked the act, and Mr. Busch at once made a deal for it. He asked if he might engage us to break another just like it for the new zoo he was building in Van Nuys, California. The act he had just bought from us was to go to Florida and be shown at the Busch Gardens there.

The restrictions on the importation of birds from Australia did not include zoos, which could buy them for display purposes but were not allowed to sell them. Mr. Busch told us he would have the birds flown in directly to us—eight white greater sulphur-crested cockatoos.

We had their quarters and training area all ready for them when they arrived and, after a few days rest, proceeded to start their training.

Now, since they were perfectly matched, telling them apart was a problem. I solved this by placing a few drops of vegetable dye on each of their tails, then I made out a chart to keep track of what each one was being trained to do. I also put some of the same color dye on each perch where they were to sit, making it easy to know where they were to go.

A. W. had the props built for the act and helped me

with the training for a while before he had to get back to the business of buying and selling birds. Certainly, we had lost a number of our contacts during all of the months we had been working on the Bird Man picture. People from whom we had been buying birds had found other outlets for them, so it was no use trying to hold out any longer.

A. W. accepted an offer to go to work for the San Francisco Zoo so, once more, I was left alone, only this time with a flock of birds. I did not have much else to do, so I devoted more time to them than a person normally would do on a job of this sort.

I made a game of it.

After breakfast I would go to the barn where the cockatoos were housed, two to a cage. There was a large aviary in conjunction with the room in which they were kept. I would take each one out of its cage and place the bird on the floor of what I now called the playroom, and go on to the next cage and do the same.

After they were all in the playroom, I would clean their cages. Each cage had a wire grate in it, which I would remove. On the tray below I had placed white sand and, with a scoop, I would quickly gather up this sand and place it in a sifter, leaving the now-clean sand on the bottom. After the cages were all cleaned and serviced with fresh feed and water, the training session would begin.

At first I would get each one on a training stick (a dowel) and then I would place it on its respective perch. Later on, after all knew their places, I got the idea of having them climb up a ladder from the floor and go to their perches. This served two purposes: It eliminated having to get them on a stick and then place them on their perch, and in the event one should for some reason fall off the table during the act, I would not have to chase after it; it would run to the table and climb back up.

I gave them the following names, which I thought would be easy for the handler to remember: August, Nora, Homer, Edward, Eunice, Sam, Edna, and Robin.

The act went as follows: Two cockatoos dance the round waltz. One cockatoo pushes a wheelbarrow to the end of the table, turns it around, and brings it back. One cockatoo counts by ringing a bell. One cockatoo pushes a cart upon which another rides to the end of the table, turns it around, and brings it back to the perch. Four cockatoos ride a merry-go-round while another cockatoo pushes. On the top of the merry-go-round is a toy airplane, and another cockatoo perches on it. One cockatoo works on the horizontal bars.

Three bars complete this act. The first bird goes across, turns around and comes back, not missing a bar, going over the top of the bars. Then, another bird runs underneath the bars. One cockatoo starts from a perch position, spins around, then jumps to bar two and spins around, then jumps to bar three and spins around—like a forward somersault.

As the second part of this act, another bird grabs the bar with its mandible (lower jaw), then puts its feet on the bar and releases its mandible to turn upside down and backwards, then releases its feet to end up on the floor. The cockatoo repeats this on bars two and three, then returns the same way.

The castle act runs as follows: A bird is placed inside the castle through a downstairs door; the bird automatically climbs a ladder inside the castle to a door on the second floor, and then waits there for the door to be opened. A toy cannon is used to simulate an attack on the castle. Upon firing of the cannon, the castle starts to burn. A cockatoo climbs an outside portable ladder to release the cockatoo waiting inside. The cockatoo inside comes out and returns to its perch, as does the one that has opened the door. Then a cockatoo climbs the ladder to extinguish the fire. To complete the act, a cockatoo raises the American flag in victory.

It took a little more than a year to break the act and teach someone to work it. After the act had been delivered to Busch Gardens in Van Nuys, I went to San Francisco to visit A. W.

○

Alaska

*P*rior to A. W.'s retirement from the San Francisco Zoo, and having no special objective in mind, but knowing that some sort of transportation was going to be necessary for all of the animals we had accumulated, he shopped around and located a Dodge truck, in which he installed cages for the dogs and stalls for the horse and ponies.

Upon arriving back in Thousand Oaks, we took all of the animals to Jungle Land, which belonged to our good friends the Goebels, and where we knew we would be welcome. Now we had to figure out what we were going to do next. The decision was made for us.

A gentleman rode into Jungle Land one day, shortly after our return from San Francisco. He was driving the most flamboyant car I had ever seen. Wild animals were painted all over it, and signs on the doors proclaimed "Hollywood Movie Land Animals." He looked like a movie star himself, so handsome was he—Gene Holter.

After making his identity known, he asked if he might look around, then he asked if we would work our dogs and ponies for him. He had little or nothing to say. After the acts were over, he asked, "How would you like to go to Alaska?"

Well, we had never been there, so why not? We went to a nearby restaurant for lunch and during the meal made a deal. He told us that any animals we would not be using could stay at his place.

We still had a few of our motion picture cockatoos, macaws, and parrots, along with Wango, our gibbon ape. These we left at Holter's ranch, where he had a small zoo. We gave the pigeons from the show in San Francisco to a little boy we knew. We no longer had a house trailer, nor would we have attempted to take one down the Alcan Highway if we had. It was the roughest road anyone could imagine. The freezing and thawing causes the land to sink, making big chuckholes. Road gangs worked constantly, weather permitting, but never caught up. The melting snow turned to water, which rushed down the mountains, flooded the roads, and washed out the attempts they made to repair the latest damage.

I find that I have not mentioned how we cared for our animals while traveling. When on a circus or fairgrounds, we would put up two picket lines, one for the ponies and one for the dogs. The dogs were allowed to remain out as long as feasible; then, each had a separate cage. The exceptions were the Chihuahuas, of which I usually carried two or three; they seemed to like to bunk together.

When traveling overland, the dogs were taken out early in the morning for a run, and again at noon. We tried to coordinate this with our lunch break. After picking up our lunch at a restaurant, we would find a nice spot, tie out the dogs, and eat in the truck, thus saving traveling time. After each dog had been watered, we would drive on. In the evening, after they had been watered and fed, they were allowed to remain out during the time we were attending the other animals' needs.

Having been told that eating establishments were few and far between on the Alcan Highway, I bought an ice chest and, just before that long journey down that never-to-be-forgotten trail, filled it to overflowing.

As the ponies, dog cages, and props took up all of the room in the truck, the only thing left to do was pack one trunk with wardrobe and load it with the props. Our personal suitcases had to ride in the cab of the truck with us.

We stacked them all up on the floor on the side where I was to ride, placed the ice chest on the seat between us, locked the door on my side, and filled every available space with canned goods, crackers, and other assorted things. I took along an electric hot plate, coffee pot, and plenty of instant coffee and Coffee Mate. This stood us in good stead later on.

On top of this conglomeration, I threw in a couple of pillows and blankets, but it still did not look too comfortable to me. This was how we made the trip to Alaska and back. I got used to the strange half-bed, with my feet on the dashboard and, later on, even managed to get some sleep while curled up into a ball.

Despite this inconvenience, and many others, at the moment I felt exhilarated, like a bird set free, or a prisoner who had been handed a reprieve. I think I had been born to travel, and for so many years I had missed it so.

Always before, I had accepted the journeys as a matter of course; now, heeding the words of a song, "You may never pass this way again," I was determined to enjoy every moment of it. Every new and pleasant sight along the way I tried to index in my mind so that I would have them to remember in the years to come. I felt young again, and happy, happy, happy.

My rejuvenation must have been obvious, because A. W. remarked, "You know, with a face lift and a manicure you would look like the girl I married," which, for him, was pretty close to a compliment.

After hitting the snow country, on the first afternoon we unloaded the dogs for their run, I was in for a surprise. When I was a child in Michigan, I had a dog that ran and played in the snow with me, and seemed to enjoy it as much as I. Then, when Mother and I were living in Scottsburg, my German shepherd, Pat, loved to follow me through the snow when I went horseback riding.

We had pulled over to the side of the road, and for miles all we could see was a blanket of snow, although it was only two or three inches deep. The antics of my California canines were delightful to watch. Several of them let out a yelp, as though they had been set down on a hot stove lid; others shook one leg and then another, like a cat that had stepped on flypaper. After a few minutes, the more aggressive ones started to romp and play, and several delighted in rolling in the snow. Ere long, all were having great fun, with the exception of the Chihuahuas, who sat huddled in their little wool sweaters I had knitted for them. Down the road I noticed a tree with a brown space around the trunk where no snow had fallen. I gathered up my three little pooches and carried them to that area to let them answer the call of nature.

Mr. Holter had two drivers for each of his semis, with a sleeping compartment in each cab. They, of course, made far better time than we could. They had to take some of their stock back to the nearest zoo to board until his return to the States, so he suggested we go on ahead.

The drive through Canada took several days and, as a whole, was uneventful, except for one very unpleasant experience. At our first night's stop, after arranging to stable our ponies at a fairground, we fed and watered the animals and put them up for the night. Then we drove to a motel and checked in.

Now, we had a replacement in the dog act, a pretty fox terrier. He was very smart, and A. W. had taught him a number of tricks, including a high dive after climbing up a ladder. Well, said dog began to bark, and he would not stop. A. W. got up a couple of times to see if he could get the dog to shut up, but to no avail.

Then the motel manager came and requested that we leave. We were tired and needed some rest. We drove around until we found a vacant lot with nothing nearby, parked the truck there, and walked several blocks to another motel.

But it was obvious we could not go on in this manner for the entire trip.

The next night, when we arrived at a fairground, they said they could accommodate us, but we would have to use some stalls far in the rear, as a carnival was in progress in the front of the grounds. After feeding and watering the animals, we put the dogs back into the truck and, because there was no one around that the barker might disturb, we left the truck and walked to the front of the fairgrounds and called a taxi to take us to a motel.

Next morning, while we were feeding the animals, an elderly man came by. He told us he had a small sideshow with the carnival and he put on a little trained animal circus. He asked if we might know someone in the States who would sell him trained dogs.

A. W. explained all of the red tape connected with bringing them over, and then said, "But, I have one I will give you that does a number of tricks. Frankly, though, he barks all of the time."

The old man was delighted, and we unloaded the high diving ladder and gave him that, too.

Many weeks later, on our way back to the United States, we happened to pass by a fair where that same carnival was working. We stopped, on the chance that the old man might still be with it. He was, and could not thank us enough for the dog, which he said was now the feature of his dog act.

A. W. asked him how he had stopped the dog from barking. The old man laughed and said, "Oh, that was easy." He opened the door to his trailer and there, fast asleep on the old man's bed, was Skipper.

But, to get on with our journey . . . We were winding slowly up a steep mountain when, suddenly, Gene Holter's big semis overtook us and, with much friendly honking and hand waving, continued on their way. Gene, who was close behind them in his beautiful car, flagged us down at the next rest area and asked if we needed anything. After we had assured him everything was fine, he said, "We will be seeing you in Fairbanks."

As long as the rest of Gene's outfit had been behind us, we had a feeling of security; but now they were gone, and we had all those many miles ahead of us. We seldom saw another car, and could go for miles without any signs of civilization.

The road signs told us we were coming into White Horse, quite a large town for that part of the world. At least we could find nice lodgings and a good meal for a change. To say we were surprised would be putting it mildly, for what did we see but Gene Holter's trucks parked by the side of the road.

We knew they always traveled together, and if one stopped they all stopped. Something must be wrong. Something was. One of the trucks had broken down and it had been necessary to send back to the United States for the necessary parts.

We drove to where they had unloaded all of their stock and left our ponies there. After caring for all of our charges, we went to a motel. Gene met us for breakfast the next morning and told us to go on ahead . . . sort of like the tortoise and the hare.

The scenery was awesome, the roads horrible. Maintenance crews worked on them constantly. The roads froze solid during the winter and, then, when the "big thaw" came and the ice started to melt, great sections caved in. The roads were often flooded, and we would be towed through the water by trucks stationed there for that purpose.

It was getting late. We were tired, hungry, and irritable when we arrived at Watson Lake, an inspection station. A. W. went into the office, and, before long, got into quite an argument with an inspector. It seemed that no one had bothered to inform him in advance of our pending arrival. All of the necessary papers pertaining to our expedition were far behind, with Gene Holter.

I was huddled in the cab of the truck with a blanket over me. The inspector, after looking things over to see what was in the back of the truck, came to where I was seated and demanded that the door be opened on my side. At that time, A. W. used a shaving cream called Hot Lather, which really made a lot of suds. Being too tired to put up an argument, I unlocked the door, which had not been opened since leaving California.

The inspector opened the door and, just as he did, I removed the blankets preparatory to getting out, and soap bubbles started coming from everywhere. The cap had come off the container, and the bumpy road had caused it to foam up. To add to the confusion, canned goods from behind the seat started falling out and rolling everywhere.

The inspector had to laugh.

He invited me inside. His wife was in another room waiting to drive home with him. She took me into the restroom, and we tried to rinse off the soap. A bubble bath like that you have never seen. The more water we used, the soapier I got, and I had it all over me. The washroom itself became a mess. We both got to laughing so hard, her husband came to see what was the matter.

Mr. Brown, the inspector, asked us where we had intended to unload and spend the night. When we said we hadn't the least idea, he insisted we stay at his place, and his wife joined in.

The next man on duty arrived shortly thereafter, and we told him that if the rest of our outfit came through, to please let them know where we were.

We followed the Browns to their home, a lovely place made completely of logs. When we arrived, their son helped A. W. to unload and feed and water the stock while I changed clothes and got cleaned up. We had a great dinner—venison stew, which I had never tasted before. There was homemade bread, and a pie concocted from dried fruit. Fresh vegetables and fruit were hard to come by, and very expensive. Canned foods were also very high priced. Before we left the next morning, I gave our hostess some I had brought along.

After dinner, Mr. Brown and his son took A. W. for a walk in the moonlight down to the nearby lake. There they could watch all the wild animals come out of the woods for water.

Later, when they returned, A. W. located a bottle of spirits he had stashed away—in case of snakebite—and we all had a couple of drinks, seated in front of a huge, wood-burning fireplace. Our bed was an old-fashioned feather bed, and we slept like logs. Gene stopped by in the morning to let us know they had caught up with us, and stayed for a breakfast of fresh-caught fish and homemade biscuits. We loaded up, promising to stop by on our way back to the States.

So once more we were behind and on our own, but not for long. Later in the day we again sighted the Holter trucks lined up by the side of the road. We stopped to see what the matter might be.

They were parked across from a very picturesque lake, which had seemed an ideal spot to water the animals. The elephant and the hippo had enjoyed their swim immensely, so much so that the hippo had refused to leave. Now, you do not buy a hippopotamus with small change, so there was nothing they could do but wait until it finished a prolonged swim.

We made the rest of the trip without mishap, and shortly before reaching our destination, the Holter gang again overtook us and crossed the finish line in the lead.

Since we did not have a groom, we had been wondering if we might encounter difficulty in hiring someone to help out. This proved to be no problem whatsoever; there was never any shortage of help. Everywhere we went, the kids all wanted to help feed and groom the ponies. There were horses in Alaska, but ponies were new to them.

I will never forget the opening day of the Gene Holter Trained Wild Animal Show. Of course I had heard of Gene's show, everyone in our profession had, but to witness it was something else.

Gene made out a program as to the running order of the show, but, other than that, no two shows were ever alike. Anything could happen, and usually did.

His employees saw to it that the animals were available, but, from that point on, the audience itself put on most of the show. Before each event, people were invited to participate; not only did they respond, but had a whale of a time to boot.

There were camel races; sulky races with ostriches taking the place of horses, a sight to behold; zebra races; elephant races; an unrideable donkey that pitched everyone off; and a wrestling tiger, with a prize to anyone from the audience who might be able to throw it. Sandwiched in between were acts such as ours, for a change of pace. For a climax, a real showstopper: All of the animals, with the exception of the ostriches and the tiger, were brought out, and a free-for-all race was held. To be sure, many of them bit the dust, but nobody seemed to mind.

We played all of the towns in Alaska that were big enough to accommodate us, and some that looked as though they weren't, but we had crowds wherever we went. When the Alaskan tour was over, we returned to the lower forty-eight, stopping on the way back for a nice visit with our friends the Browns in Watson Lake.

The first show was in Milwaukee. We were joined in July of 1971 by another of Gene's units, consisting of several more large semis, and many more animals.

Each year the Circus World Museum, located in Baraboo, Wisconsin, in conjunction with the Schlitz Brewery, put on a parade rivaled only by the renowned Rose Parade in Pasadena, California.

Circus wagons of bygone years, from all of the various circuses, are drawn by teams of horses brought by proud owners from all over the country. All sorts of animals are needed to ride in the circus cage wagons, and Gene furnished these, along with his herd of elephants, which were ridden by pretty local girls. Two other herds were also in the parade.

For ten days preceding the parade, a big celebration was held, which included a circus program that Gene produced. We presented our pony drill as part of the Holter program. No races; just circus acts this time.

Then it was on to the fair dates, and back to the Wild West animal show.

Working with the Holter show was great fun for us. We no longer had the responsibility connected with a large unit, such as we had had when playing fairs on our own. True, we were not making the big money, but we were not having the worries either. With just two acts to put on twice a day, there was time left to enjoy ourselves.

Basically, it was a family show. Gene's son, daughters, and son-in-law were the backbone of the show; the rest of the crew felt as though they were family, too, and were treated as such.

Shortly after returning from Alaska, we bought a house trailer. After that, traveling was much easier for us.

The season ended, as all seasons do, and we went home to Thousand Oaks for the winter. We played a few television shows and some spot dates during the Christmas holidays, but, other than that, not much was in the offing.

Then, one day the phone rang. It was Gene. He asked if we were going back to Alaska with him, and we said, "Sure."

Forgotten were the bad roads, flat tires, bad accommodations on the Alcan Highway, and the sometimes bitter cold. Like a couple of old fire engine horses, we were off and running when we heard the bell.

This time, we were to play a couple of dates in New Mexico before the Alaska tour, and we would cross over at a different port of entry: Sweetwater, Montana.

Also, rather than his Hollywood Trained Animal

Show, he was taking a circus. In order to maintain the proper atmosphere, he was taking a complete tent, seats, the works. All of this equipment would meet us at the border after we finished playing the New Mexico dates.

∪

The Baers

I have avoided, as much as possible, the use of names, lest someone take offense. However, I feel at liberty to include the following.

We were assembled at our first New Mexico date, preparatory to going to Alaska. From the looks of all the paraphernalia, it was going to be quite a show.

I had retired and was going along, more or less, for the trip. Before the first show, a meeting was called for all of the personnel. A. W. was busy and told me to go and see what it was all about. I found assembled a most imposing array of talent. Besides Gene's elephants and other animal acts, he had hired the popular Gentle Ben, the bear, and his trainer; and a well-known magician who, at the climax of his act, would turn his lovely assistant into Gene's wrestling tiger.

But the big surprise was his selection of aerial talent. He had hired Bob Yerkes, who produces all of the aerial numbers for the well-known television show "The Circus of the Stars." Bob was presenting, along with several other numbers, a flying return act in which he was featuring Ernestine Clarke. We had been told that some other acts would join us at the border. It looked like an awfully lot of equipment to take over the Alcan Highway.

I walked over to where the meeting was about to

take place. A formidable-looking man proceeded to lay down the law in no uncertain terms. I knew that he was a motion picture actor by profession, and could only assume that he was playing the part of Zack Terrell at his worst . . . minus the cane.

While he was busy scaring the wits out of everyone, I noticed two very lovely young ladies who were continuing to talk to each other and paying no attention to him whatsoever. I felt sorry for them, knowing that sooner or later he would let them have it. He called for everyone to be quiet. Then, when his back was turned, one of the young ladies stuck out her tongue. His daughters. They knew he was all bark and no bite, but he played his part to perfection that day.

His name was Parley Baer.

Ernestine Clarke, born to be the star she was, descended from two of the most famous families in circus history—on one side, the world-renowned Hanneford bareback riders who have never had an equal and, on the other, the great Clarke flyers.

Circus acts are rather like a tradition. They are handed down from generation to generation. Having the best of two worlds at her disposal, there was no way that she could miss.

She had the same regal walk that was characteristic of the females in the clan. I could not help but wonder if perhaps she might be a snob; however, this was not so, and from the very moment I first met her, I adored her.

Parley and Ernie have helped me through several crises these last few years, and I am grateful. This last one, the editing of my book, took all of the grit and determination that Parley could muster, and I hope he was able to endure it.

☊

On the lot with Clyde Beatty Circus in North Hollywood, California, 1948. *Courtesy of David Reddy.*

The Final Journey

The second trip up the Alcan Highway was not to be without incident either. This time, we were crossing over into Canada via Sweetwater, Montana. The tent, pole wagon, seats, sideshow, and concession wagons were all there, awaiting our arrival. They had passed inspection and were all set to continue on, pending Gene's posting of the necessary bonds. This matter taken care of, they went on ahead. Some of the trucks seemed to be very heavily loaded, and I wondered how they would make out on the rough road ahead.

Plenty of corrals were available, and all of the stock was unloaded. We had a long wait, as the inspector was busy elsewhere. It was beastly hot, but this was not too bad as we still had our house trailers with us; we would store them later. Arrangements had been made to leave them at a trailer camp just before starting up the Alcan Highway.

In retrospect, many things that happened seem hard to believe . . . this was one of them. When the inspector arrived, at long last, he passed all of the animals and they started on their way—with the exception of ours.

Our papers were in order, but there was no way of telling the ponies apart because they were so perfectly matched. After you were around them for awhile, of course, you could tell, but the inspector would not take our word for which was which. As he had agreed that all were in perfect health, we could not see why it would matter, but he was adamant.

A. W. offered to set up the ring curb and work the act for him (the harnesses had numbers on them), but he declined.

He said he would have to talk long distance to our veterinarian in Thousand Oaks to make sure these were the same ponies for which he had made out the papers.

But this was on a Friday, and he was now ready to leave and would not be back again until Monday, so we would just have to wait.

Monday morning, while we were eating at a local restaurant, A. W. struck up a conversation with some men who were taking a load of horses to a horse show in Canada. He told them about the delay and one of the men asked, "Have you shaken hands with the inspector?"

A. W. answered, "Hell, why should I? All he is doing is causing me a lot of trouble."

The man then explained what he meant by "shaking hands."

The inspector was at the border station when we arrived. A. W. put in a call to our veterinarian in Thousand Oaks. I waited until the inspector was through talking to our vet and, before he had a chance to say anything, I breezed in, held out my hand (which contained a fifty dollar bill) and said, "Good morning to you."

The inspector turned to A. W., who was standing at the counter, and said, "You had best get loaded up and on your way. You are getting a late start."

I gave A. W. a poke as I passed him, before he could say anything. We loaded up in a hurry and went on.

By now we were three days behind the others. We came to a campsite where it had been arranged for us to leave our house trailers while making that long trip up the Alcan Highway. All of the others, of course, were already there. We unloaded the trailer and put the things that we would need in the truck, and I was, once more, in my cramped position in the cab of the truck, with all of the baggage under my feet.

At the next checkpoint in Canada, A. W. was inside having our papers inspected and making the necessary arrangements. I was walking a couple of dogs.

Gene had hired the trainer with his motion picture bear Gentle Ben to go with us to Alaska. The presentation had gone over nicely at the two shows we had just played, but I overheard this conversation while walking the dogs.

"Why in the world would anyone want to take ponies and dogs to Alaska?"

"If you think that's flaky, you ought to have been here two days ago. A guy came through here with a bear, said he was going to work with a show. Who in Alaska would pay to see a bear, with them running loose all over the place?"

Someone must have told the bear trainer the same thing because, when we arrived at our destination, we found that he had not shown up for the date.

When we reached the inspection point at Watson Lake, our friend Mr. Brown was waiting for us and, having been informed of our delay by Gene Holter, rushed us right through.

By the time we, at last, drove into Anchorage, the tent was in the air and all of the riggings were up. They had encountered a problem, though. They discovered that the tent Gene had leased was not high enough to accommodate the flying act, so they had set it up outside. It showed up to great advantage, but it was pretty rough on the performers, as some of the evenings were very cold. But troopers that they were, they worked just the same.

Pulling into the back of the lot, where a tent had been erected to house the livestock, we were delighted to find the same bunch of kids who had helped us before waiting for us. The ponies and dogs had never before been greeted with such enthusiasm.

We played only two stands, Anchorage and Fairbanks. The show, this time, was too large and the overhead too high to take it into the smaller towns. The next to the last day, between shows, A. W. and I gave a party for the youngsters who had helped us.

On closing night, we packed as fast as we could, said our good-byes, and hurried to the motel. We were determined to leave long before anyone else the next day and stay ahead of the rest of them as long as we could.

This was not because we liked to be in the lead, but past experience had taught us that if we had a flat tire, and on the Alcan Highway we had many, when one of Gene's trucks caught up with us, his men, with the equipment and the manpower they had, could do in just a few minutes what would take A. W. and me a considerable time to accomplish.

We left at four o'clock in the morning, long before the working crew had started to take down and load the big top, which, of course, took quite some time. As we had encountered no difficulties so far, we were well ahead of everyone, and quite satisfied with our progress. We stopped that night at a motel that we had stopped at three times before. It was ideal for our purpose, as it had a barn and a corral where the ponies could be stabled for the night and stretch their legs.

At the break of dawn, we got up and went to the truck and let the dogs out for a run, and put the feed for the ponies in their mangers so they could munch on the way. We then returned the dogs to the cages and went to load the ponies. Where there should have been six ponies, we found only three. The three that were missing were all stallions. They worked in the act together and were used to running in a corral; never before had they ever given any trouble.

As soon as daylight would permit, the proprietor of the motel, who was also a seasoned trapper, as one needs to be in that part of the country where the meat that they eat depends on it, went out to check on the trail that they would have left behind.

It did not take him long to fit the pieces together and ascertain what had happened. During the night a herd of wild horses had come by, stopped for a drink at the lake that skirted his property, and, out of curiosity and sensing the presence of other horses, had come by the corral. Quite a number of mares were in the herd, all that was needed to excite the stallions to leap the fence and take off.

Unless one had ever experienced the vastness of a place like Alaska, they would be unable to realize the precarious position we were now in: These horses had been running free for a number of years, and, as yet, no one had caught them, though, perhaps, they had not extended any great effort to do so.

While we were pondering our dilemma, one and then another of Gene's trucks came by, then Gene himself.

"Stay as long as it takes," he advised. "I will leave all of the necessary papers at the border to get you back into the United States." Suddenly, everyone was gone and we were alone.

Mail, in that far-out region, is delivered by helicopter. It was left at this motel, which was also the local post office and general store, the proprietor also being the postmaster. People would pick up their mail when they came in for groceries. Outposts such as this are to found about one hundred miles apart on the Alcan Highway.

When the helicopter pilot delivered the mail this time, he received a rather peculiar request from the postmaster through a two-way radio communication system. When the pilot was back in the air, would he circle around a few times and see if he could spot a herd of running horses and ascertain if some ponies were running with them?

It did not take him long to spot them, as they were not yet too far away from the camp. Our host then had all of his available horses, which were rented out to hunters during the deer season, saddled up, and he then walked into the combination restaurant and bar and announced, "Mount up, boys, we are going hunting, and this time just for fun." After months of idleness, everyone was eager to join in the chase.

Meanwhile, overhead, the pilot, who should have been on and about his business, continued to give the exact location of the ponies, hovering over them. He seemed to be having a gay time doing something new and exciting for a change.

The runaways were brought back and, this time, tied in stalls. It was now too late to start out, so we waited until the next morning to continue on our way.

After stopping to pick up our house trailer in Canada, we continued on to Milwaukee, where, as usual, Gene was furnishing the show and the animals for the street parade.

During the long ride down the Alcan Highway on the return trip, I had plenty of time to reminisce. I knew, instinctively, this was to be my last tour. That chapter was about to end. I looked back into the past.

Before leaving the Ringling Bros. Circus, I had extracted a promise from Pat Valdo that he would see to it that Satan was taken care of. When I did not return to the show, he kept his word. Satan was turned out in a lovely pasture to spend the rest of his days, and no one ever rode him again. He had more than paid into "equine security" enough to cover his retirement.

When it came time to leave the circus for the last time and go to work at Bird Wonderland, knowing that he would not be happy with nothing to do and no horses to care for, I had turned my ever-faithful Jimmy over to my good friend, Jack Gibson, who was then ring stock boss on the Clyde Beatty show. Jack looked after him all season like a mother hen with one baby chick, but Jimmy was now well along in years and, when the show closed, he went to live in the Veterans' Home in Los Angeles. He came to visit with me and spend the day quite often when I was at the bird farm in Encino.

Then, one day, they called to tell me he would not be coming any more. He had gone to join the horses he had loved so very much.

One by one they seemed to come prancing by, in reverie, all of the horses that I had owned or ridden—some to nod their head in recognition, others to drop to one knee and bow, in what I hoped with all my heart was affection. I looked up into the vastness of the sky, which is so awesome in the wilds of Alaska, and wondered if far away, up there, there might just be a place for them and me. If so, then we would all know there is a heaven after all—not only for people, but animals as well.

When the Milwaukee date was over, we went back to the forever-popular trained wild animal show. We continued to play fairs all the rest of the season. It was a lovely tour, with congenial people and a grand family, the Holters.

I am glad that our last trip was filled with such pleasant memories.

And So It Has

When I started out on these memories, they were intended to be sort of a fun thing, a little memento to leave to my friends so they may have a laugh or two. In order to see my wish carried out, it was necessary that I let certain people know of its existence; then, if some points were not quite clear, I could make the necessary corrections.

It has been assembled with mixed emotions, but the general consensus seems to be that it ought to be published now, not at some date in the future. A wide variety of reasons have been offered—one, that it be made available to the here/now generation so they might make use of the information pertaining to the training of horses. Others think it might be of interest to the circus fans for its historical value. Most agree that it ought to be printed for no particular reason at all.